# The Complete Diabetic Diet
# Cookbook After 50

2000-Day Super Easy, Low-Carb, Low-Sugar Recipes for Better Managing Pre-Diabetes and Type 2 Diabetes in People Over 50 | Includes 30-Day Meal Plan

## Julia R. Aguilar

# TABLE OF
# CONTENTS

# Introduction

We all know that people with diabetes need to be thoughtful about their diet and nutrition. Every bite of food we eat plays a vital role in controlling blood sugar levels and overall health. Therefore, having access to a wide range of tasty and balanced recipes tailored specifically for diabetics is invaluable.

This recipe book aims to be a guiding light for those navigating the complex terrain of diabetic-friendly cooking. It's more than just a collection of recipes; it's a roadmap to a healthier lifestyle. By combining wholesome ingredients with innovative culinary techniques, we endeavor to show that managing diabetes doesn't mean sacrificing flavor or enjoyment in your meals.

Whether you're newly diagnosed or have been managing diabetes for years, this book offers something for everyone. From hearty breakfast options to satisfying main courses and delightful desserts, each recipe is crafted with care to ensure it not only meets dietary requirements but also tantalizes the taste buds.

Moreover, we understand the importance of simplicity and accessibility. Many of the recipes featured herein utilize readily available ingredients and straightforward cooking methods, making them suitable for even the busiest of schedules. Additionally, nutritional information is provided for each dish, empowering individuals to make informed choices about their dietary intake.

It's our belief that food should be a source of nourishment, pleasure, and community, regardless of dietary restrictions. With this recipe book, we hope to inspire and empower individuals with diabetes to take charge of their health and embrace a flavorful approach to eating that enhances both physical well-being and culinary enjoyment. So, let's embark on this journey together, one delicious recipe at a time.

## Chapter 1 Knowing Diabetes Before You Get

Diabetes, a chronic condition affecting millions worldwide, requires diligent management and mindful lifestyle choices. From monitoring blood sugar levels to making informed dietary decisions, individuals with diabetes navigate a unique path toward wellness each day.

Managing diabetes is vital for controlling blood sugar levels and preventing complications like heart disease and nerve damage. It enables individuals to lead healthier lives, reducing the risk of long-term health issues and enhancing overall well-being.

### What is Diabetes?

Diabetes is a chronic medical condition characterized by elevated levels of glucose (sugar) in the blood. It occurs when the body either doesn't produce enough insulin (a hormone that regulates blood sugar) or can't effectively use the insulin it produces. There are several types of diabetes, including type 1, type 2, and gestational diabetes, each with its own causes and management strategies. Uncontrolled diabetes can lead to serious complications such as heart disease, kidney damage, nerve damage, and vision problems.

The three main types of diabetes:

Type 1 Diabetes: It is an autoimmune disease in which the pancreas produces little or no insulin because the body's immune system attacks and destroys insulin-producing cells. It usually develops in childhood or adolescence, but can occur at any age. Treatment includes lifelong insulin therapy, dietary monitoring and regular physical activity to control blood sugar levels and prevent complications.

Type 2 Diabetes: This is a chronic condition that affects the way the body processes blood sugar (glucose), leading to high blood sugar levels. It occurs when the body becomes resistant to insulin or when the pancreas is unable to produce enough insulin. Management typically involves lifestyle changes, such as improved diet and increased physical activity, along with medication to control blood sugar levels and prevent complications.

Gestational Diabetes: Gestational diabetes is a form of diabetes that occurs exclusively during pregnancy, characterized by high blood sugar levels that develop during pregnancy in women who didn't previously have diabetes. It is diagnosed through glucose testing and is managed by monitoring blood sugar levels, adopting a healthy diet, exercising, and sometimes

using insulin or other medications. Although it usually resolves after giving birth, it increases the risk of developing type 2 diabetes later in life for both the mother and the child.

High blood sugar, if not properly controlled, can cause complications in major organs such as the heart, kidneys, eyes and nerves. However, people with diabetes can effectively control their blood sugar, reduce the risk of these complications and build a healthier lifestyle by following a proper management plan that includes a healthy diet, regular exercise, adherence to medication (if prescribed) and regular checking of blood glucose levels in co-operation with their doctors.

## Benefits of the Diabetic Diet

The benefits of a diabetes-friendly diet are multifaceted and crucial for managing both type 1 and type 2 diabetes. This type of diet focuses on controlling blood sugar levels to keep them within a healthy range, which is essential to preventing the short- and long-term complications associated with uncontrolled diabetes. Here are the key benefits:

Improved Blood Sugar Control: By balancing carbohydrate intake and incorporating low glycemic index foods that have a more gradual effect on blood sugar levels, individuals can achieve better glucose control. This helps in reducing the risk of hyperglycemia (high blood sugar) and hypoglycemia (low blood sugar).

Weight Management: Many people with diabetes may need to manage their weight to control the disease. A diabetes-friendly diet, often rich in fiber and low in unhealthy fats and calories, can help in maintaining a healthy weight or losing weight if necessary. This is particularly important since obesity is a significant risk factor for developing type 2 diabetes.

Lowered Risk of Diabetes Complications: Consistently high blood sugar levels can lead to various complications, including heart disease, kidney damage, and nerve damage. A diet that helps manage blood sugar levels can reduce the risk of these complications.

Increased Energy Levels: Proper nutrition helps in maintaining stable blood sugar levels, which can significantly increase energy levels and overall well-being. When blood sugar levels are stable, people with diabetes often experience fewer episodes of fatigue and have more energy throughout the day.

Improved Heart Health: A diabetes-friendly diet is not only about controlling sugar intake but also about promoting overall heart health. By limiting intake of saturated and trans fats, and increasing consumption of fruits, vegetables, and whole grains, individuals can lower their blood pressure and cholesterol levels, reducing the risk of heart disease.

Enhanced Nutrient Intake: Diets tailored for diabetes management emphasize the consumption of nutrient-dense foods, which ensures that individuals receive a broad spectrum of vitamins, minerals, and antioxidants. These nutrients are essential for supporting overall health and preventing nutritional deficiencies.

Support for Immune Function: Eating a balanced and healthy diet can also bolster the immune system, making it easier for the body to fight off infections, which is particularly important for people with diabetes as they may have a higher risk of infections due to high blood sugar levels.

## Food To Eat with Diabetes

Diet plays a pivotal role in controlling diabetes, so choosing your daily food and nutritional intake wisely plays a vital role in keeping your blood sugar levels stable.

Here's a roundup of the types of foods that are friendly to diabetics:

Whole Grains: Foods like brown rice, quinoa, oats, and whole wheat products are rich in fiber, which can help manage blood sugar levels.

Non-starchy vegetables: Non-starchy vegetables such as green leafy vegetables, peppers, broccoli and carrots are low in calories and carbohydrates and high in vitamins, minerals and fibre.

Fruits low in sugar: Fruits are rich in vitamins, minerals and fibre despite their sugar content. It is best to consume whole, low-sugar fruits rather than fruit juices in order to benefit from the fibre content.

Lean Proteins: Sources like chicken, turkey, fish, eggs, tofu, and legumes can help maintain muscle mass and control blood sugar spikes.

Healthy Fats: Avocados, nuts, seeds, and olive oil provide heart-healthy fats that, when consumed properly, help control cholesterol levels.

Legumes: Beans, lentils, and chickpeas are excellent sources of protein and fiber, making them great for blood sugar control.

Low-fat dairy products or dairy alternatives: Choose

low-fat or skimmed dairy products such as yoghurt, milk and cheese. Or choose dairy alternatives fortified with calcium and vitamin D, such as almond milk or soya milk.

Balancing portion sizes and nutrient intake at each meal is key to building a healthy life and will give you confidence in your blood sugar management.

Adopting a diabetes-friendly diet requires careful planning and consideration but offers significant benefits for managing diabetes and improving overall health.

## Food To Avoid with Diabetes

Knowing which foods to avoid or limit is essential to controlling blood glucose levels and overall health for people with diabetes. Individuals with diabetes are generally advised to avoid or limit the following types of foods to manage their blood sugar levels and maintain overall health:

Refined Grains: Foods like white bread, white rice, and pastries have been processed to remove the bran and germ, leading to a loss of fiber. This lack of fiber means they are digested and absorbed quickly, causing rapid spikes in blood sugar levels. Opting for whole grains instead can help maintain steadier blood sugar levels.

Sugary Beverages: Soda, fruit juice, sweetened teas, and coffees are significant sources of added sugars and calories but provide little to no nutritional value. These drinks can quickly increase blood sugar levels and contribute to weight gain, increasing the risk of diabetes complications.

High-Sugar Snacks: Candies, cookies, and ice cream are not only high in sugar but also in unhealthy fats and calories, contributing to blood sugar spikes and weight issues. These foods can also displace healthier food choices that provide the nutrients needed for overall health.

Processed Foods: Many processed foods are high in salt, sugar, and unhealthy fats. These components can interfere with blood sugar control and contribute to high blood pressure, heart disease, and obesity. Processed foods often lack essential nutrients, making them poor choices for a diabetes-friendly diet.

Fatty Meats: Meats such as bacon, sausages, and ribeye steaks are high in saturated fats, which can exacerbate heart disease risk. People with diabetes are already at an increased risk for heart disease, and consuming high amounts of saturated fats can further increase this risk.

Full-Fat Dairy Products: Products like whole milk, cheese, and cream are high in saturated fats, which can impact heart health by raising levels of LDL (bad) cholesterol. Choosing low-fat or fat-free dairy options can provide the benefits of dairy while minimizing these risks.

Trans Fats: Trans fats, sometimes listed as partially hydrogenated oils on labels, are found in some margarines, spreads, and processed snacks. They can worsen cholesterol profiles by raising LDL cholesterol and lowering HDL (good) cholesterol, increasing the risk of heart disease. Trans fats have been phased out of many products but can still be found in some foods.

Alcohol: Alcohol can affect blood sugar levels in unpredictable ways, potentially causing them to swing too high or too low. Moreover, alcoholic beverages can be high in calories, leading to weight gain. If consumed, it should be in moderation and with a meal to help stabilize blood sugar levels.

Emphasizing moderation and balance in the diet is vital for people with diabetes. Focusing on nutrient-rich foods, such as fruits, vegetables, whole grains, lean proteins, and healthy fats, can help manage blood sugar levels and support overall health. Working with a healthcare provider or a registered dietitian can help in developing a personalized eating plan that considers individual health goals, preferences, and nutritional needs.

## Chapter 2 Diabetes and Aging: Navigating Metabolic Changes After 50

Reaching the milestone of 50 years brings about significant physiological changes that can impact the management and understanding of diabetes.

### Understanding Diabetes at 50

As individuals age, particularly after the age of 50, their metabolic rate naturally declines, presenting unique challenges for those managing diabetes. This period demands an adjustment in strategies to control blood sugar levels effectively. Aging bodies become less efficient at processing glucose due to decreased insulin sensitivity and potential loss of muscle mass, which plays a critical role in glucose metabolism. Moreover, the risk of type 2 diabetes increases with age, necessitating closer monitoring of diet, physical activity, and medication. Navigating these metabolic

changes requires a tailored approach to diabetes management, focusing on dietary adjustments, regular exercise, and possibly medication modifications, to maintain blood sugar control and overall health in the later stages of life.

## How to manage diabetes after 50

Managing diabetes after the age of 50 requires a comprehensive and adaptive approach, taking into account the body's changing needs and metabolism. Here are some strategies to effectively manage diabetes in this stage of life:

Monitor Blood Sugar Regularly: As the body ages, it's crucial to keep a closer eye on blood sugar levels. This can help in making necessary adjustments to your diet, exercise, and medication in a timely manner.

Adjust Your Diet: Focus on a balanced diet rich in nutrients, fiber, and whole foods while limiting processed foods, sugar, and unhealthy fats. Portion control can also play a significant role in managing blood glucose levels.

Stay Active: Incorporate regular physical activity into your routine. Activities such as walking, swimming, or yoga can help maintain a healthy weight, improve insulin sensitivity, and boost overall well-being.

Manage Stress: Stress can significantly impact blood sugar levels. Techniques such as mindfulness, meditation, or simply engaging in hobbies can help reduce stress.

Regular Health Check-ups: Regular visits to your healthcare provider are vital. These check-ups can help in the early detection and management of potential diabetes-related complications.

Medication Management: Be open to adjusting your diabetes medications as recommended by your healthcare provider. As your body changes, your medication needs might also evolve.

Healthy Emotional Management☐Lean on a support system of family, friends, or diabetes support groups. Sharing experiences and strategies can provide valuable insights and emotional support.

Sleep Well: Quality sleep is crucial for managing stress, hunger hormones, and insulin sensitivity. Aim for 7-9 hours of sleep per night.

By adopting these strategies, individuals over 50 can manage their diabetes more effectively, leading to a healthier and more active lifestyle.

## Diabetes Diet Tips After 50

For individuals over 50 managing diabetes, diet plays a crucial role in controlling blood sugar levels and maintaining overall health. Here are some dietary tips:

Prioritize Fiber-Rich Foods: Incorporate plenty of vegetables, fruits, whole grains, and legumes into your diet. These foods can help regulate blood sugar levels and aid digestion.

Choose Healthy Fats: Focus on unsaturated fats found in nuts, seeds, avocados, and olive oil, which can help improve heart health without spiking your blood sugar.

Monitor Carbohydrate Intake: Be mindful of carbohydrate portions and opt for complex carbohydrates like whole grains over simple sugars and refined carbs to maintain steady blood sugar levels.

Stay Hydrated: Drink plenty of water throughout the day to help manage blood sugar levels and avoid sugary drinks that can cause spikes.

Lean Proteins: Include lean protein sources such as chicken, fish, tofu, and beans in your meals to support muscle health without affecting blood sugar significantly.

Regular Meal Times: Eating at consistent times helps regulate your body's insulin response and manage blood sugar levels more effectively.

Limit Salt and Sugar: Reduce intake of salt and added sugars to decrease the risk of hypertension and to avoid blood sugar spikes, respectively.

Portion Control: Pay attention to portion sizes to avoid overeating, which can lead to weight gain and increased blood sugar levels.

Consult a Dietitian: Consider consulting with a dietitian who specializes in diabetes to create a personalized eating plan that meets your nutritional needs and lifestyle.

Adapting your diet according to these tips can significantly contribute to managing diabetes after 50, promoting a healthier and more balanced life.

Embarking on a journey of dietary mindfulness after 50, especially with diabetes, can transform your health and vitality, offering a new lease on life. This cookbook is designed to guide you through the nuances of diabetic-friendly eating, providing not just recipes but a roadmap to a balanced and fulfilling lifestyle. Let each meal be a step towards better health, more energy, and a deeper appreciation for the nourishing power of food, tailored to your unique needs in this vibrant chapter of life.

# Chapter 1 Breakfasts

## Veggie-Stuffed Omelet

Prep time: 15 minutes / Cook time: 10 minutes / Serves 1

- 1 teaspoon olive or canola oil
- 2 tablespoons chopped red bell pepper
- 1 tablespoon chopped onion
- ¼ cup sliced fresh mushrooms
- 1 cup loosely packed fresh baby spinach leaves, rinsed
- ½ cup fat-free egg product or 2 eggs, beaten
- 1 tablespoon water
- Pinch salt
- Pinch pepper
- 1 tablespoon shredded reduced-fat Cheddar cheese

1. In 8-inch nonstick skillet, heat oil over medium-high heat. Add bell pepper, onion and mushrooms to oil. Cook 2 minutes, stirring frequently, until onion is tender. Stir in spinach; continue cooking and stirring just until spinach wilts. Transfer vegetables from pan to small bowl.
2. In medium bowl, beat egg product, water, salt and pepper with fork or whisk until well mixed. Reheat same skillet over medium-high heat. Quickly pour egg mixture into pan. While sliding pan back and forth rapidly over heat, quickly stir with spatula to spread eggs continuously over bottom of pan as they thicken. Let stand over heat a few seconds to lightly brown bottom of omelet. Do not overcook; omelet will continue to cook after folding.
3. Place cooked vegetable mixture over half of omelet; top with cheese. With spatula, fold other half of omelet over vegetables. Gently slide out of pan onto plate. Serve immediately.

*Per Serving:calorie: 140 / fat: 5g / protein: 16g / carbs: 6g / sugars: 3g / fiber: 2g / sodium: 470mg*

## Breakfast Hash

Prep time: 10 minutes / Cook time: 30 minutes / Serves 6

- Oil, for spraying
- 3 medium russet potatoes, diced
- ½ yellow onion, diced
- 1 green bell pepper, seeded and diced
- 2 tablespoons olive oil
- 2 teaspoons granulated garlic
- 1 teaspoon salt
- ½ teaspoon freshly ground black pepper

1. Line the air fryer basket with parchment and spray lightly with oil.
2. In a large bowl, mix together the potatoes, onion, bell pepper, and olive oil.
3. Add the garlic, salt, and black pepper and stir until

evenly coated.
4. Transfer the mixture to the prepared basket.
5. Air fry at 400°F (204°C) for 20 to 30 minutes, shaking or stirring every 10 minutes, until browned and crispy. If you spray the potatoes with a little oil each time you stir, they will get even crispier.

*Per Serving:calories: 133 / fat: 5g / protein: 3g / carbs: 21g / fiber: 2g / sodium: 395mg*

## Sausage, Sweet Potato, and Kale Hash

Prep time: 10 minutes / Cook time: 15 minutes / Serves 4

- Avocado oil cooking spray
- 1⅓ cups peeled and diced sweet potatoes
- 8 cups roughly chopped kale, stemmed and loosely packed (about 2 bunches)
- 4 links chicken or turkey breakfast sausage
- 4 large eggs
- 4 lemon wedges

1. Heat a large skillet over medium heat. When hot, coat the cooking surface with cooking spray. Cook the sweet potatoes for 4 minutes, stirring once halfway through.
2. Reduce the heat to medium-low and move the potatoes to one side of the skillet. Arrange the kale and sausage in a single layer. Cover and cook for 3 minutes.
3. Stir the vegetables and sausage together, then push them to one side of the skillet to create space for the eggs. Add the eggs and cook them to your liking. Cover the skillet and cook for 3 minutes.
4. Divide the sausage and vegetables into four equal portions and top with an egg and a squeeze of lemon.

*Per Serving:calories: 160 / fat: 8g / protein: 11g / carbs: 13g / sugars: 3g / fiber: 3g / sodium: 197mg*

## Vanilla Steel-Cut Oatmeal

Prep time: 5 minutes / Cook time: 40 minutes / Serves 4

- 4 cups water
- Pinch sea salt
- 1 cup steel-cut oats
- ¾ cup skim milk
- 2 teaspoons pure vanilla extract

1. In a large pot over high heat, bring the water and salt to a boil.
2. Reduce the heat to low and stir in the oats.
3. Cook the oats for about 30 minutes to soften, stirring occasionally.
4. Stir in the milk and vanilla and cook until your desired consistency is reached, about 10 more minutes.
5. Remove the cereal from the heat. Serve topped

with sunflower seeds, chopped peaches, fresh berries, sliced almonds, or flaxseeds.

*Per Serving: calories: 79 / fat: 2g / protein: 6g / carbs: 18g / sugars: 3g / fiber: 4g / sodium: 25mg*

## Berry–French Toast Stratas

Prep time: 15 minutes / Cook time: 20 to 25 minutes / Serves 6

- 3 cups assorted fresh berries, such as blueberries, raspberries or cut-up strawberries
- 1 tablespoon granulated sugar
- 4 cups cubes (¾ inch) whole wheat bread (about 5 slices)
- 1½ cups fat-free egg product or 6 eggs
- ½ cup fat-free (skim) milk
- ½ cup fat-free half-and-half
- 2 tablespoons honey
- 1½ teaspoons vanilla
- 1 teaspoon ground cinnamon
- ¼ teaspoon ground nutmeg
- ½ teaspoon powdered sugar, if desired

1. In medium bowl, mix fruit and granulated sugar; set aside.
2. Heat oven to 350°F. Spray 12 regular-size muffin cups generously with cooking spray. Divide bread cubes evenly among muffin cups.
3. In large bowl, beat remaining ingredients, except powdered sugar, with fork or whisk until well mixed. Pour egg mixture over bread cubes, pushing down lightly with spoon to soak bread cubes. (If all egg mixture doesn't fit into cups, let cups stand up to 10 minutes, gradually adding remaining egg mixture as bread cubes soak it up.)
4. Bake 20 to 25 minutes or until centers are set. Cool 5 minutes. Remove from muffin cups, placing 2 stratas on each of 6 plates. Divide fruit mixture evenly over stratas; sprinkle with powdered sugar.

*Per Serving: calories: 218 / fat: 6g / protein: 11g / carbs: 32g / sugars: 17g / fiber: 4g / sodium: 216mg*

## Easy Breakfast Chia Pudding

Prep time: 5 minutes / Cook time: 0 minutes / Serves 4

- 4 cups unsweetened almond milk or skim milk
- ¾ cup chia seeds
- 1 teaspoon ground cinnamon
- Pinch sea salt

1. Stir together the milk, chia seeds, cinnamon, and salt in a medium bowl.
2. Cover the bowl with plastic wrap and chill in the refrigerator until the pudding is thick, about 1 hour.
3. Sweeten with your favorite sweetener and fruit.

*Per Serving: calories: 129 / fat: 3g / protein: 10g / carbs: 16g / sugars: 12g / fiber: 3g / sodium: 131mg*

## Mini Breakfast Quiches

Prep time: 10 minutes / Cook time: 20 minutes / Serves 6

- 4 ounces diced green chilies
- ¼ cup diced pimiento
- 1 small eggplant, cubed
- 3 cups precooked brown rice
- ½ cup egg whites
- ⅓ cup fat-free milk
- ½ teaspoon cumin
- 1 bunch fresh cilantro or Italian parsley, finely chopped
- 1 cup shredded reduced-fat cheddar cheese, divided

1. Preheat the oven to 400 degrees. Spray a 12-cup muffin tin with nonstick cooking spray.
2. In a large mixing bowl, combine all the ingredients except ½ cup of the cheese.
3. Add a dash of salt and pepper, if desired.
4. Spoon the mixture evenly into muffin cups, and sprinkle with the remaining cheese. Bake for 12–15 minutes or until set. Carefully remove the quiches from the pan, arrange on a platter, and serve.

*Per Serving: calories: 189 / fat: 3g / protein: 11g / carbs: 31g / sugars: 6g / fiber: 5g / sodium: 214mg*

## Bacon-and-Eggs Avocado

Prep time: 5 minutes / Cook time: 17 minutes / Serves 1

- 1 large egg
- 1 avocado, halved, peeled, and pitted
- 2 slices bacon
- Fresh parsley, for serving (optional)
- Sea salt flakes, for garnish (optional)

1. Spray the air fryer basket with avocado oil. Preheat the air fryer to 320°F (160°C). Fill a small bowl with cool water.
2. Soft-boil the egg: Place the egg in the air fryer basket. Air fry for 6 minutes for a soft yolk or 7 minutes for a cooked yolk. Transfer the egg to the bowl of cool water and let sit for 2 minutes. Peel and set aside.
3. Use a spoon to carve out extra space in the center of the avocado halves until the cavities are big enough to fit the soft-boiled egg. Place the soft-boiled egg in the center of one half of the avocado and replace the other half of the avocado on top, so the avocado appears whole on the outside.
4. Starting at one end of the avocado, wrap the bacon around the avocado to completely cover it. Use toothpicks to hold the bacon in place.
5. Place the bacon-wrapped avocado in the air fryer basket and air fry for 5 minutes. Flip the avocado over and air fry for another 5 minutes, or until the bacon is cooked to your liking. Serve on a bed of fresh parsley, if desired, and sprinkle with salt flakes, if desired.
6. Best served fresh. Store extras in an airtight container in the fridge for up to 4 days. Reheat in a

preheated 320ºF (160ºC) air fryer for 4 minutes, or until heated through.

*Per Serving:calories: 605 / fat: 54g / protein: 17g / carbs: 18g / sugars: 2g / fiber: 14g / sodium: 329mg*

## Savory Grits

Prep time: 5 minutes / Cook time: 7 minutes / Serves 4

- 2 cups water
- 1 cup fat-free milk
- 1 cup stone-ground corn grits

1. In a heavy-bottomed pot, bring the water and milk to a simmer over medium heat.
2. Gradually add the grits, stirring continuously.
3. Reduce the heat to low, cover, and cook, stirring often, for 5 to 7 minutes, or until the grits are soft and tender. Serve and enjoy.

*Per Serving:calories: 166 / fat: 1g / protein: 6g / carbs: 34g / sugars: 3g / fiber: 1g / sodium: 35mg*

## Breakfast Panini

Prep time: 10 minutes / Cook time: 10 minutes / Serves 2

- 2 eggs, beaten
- ½ teaspoon salt-free seasoning blend
- 2 tablespoons chopped fresh chives
- 2 whole wheat thin bagels
- 2 slices tomato
- 2 thin slices onion
- 4 ultra-thin slices reduced-sodium deli ham
- 2 thin slices reduced-fat Cheddar cheese

1. Spray 8-inch skillet with cooking spray; heat skillet over medium heat. In medium bowl, beat eggs, seasoning and chives with fork or whisk until well mixed. Pour into skillet. As eggs begin to set at bottom and side, gently lift cooked portions with spatula so that thin, uncooked portion can flow to bottom. Avoid constant stirring. Cook 3 to 4 minutes or until eggs are thickened throughout but still moist and creamy; remove from heat.
2. Meanwhile, heat closed contact grill or panini maker 5 minutes.
3. For each panini, divide cooked eggs evenly between bottom halves of bagels. Top each with 1 slice each tomato and onion, 2 ham slices, 1 cheese slice and top half of bagel. Transfer filled panini to heated grill. Close cover, pressing down lightly. Cook 2 to 3 minutes or until browned and cheese is melted. Serve immediately.

*Per Serving:1 Panini: calories: 260 / fat: 7g / protein: 15g / carbs: 32g / sugars: 5g / fiber: 2g / sodium: 410mg*

## Cherry, Chocolate, and Almond Shake

Prep time: 5 minutes / Cook time: 0 minutes / Serves 2

- 10 ounces frozen cherries
- 2 tablespoons cocoa powder
- 2 tablespoons almond butter
- 2 tablespoons hemp seeds
- 8 ounces unsweetened almond milk

1. Combine the cherries, cocoa, almond butter, hemp seeds, and almond milk in a blender and blend on high speed until smooth. Use a spatula to scrape down the sides as needed. Serve immediately.

*Per Serving:calories: 243 / fat: 16g / protein: 8g / carbs: 24g / sugars: 13g / fiber: 7g / sodium: 85mg*

## Ginger Blackberry Bliss Smoothie Bowl

Prep time: 5 minutes / Cook time: 0 minutes / Serves 2

- ½ cup frozen blackberries
- 1 cup plain Greek yogurt
- 1 cup baby spinach
- ½ cup unsweetened almond milk
- ½ teaspoon peeled and grated fresh ginger
- ¼ cup chopped pecans

1. In a blender or food processor, combine the blackberries, yogurt, spinach, almond milk, and ginger. Blend until smooth.
2. Spoon the mixture into two bowls.
3. Top each bowl with 2 tablespoons of chopped pecans and serve.

*Per Serving:calories: 211 / fat: 11g / protein: 10g / carbs: 18g / sugars: 13g / fiber: 4g / sodium: 149mg*

## Pumpkin–Peanut Butter Single-Serve Muffins

Prep time: 10 minutes / Cook time: 25 minutes / Serves 2

- 2 tablespoons powdered peanut butter
- 2 tablespoons coconut flour
- 2 tablespoons finely ground flaxseed
- 1 teaspoon pumpkin pie spice
- ½ teaspoon baking powder
- 1 tablespoon dried cranberries
- ½ cup water
- 1 cup canned pumpkin
- 2 large eggs
- ½ teaspoon vanilla extract
- Extra-virgin olive oil cooking spray

1. Preheat the oven to 350°F.
2. In a medium bowl, stir together the powdered peanut butter, coconut flour, flaxseed, pumpkin pie spice, baking powder, dried cranberries, and water.
3. In a separate medium bowl, whisk together the pumpkin and eggs until smooth.
4. Add the pumpkin mixture to the dry ingredients. Stir to combine.
5. Add the vanilla. Mix together well.
6. Spray 2 (8-ounce) ramekins with cooking spray.
7. Spoon half of the batter into each ramekin.
8. Place the ramekins on a baking and carefully

transfer the sheet to the preheated oven. Bake for 25 minutes, or until a toothpick in the center comes out clean. Enjoy immediately!

*Per Serving:calories: 286 / fat: 16g / protein: 15g / carbs: 24g / sugars: 9g / fiber: 7g / sodium: 189mg*

## Coddled Eggs and Smoked Salmon Toasts

Prep time: 5 minutes / Cook time: 10 minutes / Serves 4

- 2 teaspoons unsalted butter
- 4 large eggs
- 4 slices gluten-free or whole-grain rye bread
- ½ cup plain 2 percent Greek yogurt
- 4 ounces cold-smoked salmon, or 1 medium avocado, pitted, peeled, and sliced
- 2 radishes, thinly sliced
- 1 Persian cucumber, thinly sliced
- 1 tablespoon chopped fresh chives
- ¼ teaspoon freshly ground black pepper

1. Pour 1 cup water into the Instant Pot and place a long-handled silicone steam rack into the pot. (If you don't have the long-handled rack, use the wire metal steam rack and a homemade sling)
2. Coat each of four 4-ounce ramekins with ½ teaspoon butter. Crack an egg into each ramekin. Place the ramekins on the steam rack in the pot.
3. Secure the lid and set the Pressure Release to Sealing. Select the Steam setting and set the cooking time for 3 minutes at low pressure. (The pot will take about 5 minutes to come up to pressure before the cooking program begins. )
4. While eggs are cooking, toast the bread in a toaster until golden brown. Spread the yogurt onto the toasted slices, put the toasts onto plates, and then top each toast with the smoked salmon, radishes, and cucumber.
5. When the cooking program ends, let the pressure release naturally for 5 minutes, then move the Pressure Release to Venting to release any remaining steam. Open the pot and, wearing heat-resistant mitts, grasp the handles of the steam rack and lift it out of the pot.
6. Run a knife around the inside edge of each ramekin to loosen the egg and unmold one egg onto each toast. Sprinkle the chives and pepper on top and serve right away.
7. Note 8. The yolks of these eggs are fully cooked through. If you prefer the yolks slightly less solid, perform a quick pressure release rather than letting the pressure release naturally for 5 minutes.

*Per Serving:calories: 275 / fat: 12g / protein: 21g / carbs: 21g / sugars: 4g / fiber: 5g / sodium: 431mg*

## Plum Smoothie

Prep time: 5 minutes / Cook time: 0 minutes / Serves 2

- 4 ripe plums, pitted
- 1 cup skim milk
- 6 ounces 2 percent plain Greek yogurt
- 4 ice cubes
- ¼ teaspoon ground nutmeg

1. Put the plums, milk, yogurt, ice, and nutmeg in a blender and blend until smooth.
2. Pour into two glasses and serve.

*Per Serving:calories: 144 / fat: 1g / protein: 14g / carbs: 20g / sugars: 17g / fiber: 2g / sodium: 82mg*

## Pumpkin Walnut Smoothie Bowl

Prep time: 5 minutes / Cook time: 0 minutes / Serves 2

- 1 cup plain Greek yogurt
- ½ cup canned pumpkin purée (not pumpkin pie mix)
- 1 teaspoon pumpkin pie spice
- 2 (1-gram) packets stevia
- ½ teaspoon vanilla extract
- Pinch sea salt
- ½ cup chopped walnuts

1. In a bowl, whisk together the yogurt, pumpkin purée, pumpkin pie spice, stevia, vanilla, and salt (or blend in a blender).
2. Spoon into two bowls. Serve topped with the chopped walnuts.

*Per Serving:calories: 277 / fat: 19g / protein: 12g / carbs: 18g / sugars: 11g / fiber: 3g / sodium: 96mg*

## Mandarin Orange–Millet Breakfast Bowl

Prep time: 5 minutes / Cook time: 30 minutes / Serves 2

- ⅓ cup millet
- 1 cup nonfat milk
- ½ cup water
- ¼ teaspoon cinnamon
- ¼ teaspoon ground cardamom
- 1 teaspoon vanilla extract
- Pinch salt
- Stevia, for sweetening
- ½ cup canned mandarin oranges, drained
- 2 tablespoons sliced almonds

1. In a small saucepan set over medium-high heat, stir together the millet, milk, water, cinnamon, cardamom, vanilla, salt, and stevia. Bring to a boil. Reduce the heat to low. Cover and simmer for 25 minutes, without stirring. If the liquid is not completely absorbed, cook for 3 to 5 minutes longer, partially covered.
2. Stir in the oranges. Remove from the heat.
3. Top with the sliced almonds and serve.

*Per Serving:calories: 254 / fat: 7g / protein: 10g / carbs: 38g / sugars: 12g / fiber: 5g / sodium: 73mg*

## Cynthia's Yogurt

Prep time: 10 minutes / Cook time: 8 hours / Serves 16

- 1 gallon low-fat milk
- ¼ cup low-fat plain yogurt with active cultures

1. Pour milk into the inner pot of the Instant Pot.
2. Lock lid, move vent to sealing, and press the yogurt button. Press Adjust till it reads "boil." 3. When boil cycle is complete (about 1 hour), check the temperature. It should be at 185°F. If it's not, use the Sauté function to warm to 185.
4. After it reaches 185°F, unplug Instant Pot, remove inner pot, and cool. You can place on cooling rack and let it slowly cool. If in a hurry, submerge the base of the pot in cool water. Cool milk to 110°F.
5. When mixture reaches 110, stir in the ¼ cup of yogurt. Lock the lid in place and move vent to sealing.
6. Press Yogurt. Use the Adjust button until the screen says 8:00. This will now incubate for 8 hours.
7. After 8 hours (when the cycle is finished), chill yogurt, or go immediately to straining in step 8.
8. After chilling, or following the 8 hours, strain the yogurt using a nut milk bag. This will give it the consistency of Greek yogurt.

*Per Serving:calories: 141 / fat: 5g / protein: 10g / carbs: 14g / sugars: 1g / fiber: 0g / sodium: 145mg*

## Tropical Fruit 'n Ginger Oatmeal

Prep time: 15 minutes / Cook time: 25 to 30 minutes / Serves 4

- 2¼ cups water
- ¾ cup steel-cut oats
- 2 teaspoons finely chopped gingerroot
- ⅛ teaspoon salt
- ½ medium banana, mashed
- 1 container (6 ounces) vanilla low-fat yogurt
- 1 medium mango, pitted, peeled and chopped (1 cup)
- ½ cup sliced fresh strawberries
- 2 tablespoons shredded coconut, toasted
- 2 tablespoons chopped walnuts

1. In 1½-quart saucepan, heat water to boiling. Stir in oats, gingerroot and salt. Reduce heat; simmer gently uncovered 25 to 30 minutes, without stirring, until oats are tender yet slightly chewy; stir in banana. Divide oatmeal evenly among 4 bowls.
2. Top each serving with yogurt, mango, strawberries, coconut and walnuts. Serve immediately.

*Per Serving:calories: 200 / fat: 6g / protein: 5g / carbs: 31g / sugars: 16g / fiber: 4g / sodium: 110mg*

## Green Eggs and Ham

Prep time: 5 minutes / Cook time: 10 minutes / Serves 2

- 1 large Hass avocado, halved and pitted
- 2 thin slices ham
- 2 large eggs
- 2 tablespoons chopped green onions, plus more for garnish
- ½ teaspoon fine sea salt
- ¼ teaspoon ground black pepper
- ¼ cup shredded Cheddar cheese (omit for dairy-free)

1. Preheat the air fryer to 400°F (204°C).
2. Place a slice of ham into the cavity of each avocado half. Crack an egg on top of the ham, then sprinkle on the green onions, salt, and pepper.
3. Place the avocado halves in the air fryer cut side up and air fry for 10 minutes, or until the egg is cooked to your desired doneness. Top with the cheese (if using) and air fry for 30 seconds more, or until the cheese is melted. Garnish with chopped green onions.
4. Best served fresh. Store extras in an airtight container in the fridge for up to 4 days. Reheat in a preheated 350°F (177°C) air fryer for a few minutes, until warmed through.

*Per Serving:calories: 316 / fat: 25g / protein: 16g / carbs: 10g / sugars: 1g / fiber: 7g / sodium: 660mg*

## Spaghetti Squash Fritters

Prep time: 15 minutes / Cook time: 8 minutes / Serves 4

- 2 cups cooked spaghetti squash
- 2 tablespoons unsalted butter, softened
- 1 large egg
- ¼ cup blanched finely ground almond flour
- 2 stalks green onion, sliced
- ½ teaspoon garlic powder
- 1 teaspoon dried parsley

1. Remove excess moisture from the squash using a cheesecloth or kitchen towel.
2. Mix all ingredients in a large bowl. Form into four patties.
3. Cut a piece of parchment to fit your air fryer basket. Place each patty on the parchment and place into the air fryer basket.
4. Adjust the temperature to 400°F (204°C) and set the timer for 8 minutes.
5. Flip the patties halfway through the cooking time. Serve warm.

*Per Serving:calories: 146 / fat: 12g / protein: 4g / carbs: 7g / sugars: 3g / fiber: 2g / sodium: 36mg*

## Biscuits

Prep time: 15 minutes / Cook time: 15 minutes / Serves 12

- 1½ cups gluten-free all-purpose flour
- ½ cup split pea flour or chickpea flour
- ½ cup cornmeal
- 1 teaspoon baking powder
- ½ teaspoon salt
- 1 cup low-fat buttermilk
- 1 medium egg
- 2 medium egg whites

- 4 tablespoons (½ stick) unsalted non-hydrogenated plant-based butter, cold, cut into ¼-inch chunks

1. Preheat the oven to 400°F. Line a rimmed baking sheet with parchment paper.
2. In a medium bowl, whisk the gluten-free flour, split pea flour, cornmeal, baking powder, and salt together.
3. In a large bowl, beat the buttermilk, egg, and egg whites together.
4. Gently fold the dry ingredients into the wet ingredients until just combined, taking care not to overmix.
5. Add the butter to the mixture, gently working together with clean hands. Knead the dough only once or twice.
6. Transfer the dough to a clean workspace, and pat it to a 1-inch thickness.
7. Using a biscuit cutter, cut 12 biscuits, and place them, evenly spaced, onto the prepared baking sheet.
8. Transfer the baking sheet to the oven, and bake for 10 to 15 minutes, or until golden brown.

*Per Serving:calories: 139 / fat: 4g / protein: 5g / carbs: 21g / sugars: 2g / fiber: 1g / sodium: 138mg*

## Sausage Egg Cup

Prep time: 10 minutes / Cook time: 15 minutes / Serves 6

- 12 ounces (340 g) ground pork breakfast sausage
- 6 large eggs
- ½ teaspoon salt
- ¼ teaspoon ground black pepper
- ½ teaspoon crushed red pepper flakes

1. Place sausage in six 4-inch ramekins (about 2 ounces / 57 g per ramekin) greased with cooking oil. Press sausage down to cover bottom and about ½-inch up the sides of ramekins. Crack one egg into each ramekin and sprinkle evenly with salt, black pepper, and red pepper flakes.
2. Place ramekins into air fryer basket. Adjust the temperature to 350°F (177°C) and set the timer for 15 minutes. Egg cups will be done when sausage is fully cooked to at least 145°F (63°C) and the egg is firm. Serve warm.

*Per Serving:calorie: 292 / fat: 23g / protein: 18g / carbs: 1g / sugars: 0g / fiber: 0g / sodium: 616mg*

## Blueberry Cornmeal Muffins

Prep time: 5 minutes / Cook time: 25 minutes / Makes 12 muffins

- 2 cups oat flour
- ½ cup fine corn flour
- ¼ cup coconut sugar
- 2 teaspoons baking powder
- ½ teaspoon baking soda
- ¼ teaspoon sea salt
- 1 teaspoon lemon zest
- ½ cup + 2 to 3 tablespoons plain nondairy yogurt

- ¼ cup pure maple syrup
- ½ cup plain low-fat nondairy milk
- 1 teaspoon lemon juice or apple cider vinegar
- 1 cup frozen or fresh blueberries
- 1 tablespoon oat flour

1. Preheat the oven to 350°F. Line a muffin pan with 12 parchment cupcake liners.
2. In a large bowl, combine the oat flour, corn flour, sugar, baking powder, baking soda, salt, and lemon zest. Stir well. In a medium bowl, combine the yogurt, syrup, milk, and lemon juice or apple cider vinegar, and stir to combine. Add the wet ingredients to the dry and mix until just combined. Toss the berries with the oat flour, and fold them into the batter. Spoon the batter into the muffin liners. Bake for 25 minutes. Remove from the oven and let the muffins cool in the pan for a couple of minutes, then transfer to a cooling rack.

*Per Serving:1 muffin: calorie: 152 / fat: 2g / protein: 4g / carbs: 31g / sugars: 11g / fiber: 3g / sodium: 191mg*

## Polenta Porridge with Berry Swirl

Prep time: 5 minutes / Cook time: 8 minutes / Serves 4

- 1 cup frozen raspberries
- ¼ cup + 1 tablespoon pure maple syrup
- 2 cups vanilla or plain low-fat nondairy milk
- 1 cup water
- ¼ teaspoon nutmeg
- Couple pinches of sea salt
- 1 cup cornmeal
- 1 cup fresh berries for serving or 1 cup sliced ripe banana (optional)
- Sprinkle of coconut sugar for serving (optional)

1. In a blender, combine the raspberries and ¼ cup of the syrup. Blend until pureed. In a saucepan over medium-high heat, bring the milk, water, nutmeg, and salt to a boil. Reduce the heat to medium and slowly whisk in the cornmeal. Stir frequently for about 5 minutes, until the cornmeal comes to a slow bubble and thickens. Add the remaining 1 tablespoon syrup and stir to combine. Remove from the heat. Pour the porridge into bowls, and add the raspberry sauce, swirling it through the porridge with a butter knife or spoon. Serve, topping with the berries or banana (if using) and a sprinkle of coconut sugar (if using).

*Per Serving:calorie: 300 / fat: 2g / protein: 6g / carbs: 65g / sugars: 23g / fiber: 6g / sodium: 207mg*

## Cottage Cheese Almond Pancakes

Prep time: 10 minutes / Cook time: 20 minutes / Serves 4

- 2 cups low-fat cottage cheese
- 4 egg whites
- 2 eggs

- 1 tablespoon pure vanilla extract
- 1½ cups almond flour
- Nonstick cooking spray

1. Place the cottage cheese, egg whites, eggs, and vanilla in a blender and pulse to combine.
2. Add the almond flour to the blender and blend until smooth.
3. Place a large nonstick skillet over medium heat and lightly coat it with cooking spray.
4. Spoon ¼ cup of batter per pancake, 4 at a time, into the skillet. Cook the pancakes until the bottoms are firm and golden, about 4 minutes.
5. Flip the pancakes over and cook the other side until they are cooked through, about 3 minutes.
6. Remove the pancakes to a plate and repeat with the remaining batter.
7. Serve with fresh fruit.

*Per Serving:calories: 441 / fat: 32g / protein: 30g / carbs: 9g / sugars: 3g / fiber: 5g / sodium: 528mg*

## Breakfast Meatballs

Prep time: 10 minutes / Cook time: 15 minutes / Makes 18 meatballs

- 1 pound (454 g) ground pork breakfast sausage
- ½ teaspoon salt
- ¼ teaspoon ground black pepper
- ½ cup shredded sharp Cheddar cheese
- 1 ounce (28 g) cream cheese, softened
- 1 large egg, whisked

1. Combine all ingredients in a large bowl. Form mixture into eighteen 1-inch meatballs.
2. Place meatballs into ungreased air fryer basket. Adjust the temperature to 400°F (204°C) and air fry for 15 minutes, shaking basket three times during cooking. Meatballs will be browned on the outside and have an internal temperature of at least 145°F (63°C) when completely cooked. Serve warm.

*Per Serving:1 meatball: calories: 106 / fat: 9g / protein: 5g / carbs: 0g / sugars: 0g / fiber: 0g / sodium: 284mg*

## Veggie And Egg White Scramble With Pepper Jack Cheese

Prep time: 5 minutes / Cook time: 10 minutes / Serves 2

- 2 tablespoons extra-virgin olive oil
- ½ red onion, finely chopped
- 1 green bell pepper, seeded and finely chopped
- 8 large egg whites (or 4 whole large eggs), beaten
- ½ teaspoon sea salt
- 2 ounces grated pepper Jack cheese
- Salsa (optional, for serving)

1. In a medium nonstick skillet over medium-high heat, heat the olive oil until it shimmers.
2. Add the onion and bell pepper and cook, stirring occasionally, until the vegetables begin to brown, about 5 minutes.
3. Meanwhile, in a small bowl, whisk together the egg whites and salt.
4. Add the egg whites to the pan and cook, stirring, until the whites set, about 3 minutes. Add the cheese. Cook, stirring, 1 minute more.
5. Serve topped with salsa, if desired.

*Per Serving:calories: 320 / fat: 23g / protein: 22g / carbs: 7g / sugars: 4g / fiber: 2g / sodium: 584mg*

## Crepe Cakes

Prep time: 5 minutes / Cook time: 20 minutes / Serves 4

- Avocado oil cooking spray
- 4 ounces reduced-fat plain cream cheese, softened
- 2 medium bananas
- 4 large eggs
- ½ teaspoon vanilla extract
- ⅛ teaspoon salt

1. Heat a large skillet over low heat. Coat the cooking surface with cooking spray, and allow the pan to heat for another 2 to 3 minutes.
2. Meanwhile, in a medium bowl, mash the cream cheese and bananas together with a fork until combined. The bananas can be a little chunky.
3. Add the eggs, vanilla, and salt, and mix well.
4. For each cake, drop 2 tablespoons of the batter onto the warmed skillet and use the bottom of a large spoon or ladle to spread it thin. Let it cook for 7 to 9 minutes.
5. Flip the cake over and cook briefly, about 1 minute.

*Per Serving:calories: 183 / fat: 9g / protein: 9g / carbs: 16g / sugars: 9g / fiber: 2g / sodium: 251mg*

## Coconut Pancakes

Prep time: 5 minutes / Cook time: 15 to 20 minutes / Serves 4

- ½ cup coconut flour
- 1 teaspoon baking powder
- ½ teaspoon ground cinnamon
- ⅛ teaspoon salt
- 8 large eggs
- ⅓ cup unsweetened almond milk
- 2 tablespoons avocado or coconut oil
- 1 teaspoon vanilla extract

1. Heat a large skillet over medium-low heat.
2. In a large bowl, whisk together the flour, baking powder, cinnamon, and salt. Set aside.
3. In a medium bowl, whisk together the eggs, almond milk, oil, and vanilla. Pour the wet mixture into the dry ingredients and stir until combined.
4. Pour ⅓ cup of the batter onto the skillet for each pancake. Cook until bubbles appear on the surface of the pancake, about 7 minutes, then flip and cook for 1 minute more.

*Per Serving:calories: 238 / fat: 18g / protein: 13g / carbs: 4g / sugars: 1g / fiber: 3g / sodium: 236mg*

## Spinach and Mushroom Mini Quiche

Prep time: 10 minutes / Cook time: 15 minutes / Serves 4

- 1 teaspoon olive oil, plus more for spraying
- 1 cup coarsely chopped mushrooms
- 1 cup fresh baby spinach, shredded
- 4 eggs, beaten
- ½ cup shredded Cheddar cheese
- ½ cup shredded Mozzarella cheese
- ¼ teaspoon salt
- ¼ teaspoon black pepper

1. Spray 4 silicone baking cups with olive oil and set aside.
2. In a medium sauté pan over medium heat, warm 1 teaspoon of olive oil. Add the mushrooms and sauté until soft, 3 to 4 minutes.
3. Add the spinach and cook until wilted, 1 to 2 minutes. Set aside.
4. In a medium bowl, whisk together the eggs, Cheddar cheese, Mozzarella cheese, salt, and pepper.
5. Gently fold the mushrooms and spinach into the egg mixture.
6. Pour ¼ of the mixture into each silicone baking cup.
7. Place the baking cups into the air fryer basket and air fry at 350°F (177°C) for 5 minutes. Stir the mixture in each ramekin slightly and air fry until the egg has set, an additional 3 to 5 minutes.

*Per Serving:calorie: 174 / fat: 12g / protein: 13g / carbs: 3g / sugars: 1g / fiber: 1g / sodium: 346mg*

## Oatmeal Strawberry Smoothie

Prep time: 5 minutes / Cook time: 0 minutes / Serves 2

- 2 tablespoons instant oats
- 1 cup frozen strawberries
- 3 cups skim milk
- ½ teaspoon pure vanilla extract

1. Put the oats, strawberries, milk, and vanilla in a blender and blend until smooth.
2. Pour into two glasses and serve.

*Per Serving:calories: 179 / fat: 1g / protein: 14g / carbs: 27g / sugars: 18g / fiber: 3g / sodium: 156mg*

## Italian Frittata

Prep time: 10 minutes / Cook time: 30 minutes / Serves 6

- 2 tablespoons extra-virgin olive oil
- 2 medium yellow onions, sliced thinly
- 6 large eggs, beaten until foamy
- 2 cups mixed steamed vegetables (try chopped broccoli, asparagus, and red bell peppers)
- 2 teaspoons garlic, minced
- 1 bunch fresh basil, finely chopped
- ½ teaspoon freshly ground black pepper

- ¼ cup freshly grated Parmigiano-Reggiano cheese, for garnish

1. Preheat the oven to 350 degrees. Add the oil to a large, wide, ovenproof skillet and heat over medium heat.
2. Add the onions and sauté until lightly golden, approximately 5 to 10 minutes.
3. In a large bowl, combine the remaining ingredients (except the cheese), and add to the skillet.
4. Place the skillet in the oven and bake the frittata for 14 to 17 minutes until set. Remove from the oven and loosen the edges with a spatula. Sprinkle with grated cheese, cut into wedges, and serve.

*Per Serving:calories: 160 / fat: 11g / protein: g9 / carbs: 8g / sugars: 3g / fiber: 2g / sodium: 159mg*

## Cheesy Quinoa-Crusted Spinach Frittata

Prep time: 10 minutes / Cook time: 50 minutes / Serves 4

- 1 cup (170 g) uncooked quinoa
- Cooking oil spray, as needed
- ½ cup (120 ml) egg whites
- ¾ cup (90 g) shredded Cheddar cheese
- ½ tablespoon (8 ml) cooking oil of choice
- ½ medium yellow onion, diced
- 5 ounces (142 g) baby spinach
- 6 large eggs
- ⅔ cup (160 ml) 2% milk
- ½ teaspoon mustard powder
- ½ teaspoon sea salt
- ¼ teaspoon black pepper

1. In a medium pot, cook the quinoa according to the package instructions. Set the quinoa aside to cool in the pot.
2. Preheat the oven to 375°F (191°C). Spray a 9-inch (23-cm) pie dish with the cooking oil spray.
3. Once the quinoa has cooled, add the egg whites and Cheddar cheese, stirring to combine the ingredients. Carefully press the quinoa mixture into the prepared pie dish. Bake the crust for 15 minutes. Remove the crust from the oven and allow it to cool.
4. While the crust is baking, heat the oil in a medium skillet over medium heat. Add the onion and spinach and sauté them for 10 to 15 minutes, until the onion is translucent and the spinach is wilted. Set the vegetables aside to cool.
5. Meanwhile, combine the eggs, milk, mustard powder, salt, and black pepper in a medium bowl and whisk to combine the ingredients.
6. Add the sautéed vegetables to the crust and spread them into an even layer. Pour the egg mixture over the vegetables.
7. Return the frittata to the oven and bake it for 35 to 40 minutes, or until the eggs have set in the middle.

*Per Serving:calorie: 414 / fat: 19g / protein: 26g / carbs: 33g / sugars: 4g / fiber: 4g / sodium: 624mg*

# Chapter 2 Beans and Grains

## Red Beans

Prep time: 10 minutes / Cook time: 45 minutes / Serves 8

- 1 cup crushed tomatoes
- 1 medium yellow onion, chopped
- 2 garlic cloves, minced
- 2 cups dried red kidney beans
- 1 cup roughly chopped green beans
- 4 cups store-bought low-sodium vegetable broth
- 1 teaspoon smoked paprika

1. Select the Sauté setting on an electric pressure cooker, and combine the tomatoes, onion, and garlic. Cook for 3 to 5 minutes, or until softened.
2. Add the kidney beans, green beans, broth, and paprika. Stir to combine.
3. Close and lock the lid, and set the pressure valve to sealing.
4. Change to the Manual/Pressure Cook setting, and cook for 35 minutes.
5. Once cooking is complete, quick-release the pressure. Carefully remove the lid.
6. Serve.

*Per Serving:calorie: 73 / fat: 0g / protein: 4g / carbs: 14g / sugars: 4g / fiber: 4g / sodium: 167mg*

## Texas Caviar

Prep time: 10 minutes / Cook time: 0 minutes / Serves 6

- 1 cup cooked black-eyed peas
- 1 cup cooked lima beans
- 1 ear fresh corn, kernels removed
- 2 celery stalks, chopped
- 1 red bell pepper, chopped
- ½ red onion, chopped
- 3 tablespoons apple cider vinegar
- 2 tablespoons extra-virgin olive oil
- 1 teaspoon paprika

1. In a large bowl, combine the black-eyed peas, lima beans, corn, celery, bell pepper, and onion.
2. In a small bowl, to make the dressing, whisk the vinegar, oil, and paprika together.
3. Pour the dressing over the bean mixture, and gently mix. Set aside for 15 to 30 minutes, allowing the flavors to come together.

*Per Serving:calorie: 142 / fat: 5g / protein: 6g / carbs: 19g / sugars: 3g / fiber: 6g / sodium: 10mg*

## Whole-Wheat Linguine with Kale Pesto

Prep time: 10 minutes / Cook time: 20 minutes / Serves 6

- ½ cup shredded kale
- ½ cup fresh basil
- ½ cup sun-dried tomatoes
- ¼ cup chopped almonds
- 2 tablespoons extra-virgin olive oil
- 8 ounces dry whole-wheat linguine
- ½ cup grated Parmesan cheese

1. Place the kale, basil, sun-dried tomatoes, almonds, and olive oil in a food processor or blender, and pulse until a chunky paste forms, about 2 minutes. Scoop the pesto into a bowl and set it aside.
2. Place a large pot filled with water on high heat and bring to a boil.
3. Cook the pasta al dente, according to the package directions.
4. Drain the pasta and toss it with the pesto and the Parmesan cheese.
5. Serve immediately.

*Per Serving:calorie: 365 / fat: 19g / protein: 15g / carbs: 38g / sugars: 3g / fiber: 7g / sodium: 299mg*

## Coconut-Ginger Rice

Prep time: 10 minutes / Cook time: 20 minutes / Serves 8

- 2½ cups reduced-sodium chicken broth
- ⅔ cup reduced-fat (lite) coconut milk (not cream of coconut)
- 1 tablespoon grated gingerroot
- ½ teaspoon salt
- 1⅓cups uncooked regular long-grain white rice
- 1 teaspoon grated lime peel
- 3 medium green onions, chopped (3 tablespoons)
- 3 tablespoons flaked coconut, toasted*
- Lime slices

1. In 3-quart saucepan, heat broth, coconut milk, gingerroot and salt to boiling over medium-high heat. Stir in rice. Return to boiling. Reduce heat; cover and simmer about 15 minutes or until rice is tender and liquid is absorbed. Remove from heat.
2. Add lime peel and onions; fluff rice mixture lightly with fork to mix. Garnish with coconut and lime slices.

*Per Serving:calorie: 150 / fat: 2g / protein: 3g / carbs: 30g / sugars: 1g / fiber: 0g / sodium: 340mg*

## Southwestern Quinoa Salad

Prep time: 15 minutes / Cook time: 25 minutes / Serves 6

- Salad
- 1 cup uncooked quinoa
- 1 large onion, chopped (1 cup)
- 1½ cups reduced-sodium chicken broth
- 1 cup packed fresh cilantro leaves
- ¼ cup raw unsalted hulled pumpkin seeds (pepitas)
- 2 cloves garlic, sliced

- ⅛ teaspoon ground cumin
- 2 tablespoons chopped green chiles (from 4. 5-oz can)
- 1 tablespoon olive oil
- 1 can (15 ounces) no-salt-added black beans, drained, rinsed
- 6 medium plum (Roma) tomatoes, chopped (2 cups)
- 2 tablespoons lime juice
- Garnish
- 1 avocado, pitted, peeled, thinly sliced
- 4 small cilantro sprigs

1. Rinse quinoa thoroughly by placing in a fine-mesh strainer and holding under cold running water until water runs clear; drain well.
2. Spray 3-quart saucepan with cooking spray. Heat over medium heat. Add onion to pan; cook 6 to 8 minutes, stirring occasionally, until golden brown. Stir in quinoa and chicken broth. Heat to boiling; reduce heat. Cover and simmer 10 to 15 minutes or until all liquid is absorbed; remove from heat.
3. Meanwhile, in small food processor, place cilantro, pumpkin seeds, garlic and cumin. Cover; process 5 to 10 seconds, using quick on-and-off motions; scrape side. Add chiles and oil. Cover; process, using quick on-and-off motions, until paste forms.
4. To cooked quinoa, add pesto mixture and the remaining salad ingredients. Refrigerate at least 30 minutes to blend flavors.
5. To serve, divide salad evenly among 4 plates; top each serving with 3 or 4 slices avocado and 1 sprig cilantro.

*Per Serving:calorie: 310 / fat: 12g / protein: 13g / carbs: 38g / sugars: 5g / fiber: 9g / sodium: 170mg*

## Sunshine Burgers

Prep time: 10 minutes / Cook time: 18 to 20 minutes / Makes 10 burgers

- 2 cups sliced raw carrots
- 1 large clove garlic, sliced or quartered
- 2 cans (15 ounces each) chickpeas, rinsed and drained
- ¼ cup sliced dry-packed sun-dried tomatoes
- 2 tablespoons tahini
- 1 teaspoon red wine vinegar or apple cider vinegar
- 1 teaspoon smoked paprika
- ½ teaspoon dried rosemary
- ½ teaspoon ground cumin
- ½ teaspoon sea salt
- 1 cup rolled oats

1. In a food processor, combine the carrots and garlic. Pulse several times to mince. Add the chickpeas, tomatoes, tahini, vinegar, paprika, rosemary, cumin, and salt. Puree until well combined, scraping down the sides of the bowl once or twice. Add the oats, and pulse briefly to combine. Refrigerate the mixture for 30 minutes, if possible.
2. Preheat the oven to 400°F. Line a baking sheet

with parchment paper.
3. Use an ice cream scoop to scoop the mixture onto the prepared baking sheet, flattening to shape it into patties. Bake for 18 to 20 minutes, flipping the burgers halfway through. Alternatively, you can cook the burgers in a nonstick skillet over medium heat for 6 to 8 minutes Per side, or until golden brown. Serve.

*Per Serving:calorie: 137 / fat: 4 / protein: 6g / carbs: 21g / sugars: 4g / fiber: 6g / sodium: 278mg*

## Easy Lentil Burgers

Prep time: 10 minutes / Cook time: 20 minutes / Serves 5

- 1 medium-large clove garlic
- 2 tablespoons tamari
- 2 tablespoons tomato paste
- 1 tablespoon red wine vinegar
- 1½ tablespoons tahini
- 2 tablespoons fresh thyme or oregano
- 2 teaspoons onion powder
- ¼ teaspoon sea salt
- Few pinches freshly ground black pepper
- 3 cups cooked brown lentils
- 1 cup toasted breadcrumbs
- ½ cup rolled oats

1. In a food processor, combine the garlic, tamari, tomato paste, vinegar, tahini, thyme or oregano, onion powder, salt, pepper, and 1½ cups of the lentils. Puree until fairly smooth. Add the breadcrumbs, rolled oats, and the remaining 1½ cups of lentils. Pulse a few times. At this stage you're looking for a sticky texture that will hold together when pressed. If the mixture is still a little crumbly, pulse a few more times.
2. Preheat the oven to 400°F. Line a baking sheet with parchment paper.
3. Use an ice cream scoop to scoop the mixture onto the prepared baking sheet, flattening to shape into patties. Bake for about 20 minutes, flipping the burgers halfway through. Alternatively, you can cook the burgers in a nonstick skillet over medium heat for 4 to 5 minutes Per side, or until golden brown.

*Per Serving:calorie: 148 / fat: 2g / protein: 8g / carbs: 24g / sugars: 1g / fiber: 5g / sodium: 369mg*

## Herbed Beans and Brown Rice

Prep time: 15 minutes / Cook time: 15 minutes / Serves 8

- 2 teaspoons extra-virgin olive oil
- ½ sweet onion, chopped
- 1 teaspoon minced jalapeño pepper
- 1 teaspoon minced garlic
- 1 (15 ounces) can sodium-free red kidney beans, rinsed and drained
- 1 large tomato, chopped
- 1 teaspoon chopped fresh thyme

- Sea salt
- Freshly ground black pepper
- 2 cups cooked brown rice

1. Place a large skillet over medium-high heat and add the olive oil.
2. Sauté the onion, jalapeño, and garlic until softened, about 3 minutes.
3. Stir in the beans, tomato, and thyme.
4. Cook until heated through, about 10 minutes. Season with salt and pepper.
5. Serve over the warm brown rice.

*Per Serving:calorie: 97 / fat: 2g / protein: 3g / carbs: 18g / sugars: 2g / fiber: 4g / sodium: 20mg*

## Italian Bean Burgers

Prep time: 10 minutes / Cook time: 20 minutes / Makes 9 burgers

- 2 cans (14 or 15 ounces each) chickpeas, drained and rinsed
- 1 medium–large clove garlic, cut in half
- 2 tablespoons tomato paste
- 1½ tablespoons red wine vinegar (can substitute apple cider vinegar)
- 1 tablespoon tahini
- 1 teaspoon Dijon mustard
- ½ teaspoon onion powder
- Scant ½ teaspoon sea salt
- 2 tablespoons chopped fresh oregano
- ⅓ cup roughly chopped fresh basil leaves
- 1 cup rolled oats
- ⅓ cup chopped sun-dried tomatoes (not packed in oil)
- ½ cup roughly chopped kalamata or green olives

1. In a food processor, combine the chickpeas, garlic, tomato paste, vinegar, tahini, mustard, onion powder, and salt. Puree until fully combined. Add the oregano, basil, and oats, and pulse briefly. (You want to combine the ingredients but retain some of the basil's texture. ) Finally, pulse in the sun-dried tomatoes and olives, again maintaining some texture. Transfer the mixture to a bowl and refrigerate, covered, for 30 minutes or longer.
2. Preheat the oven to 400°F. Line a baking sheet with parchment paper. Use an ice cream scoop to scoop the mixture onto the prepared baking sheet, flattening to shape into patties. Bake for about 20 minutes, flipping the burgers halfway through. Alternatively, you can cook the burgers in a nonstick skillet over medium heat for 6 to 8 minutes Per side, or until golden brown. Serve.

*Per Serving:calorie: 148 / fat: 4g / protein: 6g / carbs: 23g / sugars: 4g / fiber: 6g / sodium: 387mg*

## Edamame-Tabbouleh Salad

Prep time: 20 minutes / Cook time: 10 minutes / Serves 6

- Salad
- 1 package (5. 8 ounces) roasted garlic and olive oil couscous mix
- 1¼ cups water
- 1 teaspoon olive or canola oil
- 1 bag (10 ounces) refrigerated fully cooked ready-to-eat shelled edamame (green soybeans)
- 2 medium tomatoes, seeded, chopped (1½ cups)
- 1 small cucumber, peeled, chopped (1 cup)
- ¼ cup chopped fresh parsley
- Dressing
- 1 teaspoon grated lemon peel
- 2 tablespoons lemon juice
- 1 teaspoon olive or canola oil

1. Make couscous mix as directed on package, using the water and oil.
2. In large bowl, mix couscous and remaining salad ingredients. In small bowl, mix dressing ingredients. Pour dressing over salad; mix well. Serve immediately, or cover and refrigerate until serving time.

*Per Serving:calorie: 200 / fat: 5g / protein: 10g / carbs: 28g / sugars: 3g / fiber: 4g / sodium: 270mg*

## Wild Rice with Blueberries and Pumpkin Seeds

Prep time: 15 minutes / Cook time: 45 minutes / Serves 4

- 1 tablespoon extra-virgin olive oil
- ½ sweet onion, chopped
- 2½ cups sodium-free chicken broth
- 1 cup wild rice, rinsed and drained
- Pinch sea salt
- ½ cup toasted pumpkin seeds
- ½ cup blueberries
- 1 teaspoon chopped fresh basil

1. Place a medium saucepan over medium-high heat and add the oil.
2. Sauté the onion until softened and translucent, about 3 minutes.
3. Stir in the broth and bring to a boil.
4. Stir in the rice and salt and reduce the heat to low. Cover and simmer until the rice is tender, about 40 minutes.
5. Drain off any excess broth, if necessary. Stir in the pumpkin seeds, blueberries, and basil.
6. Serve warm.

*Per Serving:calorie: 306 / fat: 15g / protein: 12g / carbs: 37g / sugars: 7g / fiber: 6g / sodium: 12mg*

## Sage and Garlic Vegetable Bake

Prep time: 30 minutes / Cook time: 1 hour 15 minutes / Serves 6

- 1 medium butternut squash, peeled, cut into 1-inch pieces (3 cups)
- 2 medium parsnips, peeled, cut into 1-inch pieces (2 cups)
- 2 cans (14. 5 ounces each) stewed tomatoes, undrained

- 2 cups frozen cut green beans
- 1 medium onion, coarsely chopped (½ cup)
- ½ cup uncooked quick-cooking barley
- ½ cup water
- 1 teaspoon dried sage leaves
- ½ teaspoon seasoned salt
- 2 cloves garlic, finely chopped

1. Heat oven to 375°F. In ungreased 3-quart casserole, mix all ingredients, breaking up large pieces of tomatoes.
2. Cover; bake 1 hour to 1 hour 15 minutes or until vegetables and barley are tender.

*Per Serving:calorie: 170 / fat: 0g / protein: 4g / carbs: 37g / sugars: 9g / fiber: 8g / sodium: 410mg*

## Quinoa Vegetable Skillet

Prep time: 15 minutes / Cook time: 15 minutes / Serves 6

- 2 cups vegetable broth
- 1 cup quinoa, well rinsed and drained
- 1 teaspoon extra-virgin olive oil
- ½ sweet onion, chopped
- 2 teaspoons minced garlic
- ½ large green zucchini, halved lengthwise and cut into half disks
- 1 red bell pepper, seeded and cut into thin strips
- 1 cup fresh or frozen corn kernels
- 1 teaspoon chopped fresh basil
- Sea salt
- Freshly ground black pepper

1. Place a medium saucepan over medium heat and add the vegetable broth. Bring the broth to a boil and add the quinoa. Cover and reduce the heat to low.
2. Cook until the quinoa has absorbed all the broth, about 15 minutes. Remove from the heat and let it cool slightly.
3. While the quinoa is cooking, place a large skillet over medium-high heat and add the oil.
4. Sauté the onion and garlic until softened and translucent, about 3 minutes.
5. Add the zucchini, bell pepper, and corn, and sauté until the vegetables are tender-crisp, about 5 minutes.
6. Remove the skillet from the heat. Add the cooked quinoa and the basil to the skillet, stirring to combine. Season with salt and pepper, and serve.

*Per Serving:calorie: 178 / fat: 2g / protein: 6g / carbs: 35g / sugars: 5g / fiber: 5g / sodium: 375mg*

## Stewed Green Beans

Prep time: 5 minutes / Cook time: 10 minutes / Serves 4

- 1 pound green beans, trimmed
- 1 medium tomato, chopped
- ½ yellow onion, chopped
- 1 garlic clove, minced
- 1 teaspoon Creole seasoning
- ¼ cup store-bought low-sodium vegetable broth

1. In an electric pressure cooker, combine the green beans, tomato, onion, garlic, Creole seasoning, and broth.
2. Close and lock the lid, and set the pressure valve to sealing.
3. Select the Manual/Pressure Cook setting, and cook for 10 minutes.
4. Once cooking is complete, quick-release the pressure. Carefully remove the lid.
5. Transfer the beans to a serving dish. Serve warm.

*Per Serving:calorie: 58 / fat: 0g / protein: 3g / carbs: 13g / sugars: 7g / fiber: 4g / sodium: 98mg*

## BBQ Bean Burgers

Prep time: 10 minutes / Cook time: 20 minutes / Makes 8 burgers

- 2 cups sliced carrots
- 1 medium-large clove garlic, quartered
- 1 can (15 ounces) kidney beans, rinsed and drained
- 1 cup cooked, cooled brown rice
- ¼ cup barbecue sauce
- ½ tablespoon vegan Worcestershire sauce
- ½ tablespoon Dijon mustard
- Scant ½ teaspoon sea salt
- ¼ to ½ teaspoon smoked paprika
- 1 tablespoon chopped fresh thyme
- 1¼ cups rolled oats

1. In a food processor, combine the carrots and garlic. Pulse until minced. Add the beans, rice, barbecue sauce, Worcestershire sauce, mustard, salt, paprika, and thyme. Puree until well combined. Once the mixture is fairly smooth, add the oats and pulse to combine. Chill the mixture for 30 minutes, if possible.
2. Preheat the oven to 400°F. Line a baking sheet with parchment paper.
3. Use an ice cream scoop to scoop the mixture onto the prepared baking sheet, flattening to shape it into patties. Bake for about 20 minutes, flipping the burgers halfway through. Alternatively, you can cook the burgers in a nonstick skillet over medium heat for 6 to 8 minutes Per side, or until golden brown.

*Per Serving:calorie: 152 / fat: 2g / protein: 6g / carbs: 29g / sugars: 6 / fiber: 5g / sodium: 247mg*

## Beet Greens and Black Beans

Prep time: 10 minutes / Cook time: 20 minutes / Serves 4

- 1 tablespoon unsalted non-hydrogenated plant-based butter
- ½ Vidalia onion, thinly sliced
- ½ cup store-bought low-sodium vegetable broth
- 1 bunch beet greens, cut into ribbons
- 1 bunch dandelion greens, cut into ribbons
- 1 (15-ounce) can no-salt-added black beans
- Freshly ground black pepper

1. In a medium skillet, melt the butter over low heat.

2. Add the onion, and sauté for 3 to 5 minutes, or until the onion is translucent.
3. Add the broth and greens. Cover the skillet and cook for 7 to 10 minutes, or until the greens are wilted.
4. Add the black beans and cook for 3 to 5 minutes, or until the beans are tender. Season with black pepper.

*Per Serving:calorie: 153 / fat: 3g / protein: 9g / carbs: 25g / sugars: 2g / fiber: 11g / sodium: 312mg*

## Veggies and Kasha with Balsamic Vinaigrette

Prep time: 15 minutes / Cook time: 8 minutes / Serves 4
- Salad
- 1 cup water
- ½ cup uncooked buckwheat kernels or groats (kasha)
- 4 medium green onions, thinly sliced (¼ cup)
- 2 medium tomatoes, seeded, coarsely chopped (1½ cups)
- 1 medium unpeeled cucumber, seeded, chopped (1¼ cups)
- Vinaigrette
- 2 tablespoons balsamic or red wine vinegar
- 1 tablespoon olive oil
- 2 teaspoons sugar
- ½ teaspoon salt
- ¼ teaspoon pepper
- 1 clove garlic, finely chopped

1. In 8-inch skillet, heat water to boiling. Add kasha; cook over medium-high heat 7 to 8 minutes, stirring occasionally, until tender. Drain if necessary.
2. In large bowl, mix kasha and remaining salad ingredients.
3. In tightly covered container, shake vinaigrette ingredients until blended. Pour vinaigrette over kasha mixture; toss. Cover; refrigerate 1 to 2 hours to blend flavors.

*Per Serving:calorie: 120 / fat: 4g / protein: 2g / carbs: 19g / sugars: 6g / fiber: 3g / sodium: 310mg*

## Curried Rice with Pineapple

Prep time: 5 minutes / Cook time: 35 minutes / Serves 8
- 1 onion, chopped
- 1½ cups water
- 1¼ cups low-sodium chicken broth
- 1 cup uncooked brown basmati rice, soaked in water 20 minutes and drained before cooking
- 2 red bell peppers, minced
- 1 teaspoon curry powder
- 1 teaspoon ground turmeric
- 1 teaspoon ground ginger
- 2 garlic cloves, minced
- One 8-ounce can pineapple chunks packed in juice, drained
- ¼ cup sliced almonds, toasted

1. In a medium saucepan, combine the onion, water, and chicken broth. Bring to a boil, and add the rice, peppers, curry powder, turmeric, ginger, and

garlic. Cover, placing a paper towel in between the pot and the lid, and reduce the heat. Simmer for 25 minutes.
2. Add the pineapple, and continue to simmer 5–7 minutes more until rice is tender and water is absorbed. Taste and add salt, if desired. Transfer to a serving bowl, and garnish with almonds to serve.

*Per Serving:calorie: 144 / fat: 3g / protein: 4g / carbs: 27g / sugars: 6g / fiber: 3g / sodium: 16mg*

## Colorful Rice Casserole

Prep time: 5 minutes / Cook time: 20 minutes / Serves 12
- 1 tablespoon extra-virgin olive oil
- 1½ pounds zucchini, thinly sliced
- ¾ cup chopped scallions
- 2 cups corn kernels (frozen or fresh; if frozen, defrost)
- One 14. 5-ounce can no-salt-added chopped tomatoes, undrained
- ¼ cup chopped parsley
- 1 teaspoon oregano
- 3 cups cooked brown (or white) rice
- ⅛ teaspoon freshly ground black pepper

1. In a large skillet, heat the oil. Add the zucchini and scallions, and sauté for 5 minutes.
2. Add the remaining ingredients, cover, reduce heat, and simmer for 10–15 minutes or until the vegetables are heated through. Season with salt, if desired, and pepper. Transfer to a bowl, and serve.

*Per Serving:calorie: 109 / fat: 2g / protein: 3g / carbs: 21g / sugars: 4g / fiber: 3g / sodium: 14mg*

## Rice with Spinach and Feta

Prep time: 10 minutes / Cook time: 15 minutes / Serves 4
- ¾ cup uncooked brown rice
- 1½ cups water
- 1 tablespoon extra-virgin olive oil
- 1 medium onion, diced
- 1 cup sliced mushrooms
- 2 garlic cloves, minced
- 1 tablespoon lemon juice
- ½ teaspoon dried oregano
- 9 cups fresh spinach, stems trimmed, washed, patted dry, and coarsely chopped
- ⅓ cup crumbled fat-free feta cheese
- ⅛ teaspoon freshly ground black pepper

1. In a medium saucepan over medium heat, combine the rice and water. Bring to a boil, cover, reduce heat, and simmer for 15 minutes. Transfer to a serving bowl.
2. In a skillet, heat the oil. Sauté the onion, mushrooms, and garlic for 5 to 7 minutes. Stir in the lemon juice and oregano. Add the spinach, cheese, and pepper, tossing until the spinach is slightly wilted.
3. Toss with rice and serve.

*Per Serving:calorie: 205 / fat: 5g / protein: 7g / carbs: 34g / sugars: 2g / fiber: 4g / sodium: 129mg*

# Chapter 3 Poultry

## Chicken Paprika

Prep time: 5 minutes / Cook time: 35 minutes / Serves 8

- 1 tablespoon extra-virgin olive oil
- 1 large onion, minced
- 1 medium red bell pepper, julienned
- 1 cup sliced fresh mushrooms
- 1 to 2 teaspoons smoked paprika
- 2 tablespoons lemon juice
- teaspoon salt
- ⅛ teaspoon freshly ground black pepper
- Four 8 ounces boneless, skinless chicken breasts, halved
- 8 ounces plain low-fat Greek yogurt

1. Heat the oil in a large skillet over medium heat. Add the onion, red pepper, and mushrooms, and sauté until tender, about 3 to 4 minutes.
2. Add 1 cup of water, the paprika, lemon juice, salt, and pepper, blending well. Bring the mixture to a boil over high heat, and reduce the heat to medium. Add the chicken; cover, and let simmer for 25 to 30 minutes or until the chicken is no longer pink.
3. Reduce the heat to low, quickly stir in the Greek yogurt, mixing well, and continue to cook for 1 to 2 minutes. Do not boil. Serve hot.

*Per Serving:calorie: 184 / fat: 5g / protein: 29g / carbs: 4g / sugars: 3g / fiber: 1g / sodium: 209mg*

## Sautéed Chicken with Artichoke Hearts

Prep time: 5 minutes / Cook time: 20 minutes / Serves 4

- Nonstick cooking spray
- Three 8-ounce boneless, skinless chicken breasts, halved
- ½ cup low-sodium chicken stock
- ¼ cup dry white wine
- Two 8-ounce cans artichoke hearts, packed in water, drained and quartered
- 1 medium onion, diced
- 1 medium green bell pepper, chopped
- 2 tablespoons minced fresh tarragon or mint
- ¼ teaspoon white pepper
- 2 teaspoons cornstarch
- 1 tablespoon cold water
- 2 medium tomatoes, cut into wedges

1. Coat a large skillet with nonstick cooking spray; place over medium heat until hot. Add the chicken, and sauté until lightly browned, about 3–4 minutes per side.
2. Add the chicken stock, wine, artichokes, onion, green pepper, tarragon or mint, and white pepper; stir well. Bring to a boil, cover, reduce heat, and let simmer for 10–15 minutes or until the chicken is no longer pink and the vegetables are just tender.
3. In a small bowl, combine the cornstarch and water; add to the chicken mixture along with the tomato wedges, stirring until the mixture has thickened. Remove from the heat, and serve.

*Per Serving:calorie: 310 / fat: 5g / protein: 44g / carbs: 21g / sugars: 5g / fiber: 8g / sodium: 199mg*

## Saffron-Spiced Chicken Breasts

Prep time: 10 minutes / Cook time: 10 minutes / Serves 4

- Pinch saffron (3 or 4 threads)
- ½ cup plain nonfat yogurt
- 2 tablespoons water
- ½ onion, chopped
- 3 garlic cloves, minced
- 2 tablespoons chopped fresh cilantro
- Juice of ½ lemon
- ½ teaspoon salt
- 1 pound boneless, skinless chicken breasts, cut into 2-inch strips
- 1 tablespoon extra-virgin olive oil

1. In a blender jar, combine the saffron, yogurt, water, onion, garlic, cilantro, lemon juice, and salt. Pulse to blend.
2. In a large mixing bowl, combine the chicken and the yogurt sauce, and stir to coat. Cover and refrigerate for at least 1 hour or up to overnight.
3. In a large skillet, heat the oil over medium heat. Add the chicken pieces, shaking off any excess marinade. Discard the marinade. Cook the chicken pieces on each side for 5 minutes, flipping once, until cooked through and golden brown.

*Per Serving:calories: 155 / fat: 5g / protein: 26g / carbs: 3g / sugars: 1g / fiber: 0g / sodium: 501mg*

## Kung Pao Chicken and Zucchini Noodles

Prep time: 15 minutes / Cook time: 15 minutes / Serves 2

- For the noodles:
- 2 medium zucchini, ends trimmed
- For the sauce:
- 1½ tablespoons low-sodium soy sauce
- 1 tablespoon balsamic vinegar
- 1 teaspoon hoisin sauce
- 2½ tablespoons water
- 1½ teaspoons red chili paste

- 2 teaspoons granulated stevia
- 2 teaspoons cornstarch
- For the chicken:
- 6 ounces boneless skinless chicken breast, cut into ½-inch pieces
- Salt, to season
- Freshly ground black pepper, to season
- 1 teaspoon extra-virgin olive oil
- 1 teaspoon sesame oil
- 2 garlic cloves, minced
- 1 tablespoon chopped fresh ginger
- ½ red bell pepper, cut into ½-inch pieces
- ½ (8-ounce) can water chestnuts, drained and sliced
- 1 celery stalk, cut into ¾-inch dice
- 2 tablespoons crushed dry-roasted peanuts, divided
- 2 tablespoons scallions, divided

1. To make the noodles: 1. With a spiralizer or julienne peeler, cut the zucchini lengthwise into spaghetti-like strips. Set aside. To make the sauce: 1. In a small bowl, whisk together the soy sauce, balsamic vinegar, hoisin sauce, water, red chili paste, stevia, and cornstarch. Set aside. To make the chicken: 1. Season the chicken with salt and pepper.
2. In a large, deep nonstick pan or wok set over medium-high heat, heat the olive oil.
3. Add the chicken. Cook for 4 to 5 minutes, stirring, or until browned and cooked through. Transfer the chicken to a plate. Set aside.
4. Return the pan to the stove. Reduce the heat to medium.
5. Add the sesame oil, garlic, and ginger. Cook for about 30 seconds, or until fragrant.
6. Add the red bell pepper, water chestnuts, and celery.
7. Stir in the sauce. Bring to a boil. Reduce the heat to low. Simmer for 1 to 2 minutes, until thick and bubbling.
8. Stir in the zucchini noodles. Cook for about 2 minutes, tossing, until just tender and mixed with the sauce.
9. Add the chicken and any accumulated juices. Stir to combine. Cook for about 2 minutes, or until heated through.
10. Divide the mixture between 2 bowls. Top each serving with 1 tablespoon of peanuts and 1 tablespoon of scallions. Enjoy!

*Per Serving:calorie: 322 / fat: 13g / protein: 29g / carbs: 28g / sugars: 12g / fiber: 8g / sodium: 553mg*

## Taco Stuffed Sweet Potatoes

Prep time: 5 minutes / Cook time: 15 minutes / Serves 4
- 4 medium sweet potatoes
- 2 tablespoons extra-virgin olive oil
- 1 pound 93% lean ground turkey
- 2 teaspoons ground cumin
- 1 teaspoon chili powder
- ½ teaspoon salt
- ½ teaspoon freshly ground black pepper

1. Pierce the potatoes with a fork, and microwave them on the potato setting, or for 10 minutes on high power.
2. Meanwhile, heat a medium skillet over medium heat. When hot, put the oil, turkey, cumin, chili powder, salt, and pepper into the skillet, stirring and breaking apart the meat, as needed.
3. Remove the potatoes from the microwave and halve them lengthwise. Depress the centers with a spoon, and fill each half with an equal amount of cooked turkey.

*Per Serving:calorie: 348 / fat: 17g / protein: 24g / carbs: 27g / sugars: 6g / fiber: 4g / sodium: 462mg*

## Cilantro Lime Chicken Thighs

Prep time: 15 minutes / Cook time: 22 minutes / Serves 4
- 4 bone-in, skin-on chicken thighs
- 1 teaspoon baking powder
- ½ teaspoon garlic powder
- 2 teaspoons chili powder
- 1 teaspoon cumin
- 2 medium limes
- ¼ cup chopped fresh cilantro

1. Pat chicken thighs dry and sprinkle with baking powder.
2. In a small bowl, mix garlic powder, chili powder, and cumin and sprinkle evenly over thighs, gently rubbing on and under chicken skin.
3. Cut one lime in half and squeeze juice over thighs. Place chicken into the air fryer basket.
4. Adjust the temperature to 380°F (193°C) and roast for 22 minutes.
5. Cut other lime into four wedges for serving and garnish cooked chicken with wedges and cilantro.

*Per Serving:calorie: 293 / fat: 19g / protein: 26g / carbs: 6g / sugars: 1g / fiber: 2g / sodium: 355mg*

## Turkey Chili

Prep time: 15 minutes / Cook time: 30 minutes / Serves 6
- 1 tablespoon extra-virgin olive oil
- 1 pound lean ground turkey
- 1 large onion, diced
- 3 garlic cloves, minced
- 1 red bell pepper, seeded and diced
- 1 cup chopped celery
- 2 tablespoons chili powder
- 1 tablespoon ground cumin
- 1 (28-ounce) can reduced-salt diced tomatoes

- 1 (15-ounce) can low-sodium kidney beans, drained and rinsed
- 2 cups low-sodium chicken broth
- ½ teaspoon salt
- Shredded cheddar cheese, for serving (optional)

1. In a large pot, heat the oil over medium heat. Add the turkey, onion, and garlic, and cook, stirring regularly, until the turkey is cooked through.
2. Add the bell pepper, celery, chili powder, and cumin. Stir well and continue to cook for 1 minute.
3. Add the tomatoes with their liquid, kidney beans, and chicken broth. Bring to a boil, reduce the heat to low, and simmer for 20 minutes.
4. Season with the salt and serve topped with cheese (if using).

*Per Serving:calorie: 276 / fat: 10g / protein: 23g / carbs: 27g / sugars: 7g / fiber: 8g / sodium: 556mg*

## Chicken Patties

Prep time: 15 minutes / Cook time: 12 minutes / Serves 4
- 1 pound (454 g) ground chicken thigh meat
- ½ cup shredded Mozzarella cheese
- 1 teaspoon dried parsley
- ½ teaspoon garlic powder
- ¼ teaspoon onion powder
- 1 large egg
- 2 ounces (57 g) pork rinds, finely ground

1. In a large bowl, mix ground chicken, Mozzarella, parsley, garlic powder, and onion powder. Form into four patties.
2. Place patties in the freezer for 15 to 20 minutes until they begin to firm up.
3. Whisk egg in a medium bowl. Place the ground pork rinds into a large bowl.
4. Dip each chicken patty into the egg and then press into pork rinds to fully coat. Place patties into the air fryer basket.
5. Adjust the temperature to 360ºF (182ºC) and air fry for 12 minutes.
6. Patties will be firm and cooked to an internal temperature of 165ºF (74ºC) when done. Serve immediately.

*Per Serving:calorie: 394 / fat: 26g / protein: 35g / carbs: 2g / sugars: 0g / fiber: 0g / sodium: 563mg*

## Jerk Chicken Thighs

Prep time: 30 minutes / Cook time: 15 to 20 minutes / Serves 6
- 2 teaspoons ground coriander
- 1 teaspoon ground allspice
- 1 teaspoon cayenne pepper
- 1 teaspoon ground ginger
- 1 teaspoon salt
- 1 teaspoon dried thyme
- ½ teaspoon ground cinnamon
- ½ teaspoon ground nutmeg
- 2 pounds (907 g) boneless chicken thighs, skin on
- 2 tablespoons olive oil

1. In a small bowl, combine the coriander, allspice, cayenne, ginger, salt, thyme, cinnamon, and nutmeg. Stir until thoroughly combined.
2. Place the chicken in a baking dish and use paper towels to pat dry. Thoroughly coat both sides of the chicken with the spice mixture. Cover and refrigerate for at least 2 hours, preferably overnight.
3. Preheat the air fryer to 360ºF (182ºC).
4. Working in batches if necessary, arrange the chicken in a single layer in the air fryer basket and lightly coat with the olive oil. Pausing halfway through the cooking time to flip the chicken, air fry for 15 to 20 minutes, until a thermometer inserted into the thickest part registers 165ºF (74ºC).

*Per Serving:calorie: 377 / fat: 24g / protein: 35g / carbs: 3g / sugars: 0g / fiber: 1g / sodium: 583mg*

## One-Pan Chicken Dinner

Prep time: 5 minutes / Cook time: 35 minutes / Serves 4
- 3 tablespoons extra-virgin olive oil
- 1 tablespoon red wine vinegar or apple cider vinegar
- ¼ teaspoon garlic powder
- 3 tablespoons Italian seasoning
- 4 (4-ounce) boneless, skinless chicken breasts
- 2 cups cubed sweet potatoes
- 20 Brussels sprouts, halved lengthwise

1. Preheat the oven to 400ºF.
2. In a large bowl, whisk together the oil, vinegar, garlic powder, and Italian seasoning.
3. Add the chicken, sweet potatoes, and Brussels sprouts, and coat thoroughly with the marinade.
4. Remove the ingredients from the marinade and arrange them on a baking sheet in a single layer. Roast for 15 minutes.
5. Remove the baking sheet from the oven, flip the chicken over, and bake for another 15 to 20 minutes.

*Per Serving:calorie: 346 / fat: 13g / protein: 30g / carbs: 26g / sugars: 6g / fiber: 7g / sodium: 575mg*

## Garlic Galore Rotisserie Chicken

Prep time: 5 minutes / Cook time: 3 minutes / Serves 4
- 3 pounds whole chicken
- 2 tablespoons olive oil, divided
- Salt to taste
- Pepper to taste
- 20 to 30 cloves fresh garlic, peeled and left whole
- 1 cup low-sodium chicken stock, broth, or water
- 2 tablespoons garlic powder

- 2 teaspoons onion powder
- ½ teaspoon basil
- ½ teaspoon cumin
- ½ teaspoon chili powder

1. Rub chicken with one tablespoon of the olive oil and sprinkle with salt and pepper.
2. Place the garlic cloves inside the chicken. Use butcher's twine to secure the legs.
3. Press the Sauté button on the Instant Pot, then add the rest of the olive oil to the inner pot.
4. When the pot is hot, place the chicken inside. You are just trying to sear it, so leave it for about 4 minutes on each side.
5. Remove the chicken and set aside. Place the trivet at the bottom of the inner pot and pour in the chicken stock.
6. Mix together the remaining seasonings and rub them all over the entire chicken.
7. Place the chicken back inside the inner pot, breast-side up, on top of the trivet and secure the lid to the sealing position.
8. Press the Manual button and use the +/- to set it for 25 minutes.
9. When the timer beeps, allow the pressure to release naturally for 15 minutes. If the lid will not open at this point, quick release the remaining pressure and remove the chicken.
10. Let the chicken rest for 5–10 minutes before serving.

*Per Serving:calories: 333 / fat: 23g / protein: 24g / carbs: 9g / sugars: 0g / fiber: 1g / sodium: 110mg*

## Ground Turkey Tetrazzini

Prep time: 5 minutes / Cook time: 20 minutes / Serves 6

- 1 tablespoon extra-virgin olive oil
- 2 garlic cloves, minced
- 1 yellow onion, diced
- 8 ounces cremini or button mushrooms, sliced
- ½ teaspoon fine sea salt
- ¼ teaspoon freshly ground black pepper
- 1 pound 93 percent lean ground turkey
- 1 teaspoon poultry seasoning
- 6 ounces whole-grain extra-broad egg-white pasta (such as No Yolks brand) or whole-wheat elbow pasta
- 2 cups low-sodium chicken broth
- 1½ cups frozen green peas, thawed
- 3 cups baby spinach
- Three ¾-ounce wedges Laughing Cow creamy light Swiss cheese, or 2 tablespoons Neufchâtel cheese, at room temperature
- ⅓ cup grated Parmesan cheese
- 1 tablespoon chopped fresh flat-leaf parsley

1. Select the Sauté setting on the Instant Pot and heat the oil and garlic for 2 minutes, until the garlic is bubbling but not browned. Add the onion, mushrooms, salt, and pepper and sauté for about 5 minutes, until the mushrooms have wilted and begun to give up their liquid. Add the turkey and poultry seasoning and sauté, using a wooden spoon or spatula to break up the meat as it cooks, for about 4 minutes more, until cooked through and no streaks of pink remain.
2. Stir in the pasta. Pour in the broth and use the spoon or spatula to nudge the pasta into the liquid as much as possible. It's fine if some pieces are not completely submerged.
3. Secure the lid and set the Pressure Release to Sealing. Press the Cancel button to reset the cooking program, then select the Pressure Cook or Manual setting and set the cooking time for 5 minutes at high pressure. (The pot will take about 5 minutes to come up to pressure before the cooking program begins. )
4. When the cooking program ends, let the pressure release naturally for 5 minutes, then move the Pressure Release to Venting to release any remaining steam. Open the pot and stir in the peas, spinach, Laughing Cow cheese, and Parmesan. Let stand for 2 minutes, then stir the mixture once more.
5. Ladle into bowls or onto plates and sprinkle with the parsley. Serve right away.

*Per Serving:calories: 321 / fat: 11g / protein: 26g / carbs: 35g / sugars: 4g / fiber: 5g / sodium: 488mg*

## Unstuffed Peppers with Ground Turkey and Quinoa

Prep time: 0 minutes / Cook time: 35 minutes / Serves 8

- 2 tablespoons extra-virgin olive oil
- 1 yellow onion, diced
- 2 celery stalks, diced
- 2 garlic cloves, chopped
- 2 pounds 93 percent lean ground turkey
- 2 teaspoons Cajun seasoning blend (plus 1 teaspoon fine sea salt if using a salt-free blend)
- ½ teaspoon freshly ground black pepper
- ¼ teaspoon cayenne pepper
- 1 cup quinoa, rinsed
- 1 cup low-sodium chicken broth
- One 14½-ounce can fire-roasted diced tomatoes and their liquid
- 3 red, orange, and/or yellow bell peppers, seeded and cut into 1-inch squares
- 1 green onion, white and green parts, thinly sliced
- 1½ tablespoons chopped fresh flat-leaf parsley
- Hot sauce (such as Crystal or Frank's RedHot) for serving

1. Select the Sauté setting on the Instant Pot and heat the oil for 2 minutes. Add the onion, celery,

and garlic and sauté for about 4 minutes, until the onion begins to soften. Add the turkey, Cajun seasoning, black pepper, and cayenne and sauté, using a wooden spoon or spatula to break up the meat as it cooks, for about 6 minutes, until cooked through and no streaks of pink remain.

2. Sprinkle the quinoa over the turkey in an even layer. Pour the broth and the diced tomatoes and their liquid over the quinoa, spreading the tomatoes on top. Sprinkle the bell peppers over the top in an even layer.
3. Secure the lid and set the Pressure Release to Sealing. Press the Cancel button to reset the cooking program, then select the Pressure Cook or Manual setting and set the cooking time for 8 minutes at high pressure. (The pot will take about 15 minutes to come up to pressure before the cooking program begins. )
4. When the cooking program ends, let the pressure release naturally for at least 15 minutes, then move the Pressure Release to Venting to release any remaining steam. Open the pot and sprinkle the green onion and parsley over the top in an even layer.
5. Spoon the unstuffed peppers into bowls, making sure to dig down to the bottom of the pot so each person gets an equal amount of peppers, quinoa, and meat. Serve hot, with hot sauce on the side.

*Per Serving:calories: 320 / fat: 14g / protein: 27g / carbs: 23g / sugars: 3g / fiber: 3g / sodium: 739mg*

## Lemon Chicken

Prep time: 5 minutes / Cook time: 20 to 25 minutes / Serves 4

- 8 bone-in chicken thighs, skin on
- 1 tablespoon olive oil
- 1½ teaspoons lemon-pepper seasoning
- ½ teaspoon paprika
- ½ teaspoon garlic powder
- ¼ teaspoon freshly ground black pepper
- Juice of ½ lemon

1. Preheat the air fryer to 360ºF (182ºC).
2. Place the chicken in a large bowl and drizzle with the olive oil. Top with the lemon-pepper seasoning, paprika, garlic powder, and freshly ground black pepper. Toss until thoroughly coated.
3. Working in batches if necessary, arrange the chicken in a single layer in the basket of the air fryer. Pausing halfway through the cooking time to turn the chicken, air fry for 20 to 25 minutes, until a thermometer inserted into the thickest piece registers 165ºF (74ºC).
4. Transfer the chicken to a serving platter and squeeze the lemon juice over the top.

*Per Serving:calorie: 386 / fat: 27g / protein: 30g /*

*carbs: 2g / sugars: 0g / fiber: 0g / sodium: 332mg*

## Crispy Baked Drumsticks with Mustard Sauce

Prep time: 15 minutes / Cook time: 30 minutes / Serves 2

- For The Chicken
- Extra-virgin olive oil cooking spray
- ⅓ cup almond meal
- ¼ teaspoon paprika
- ¼ teaspoon onion powder
- ¼ teaspoon salt
- 2 teaspoons extra-virgin olive oil
- 1 large egg
- 4 (4-ounce) skinless chicken drumsticks, trimmed
- For The Mustard Sauce
- 2 tablespoons plain nonfat Greek yogurt
- 1 tablespoon Dijon mustard
- ¼ teaspoon liquid stevia
- Freshly ground black pepper, to season

1. Make The Chicken: 1. Preheat the oven to 475ºF.
2. Coat a wire rack with cooking spray. Place the rack on a large rimmed baking sheet.
3. In a shallow dish, stir together the almond meal, paprika, onion powder, and salt. Drizzle with the olive oil. Mash together with a fork until the oil is thoroughly incorporated.
4. In another shallow dish, lightly beat the egg with a fork.
5. Working with 1 drumstick at a time, dip each into the egg, then press into the almond meal mixture, coating evenly on both sides. Place the chicken on the prepared rack. Repeat until all pieces are coated.
6. Place the sheet in the preheated oven. Bake for 25 to 30 minutes, or until golden and an instant-read thermometer inserted into the thickest part of a drumstick without touching the bone registers 165ºF. Make The Mustard Sauce: 1. In a small bowl, stir together the yogurt, mustard, and stevia. Season with pepper. 2. Serve the sauce with the drumsticks.

*Per Serving:calorie: 423 / fat: 22g / protein: 51g / carbs: 5g / sugars: 2g / fiber: 2g / sodium: 425mg*

## Pizza in a Pot

Prep time: 25 minutes / Cook time: 15 minutes / Serves 8

- 1 pound bulk lean sweet Italian turkey sausage, browned and drained
- 28 ounces can crushed tomatoes
- 15½ ounces can chili beans
- 2¼ ounces can sliced black olives, drained
- 1 medium onion, chopped
- 1 small green bell pepper, chopped
- 2 garlic cloves, minced
- ¼ cup grated Parmesan cheese
- 1 tablespoon quick-cooking tapioca

- 1 tablespoon dried basil
- 1 bay leaf

1. Set the Instant Pot to Sauté, then add the turkey sausage. Sauté until browned.
2. Add the remaining ingredients into the Instant Pot and stir.
3. Secure the lid and make sure the vent is set to sealing. Cook on Manual for 15 minutes.
4. When cook time is up, let the pressure release naturally for 5 minutes then perform a quick release. Discard bay leaf.

*Per Serving:calorie: 251 / fat: 10g / protein: 18g / carbs: 23g / sugars: 8g / fiber: 3g / sodium: 936mg*

## Mediterranean-Style Chicken Scaloppine

Prep time: 15 minutes / Cook time: 1 hour / Serves

- Six 3-ounce boneless, skinless chicken breast halves
- 2 cups fat-free Greek yogurt
- ¼ cup lemon juice
- Zest of 1 lemon
- ¼ cup freshly chopped baby dill
- 2 teaspoons paprika
- 2 garlic cloves, minced
- ½ teaspoon salt
- ¼ teaspoon freshly ground black pepper
- 1 cup dried whole-wheat bread crumbs
- 2½ cups frozen artichoke hearts, thawed
- 2 tablespoons extra-virgin olive oil
- ¼ cup finely chopped fresh parsley
- 1 lemon, sliced

1. Wash chicken breasts under cold running water, and pat dry.
2. In a medium bowl, combine the yogurt, lemon juice, lemon zest, baby dill, paprika, garlic, salt, and pepper. Measure out ½ cup of this marinade, and reserve the rest in the refrigerator.
3. Add the chicken to the ½ cup of marinade, and coat each piece well. Refrigerate overnight.
4. Preheat the oven to 350 degrees.
5. Remove the chicken from the marinade, discard the marinade, and roll the chicken in bread crumbs, coating evenly.
6. Arrange the chicken in a single layer in a large baking pan. Add the artichoke hearts in with the chicken. Drizzle the olive oil over the chicken and artichokes. Bake at 350 degrees, uncovered, for 45 minutes, or until the chicken is no longer pink.
7. Transfer to a serving platter, and serve with the remaining marinade as a sauce and parsley and lemon slices as a garnish.

*Per Serving:calorie: 344 / fat: 11g / protein: 40g / carbs: 23g / sugars: 11g / fiber: 6g / sodium: 502mg*

## Orange Chicken Thighs with Bell Peppers

Prep time: 15 to 20 minutes / Cook time: 7 minutes / Serves 4 to 6

- 6 boneless skinless chicken thighs, cut into bite-sized pieces
- 2 packets crystallized True Orange flavoring
- ½ teaspoon True Orange Orange Ginger seasoning
- ½ teaspoon coconut aminos
- ¼ teaspoon Worcestershire sauce
- Olive oil or cooking spray
- 2 cups bell pepper strips, any color combination (I used red)
- 1 onion, chopped
- 1 tablespoon green onion, chopped fine
- 3 cloves garlic, minced or chopped
- ½ teaspoon pink salt
- ½ teaspoon black pepper
- 1 teaspoon garlic powder
- 1 teaspoon ground ginger
- ¼ to ½ teaspoon red pepper flakes
- 2 tablespoons tomato paste
- ½ cup chicken bone broth or water
- 1 tablespoon brown sugar substitute (I use Sukrin Gold)
- ½ cup Seville orange spread (I use Crofter's brand)

1. Combine the chicken with the 2 packets of crystallized orange flavor, the orange ginger seasoning, the coconut aminos, and the Worcestershire sauce. Set aside.
2. Turn the Instant Pot to Sauté and add a touch of olive oil or cooking spray to the inner pot. Add in the orange ginger marinated chicken thighs.
3. Sauté until lightly browned. Add in the peppers, onion, green onion, garlic, and seasonings. Mix well.
4. Add the remaining ingredients; mix to combine.
5. Lock the lid, set the vent to sealing, set to 7 minutes.
6. Let the pressure release naturally for 2 minutes, then manually release the rest when cook time is up.

*Per Serving:calories: 120/ fat: 2g / protein: 12g / carbs: 8g / sugars: 10g / fiber: 2g / sodium: 315mg*

## Wine-Poached Chicken with Herbs and Vegetables

Prep time: 5 minutes / Cook time: 1 hour / Serves 8

- 4 quarts low-sodium chicken broth
- 2 cups dry white wine
- 4 large bay leaves
- 4 sprigs fresh thyme
- ¼ teaspoon freshly ground black pepper
- 4-pound chicken, giblets removed, washed and patted dry
- ½ pound carrots, peeled and julienned
- ½ pound turnips, peeled and julienned

- ½ pound parsnips, peeled and julienned
- 4 small leeks, washed and trimmed

1. In a large stockpot, combine the broth, wine, bay leaves, thyme, dash salt (optional), and pepper. Let simmer over medium heat while you prepare the chicken.
2. Stuff the cavity with ⅓ each of the carrots, turnips, and parsnips; then truss. Add the stuffed chicken to the stockpot, and poach, covered, over low heat for 30 minutes.
3. Add the remaining vegetables with the leeks, and continue to simmer for 25–30 minutes, or until juices run clear when the chicken is pierced with a fork.
4. Remove the chicken and vegetables to a serving platter. Carve the chicken, remove the skin, and surround the sliced meat with poached vegetables to serve.

*Per Serving:calorie: 476 / fat: 13g / protein: 57g / carbs: 24g / sugars: 6g / fiber: 4g / sodium: 387mg*

## Chicken with Creamy Thyme Sauce

Prep time: 15 minutes / Cook time: 30 minutes / Serves 4

- 4 (4-ounce) boneless, skinless chicken breasts
- Sea salt
- Freshly ground black pepper
- 1 tablespoon extra-virgin olive oil
- ½ sweet onion, chopped
- 1 cup low-sodium chicken broth
- 2 teaspoons chopped fresh thyme
- ¼ cup heavy (whipping) cream
- 1 tablespoon butter
- 1 scallion, white and green parts, chopped

1. Preheat the oven to 375°F.
2. Season the chicken breasts lightly with salt and pepper.
3. Place a large ovenproof skillet over medium-high heat and add the olive oil.
4. Brown the chicken, turning once, about 10 minutes in total. Transfer the chicken to a plate.
5. In the same skillet, sauté the onion until softened and translucent, about 3 minutes.
6. Add the chicken broth and thyme, and simmer until the liquid has reduced by half, about 6 minutes.
7. Stir in the cream and butter, and return the chicken and any accumulated juices from the plate to the skillet.
8. Transfer the skillet to the oven. Bake until cooked through, about 10 minutes.
9. Serve topped with the chopped scallion.

*Per Serving:calorie: 240 / fat: 12g / protein: 27g / carbs: 4g / sugars: 2g / fiber: 0g / sodium: 231mg*

## Grilled Herb Chicken with Wine and Roasted Garlic

Prep time: 5 minutes / Cook time: 45 minutes / Serves 4

- Four 3-ounce boneless, skinless chicken breast halves
- 2 tablespoons extra-virgin olive oil, divided
- 1 cup red wine
- 3 sprigs fresh thyme
- 5 garlic cloves, minced
- 5 garlic cloves, whole and unpeeled
- ⅛ teaspoon freshly ground black pepper

1. In a plastic zippered bag, place chicken, 1 tablespoon of the oil, wine, thyme, and minced garlic. Marinate for 2–3 hours in the refrigerator.
2. Preheat the oven to 375 degrees.
3. Spread the whole garlic cloves on a cookie sheet, drizzle with the remaining oil, and sprinkle with pepper. Bake for 30 minutes, stirring occasionally, until soft.
4. When cool, squeeze the garlic paste from the cloves, and mash in a small bowl with a fork.
5. Remove the chicken from the marinade, and grill for 12–15 minutes, turning frequently and brushing with garlic paste. Transfer to a platter, and serve hot.

*Per Serving:calorie: 222 / fat: 9g / protein: 20g / carbs: 4g / sugars: 0g / fiber: 0g / sodium: 40mg*

## Chicken Satay Stir-Fry

Prep time: 10 minutes / Cook time: 15 minutes / Serves 4

- 3 tablespoons extra-virgin olive oil
- 1 pound chicken breasts or thighs, cut into ¾-inch pieces
- ½ teaspoon sea salt
- 2 cups broccoli florets
- 1 red bell pepper, seeded and chopped
- 6 scallions, green and white parts, sliced on the bias (cut diagonally into thin slices)
- 1 head cauliflower, riced
- Peanut Sauce

1. In a large skillet over medium-high heat, heat the olive oil until it shimmers.
2. Season the chicken with the salt. Add the chicken to the oil and cook, stirring occasionally, until opaque, about 5 minutes. Remove the chicken from the oil with a slotted spoon and set it aside on a plate. Return the pan to the heat.
3. Add the broccoli, bell pepper, and scallions. Cook, stirring, until the vegetables are crisp-tender, 3 to 5 minutes. Add the cauliflower and cook for 3 minutes more.
4. Return the chicken to the skillet. Stir in the Peanut Sauce. Bring to a simmer and reduce heat to

medium-low. Simmer to heat through, about 2 minutes more.

*Per Serving:calorie: 283 / fat: 15g / protein: 26g / carbs: 11g / sugars: 4g / fiber: 4g / sodium: 453mg*

## Chicken Provençal

Prep time: 5 minutes / Cook time: 25 minutes / Serves 4

- 2 tablespoons extra-virgin olive oil
- Two 8-ounce boneless, skinless chicken breasts, halved
- 1 medium garlic clove, minced
- ¼ cup minced onion
- ¼ cup minced green bell pepper
- ½ cup dry white wine
- 1 cup canned diced tomatoes
- ¼ cup pitted Kalamata olives
- ¼ cup finely chopped fresh basil
- ⅛ teaspoon freshly ground black pepper

1. Heat the oil in a skillet over medium heat. Add the chicken, and brown about 3–5 minutes.
2. Add the remaining ingredients, and cook uncovered over medium heat for 20 minutes or until the chicken is no longer pink. Transfer to a serving platter and season with additional pepper to taste, if desired, before serving.

*Per Serving:calorie: 245 / fat: 11g / protein: 26g / carbs: 5g / sugars: 2g / fiber: 2g / sodium: 121mg*

## Pulled BBQ Chicken and Texas-Style Cabbage Slaw

Prep time: 5 minutes / Cook time: 20 minutes / Serves 6

- Chicken
- 1 cup water
- ¼ teaspoon fine sea salt
- 3 garlic cloves, peeled
- 2 bay leaves
- 2 pounds boneless, skinless chicken thighs (see Note)
- Cabbage Slaw
- ½ head red or green cabbage, thinly sliced
- 1 red bell pepper, seeded and thinly sliced
- 2 jalapeño chiles, seeded and cut into narrow strips
- 2 carrots, julienned
- 1 large Fuji or Gala apple, julienned
- ½ cup chopped fresh cilantro
- 3 tablespoons fresh lime juice
- 3 tablespoons extra-virgin olive oil
- ½ teaspoon ground cumin
- ¼ teaspoon fine sea salt
- ¾ cup low-sugar or unsweetened barbecue sauce
- Cornbread, for serving

1. To make the chicken: Combine the water, salt, garlic, bay leaves, and chicken thighs in the Instant Pot, arranging the chicken in a single layer.
2. Secure the lid and set the Pressure Release to Sealing. Select the Poultry, Pressure Cook, or Manual setting and set the cooking time for 10 minutes at high pressure. (The pot will take about 10 minutes to come up to pressure before the cooking program begins. )
3. To make the slaw: While the chicken is cooking, in a large bowl, combine the cabbage, bell pepper, jalapeños, carrots, apple, cilantro, lime juice, oil, cumin, and salt and toss together until the vegetables and apples are evenly coated.
4. When the cooking program ends, perform a quick pressure release by moving the Pressure Release to Venting, or let the pressure release naturally. Open the pot and, using tongs, transfer the chicken to a cutting board. Using two forks, shred the chicken into bite-size pieces. Wearing heat-resistant mitts, lift out the inner pot and discard the cooking liquid. Return the inner pot to the housing.
5. Return the chicken to the pot and stir in the barbecue sauce. You can serve it right away or heat it for a minute or two on the Sauté setting, then return the pot to its Keep Warm setting until ready to serve.
6. Divide the chicken and slaw evenly among six plates. Serve with wedges of cornbread on the side.

*Per Serving:calories: 320 / fat: 14g / protein: 32g / carbs: 18g / sugars: 7g / fiber: 4g / sodium: 386mg*

## Herbed Whole Turkey Breast

Prep time: 10 minutes / Cook time:30 minutes / Serves 12

- 3 tablespoons extra-virgin olive oil
- 1½ tablespoons herbes de Provence or poultry seasoning
- 2 teaspoons minced garlic
- 1 teaspoon lemon zest (from 1 small lemon)
- 1 tablespoon kosher salt
- 1½ teaspoons freshly ground black pepper
- 1 (6 pounds) bone-in, skin-on whole turkey breast, rinsed and patted dry

1. In a small bowl, whisk together the olive oil, herbes de Provence, garlic, lemon zest, salt, and pepper.
2. Rub the outside of the turkey and under the skin with the olive oil mixture.
3. Pour 1 cup of water into the electric pressure cooker and insert a wire rack or trivet.
4. Place the turkey on the rack, skin-side up.
5. Close and lock the lid of the pressure cooker. Set the valve to sealing.
6. Cook on high pressure for 30 minutes.
7. When the cooking is complete, hit Cancel. Allow the pressure to release naturally for 20 minutes, then quick release any remaining pressure.

8. Once the pin drops, unlock and remove the lid.
9. Carefully transfer the turkey to a cutting board. Remove the skin, slice, and serve.

*Per Serving:calorie: 389 / fat: 19g / protein: 50g / carbs: 1g / sugars: 0g / fiber: 0g / sodium: 582mg*

## Greek Chicken

Prep time: 25 minutes / Cook time: 20 minutes / Serves 6

- 4 potatoes, unpeeled, quartered
- 2 pounds chicken pieces, trimmed of skin and fat
- 2 large onions, quartered
- 1 whole bulb garlic, cloves minced
- 3 teaspoons dried oregano
- ¾ teaspoons salt
- ½ teaspoons pepper
- 1 tablespoon olive oil
- 1 cup water

1. Place potatoes, chicken, onions, and garlic into the inner pot of the Instant Pot, then sprinkle with seasonings. Top with oil and water.
2. Secure the lid and make sure vent is set to sealing. Cook on Manual mode for 20 minutes.
3. When cook time is over, let the pressure release naturally for 5 minutes, then release the rest manually.

*Per Serving:calorie: 278 / fat: 6g / protein: 27g / carbs: 29g / sugars: 9g / fiber: 4g / sodium: 358mg*

## Speedy Chicken Cacciatore

Prep time: 5 minutes / Cook time: 30 minutes / Serves 6

- 2 pounds boneless, skinless chicken thighs
- 1½ teaspoons fine sea salt
- ½ teaspoon freshly ground black pepper
- 2 tablespoons extra-virgin olive oil
- 3 garlic cloves, chopped
- 2 large red bell peppers, seeded and cut into ¼ by 2-inch strips
- 2 large yellow onions, sliced
- ½ cup dry red wine
- 1½ teaspoons Italian seasoning
- ½ teaspoon red pepper flakes (optional)
- One 14½ ounces can diced tomatoes and their liquid
- 2 tablespoons tomato paste
- Cooked brown rice or whole-grain pasta for serving

1. Season the chicken thighs on both sides with 1 teaspoon of the salt and the black pepper.
2. Select the Sauté setting on the Instant Pot and heat the oil and garlic for 2 minutes, until the garlic is bubbling but not browned. Add the bell peppers, onions, and remaining ½ teaspoon salt and sauté for 3 minutes, until the onions begin to soften. Stir in the wine, Italian seasoning, and pepper flakes (if using). Using tongs, add the chicken to the pot,

turning each piece to coat it in the wine and spices and nestling them in a single layer in the liquid. Pour the tomatoes and their liquid on top of the chicken and dollop the tomato paste on top. Do not stir them in.
3. Secure the lid and set the Pressure Release to Sealing. Press the Cancel button to reset the cooking program, then select the Poultry, Pressure Cook, or Manual setting and set the cooking time for 12 minutes at high pressure. (The pot will take about 15 minutes to come up to pressure before the cooking program begins. )
4. When the cooking program ends, perform a quick pressure release by moving the Pressure Release to Venting, or let the pressure release naturally. Open the pot and, using tongs, transfer the chicken and vegetables to a serving dish.
5. Spoon some of the sauce over the chicken and serve hot, with the rice on the side.

*Per Serving:calories: 297 / fat: 11g / protein: 32g / carbs: 16g / sugars: 3g / fiber: 3g / sodium: 772mg*

## Teriyaki Turkey Meatballs

Prep time: 20 minutes / Cook time: 20 minutes / Serves 6

- 1 pound lean ground turkey
- ¼ cup finely chopped scallions, both white and green parts
- 1 egg
- 2 garlic cloves, minced
- 1 teaspoon grated fresh ginger
- 2 tablespoons reduced-sodium tamari or gluten-free soy sauce
- 1 tablespoon honey
- 2 teaspoons mirin
- 1 teaspoon toasted sesame oil

1. Preheat the oven to 400°F. Line a baking sheet with parchment paper.
2. In a large mixing bowl, combine the turkey, scallions, egg, garlic, ginger, tamari, honey, mirin, and sesame oil. Mix well.
3. Using your hands, form the meat mixture into balls about the size of a tablespoon. Arrange on the prepared baking sheet.
4. Bake for 10 minutes, flip with a spatula, and continue baking for an additional 10 minutes until the meatballs are cooked through.

*Per Serving:calories: 153 / fat: 8g / protein: 16g / carbs: 5g / sugars: 4g / fiber: 0g / sodium: 270mg*

## Baked Chicken Stuffed with Collard Greens

Prep time: 10 minutes / Cook time: 30 minutes / Serves 4

- For the gravy
- 2½ cups store-bought low-sodium chicken broth, divided

- 4 tablespoons whole-wheat flour, divided
- 1 medium yellow onion, chopped
- ½ bunch fresh thyme, roughly chopped
- 2 garlic cloves, minced
- 1 bay leaf
- ½ teaspoon celery seeds
- 1 teaspoon Worcestershire sauce
- Freshly ground black pepper
- For the chicken
- 2 boneless, skinless chicken breasts
- Juice of 1 lime
- 1 teaspoon sweet paprika
- ½ teaspoon onion powder
- ½ teaspoon garlic powder
- 2 medium tomatoes, chopped
- 1 bunch collard greens, center stem removed, cut into 1-inch ribbons
- ¼ cup chicken broth (optional)
- Generous pinch red pepper flakes

1. To make the gravy 1. In a shallow stockpot, combine ½ cup of broth and 1 tablespoon of flour and cook over medium-low heat, whisking until the flour is dissolved. Continue to add 1 cup of broth and the remaining 3 tablespoons of flour in increments until a thick sauce is formed.
2. Add the onion, thyme, garlic, bay leaf, and ½ cup of broth, stirring well. To make the chicken 1. Cut a slit in each chicken breast deep enough for stuffing along its entire length.
2. In a small mixing bowl, massage the chicken all over with the lime juice, paprika, onion powder, and garlic powder.
3. In an electric pressure cooker, combine the tomatoes and collard greens. If the mixture looks dry, add the chicken broth.
4. Close and lock the lid, and set the pressure valve to sealing.
5. Select the Manual/Pressure Cook setting, and cook for 2 minutes.
6. Once cooking is complete, quick-release the pressure. Carefully remove the lid.
7. Using tongs or a slotted spoon, remove the greens while leaving the tomatoes behind.
8. Stuff the chicken breasts with the greens. Lay on the bed of tomatoes in the pressure cooker, with the side with greens facing up.
9. Spoon half of the gravy over the stuffed chicken.
10. Close and lock the lid, and set the pressure valve to sealing.
11. Select the Manual/Pressure Cook setting, and cook for 10 minutes.
12. Once cooking is complete, quick-release the pressure. Carefully remove the lid.
13. Remove the chicken and tomatoes from pressure cooker, and transfer to a serving dish. Season with

the red pepper flakes.

*Per Serving:calorie: 301 / fat: 6g / protein: 41g / carbs: 24g / sugars: 4g / fiber: 9g / sodium: 155mg*

## Greek Chicken Stuffed Peppers

Prep time: 5 minutes / Cook time: 30 minutes / Serves 4

- 2 large red bell peppers
- 2 teaspoons extra-virgin olive oil, divided
- ½ cup uncooked brown rice or quinoa
- 4 (4-ounce) boneless, skinless chicken breasts
- ¼ teaspoon garlic powder
- ¼ teaspoon onion powder
- ⅛ teaspoon dried thyme
- ½ teaspoon dried oregano
- ½ cup crumbled feta

1. Cut the bell peppers in half and remove the seeds.
2. In a large skillet, heat 1 teaspoon of olive oil over low heat. When hot, place the bell pepper halves cut-side up in the skillet. Cover and cook for 20 minutes.
3. Cook the rice according to the package instructions.
4. Meanwhile, cut the chicken into 1-inch pieces.
5. In a medium skillet, heat the remaining 1 teaspoon of olive oil over medium-low heat. When hot, add the chicken.
6. Season the chicken with the garlic powder, onion powder, thyme, and oregano.
7. Cook for 5 minutes, stirring occasionally, until cooked through.
8. In a large bowl, combine the cooked rice and chicken. Scoop one-quarter of the chicken and rice mixture into each pepper half, cover, and cook for 10 minutes over low heat.
9. Top each pepper half with 2 tablespoons of crumbled feta.

*Per Serving:calorie: 311 / fat: 11g / protein: 32g / carbs: 20g / sugars: 4g / fiber: 3g / sodium: 228mg*

## Thai Yellow Curry with Chicken Meatballs

Prep time: 5 minutes / Cook time: 30 minutes / Serves 4

- 1 pound 95 percent lean ground chicken
- ⅓ cup gluten-free panko (Japanese bread crumbs)
- 1 egg white
- 1 tablespoon coconut oil
- 1 yellow onion, cut into 1-inch pieces
- One 14-ounce can light coconut milk
- 3 tablespoons yellow curry paste
- ¾ cup water
- 8 ounces carrots, halved lengthwise, then cut crosswise into 1-inch lengths (or quartered if very large)
- 8 ounces zucchini, quartered lengthwise, then cut crosswise into 1-inch lengths (or cut into halves, then thirds if large)

- 8 ounces cremini mushrooms, quartered
- Fresh Thai basil leaves for serving (optional)
- Fresno or jalapeño chile, thinly sliced, for serving (optional)
- 1 lime, cut into wedges
- Cooked cauliflower "rice" for serving

1. In a medium bowl, combine the chicken, panko, and egg white and mix until evenly combined. Set aside.
2. Select the Sauté setting on the Instant Pot and heat the oil for 2 minutes. Add the onion and sauté for 5 minutes, until it begins to soften and brown. Add ½ cup of the coconut milk and the curry paste and sauté for 1 minute more, until bubbling and fragrant. Press the Cancel button to turn off the pot, then stir in the water.
3. Using a 1½-tablespoon cookie scoop, shape and drop meatballs into the pot in a single layer.
4. Secure the lid and set the Pressure Release to Sealing. Select the Pressure Cook or Manual setting and set the cooking time for 5 minutes at high pressure. (The pot will take about 5 minutes to come up to pressure before the cooking program begins. )
5. When the cooking program ends, perform a quick pressure release by moving the Pressure Release to Venting, or let the pressure release naturally. Open the pot and stir in the carrots, zucchini, mushrooms, and remaining 1¼ cups coconut milk.
6. Press the Cancel button to reset the cooking program, then select the Sauté setting. Bring the curry to a simmer (this will take about 2 minutes), then let cook, uncovered, for about 8 minutes, until the carrots are fork-tender. Press the Cancel button to turn off the pot.
7. Ladle the curry into bowls. Serve piping hot, topped with basil leaves and chile slices, if desired, and the lime wedges and cauliflower "rice" on the side.

*Per Serving:calories: 349 / fat: 15g / protein: 30g / carbs: 34g / sugars: 8g / fiber: 5g / sodium: 529mg*

## Greek Chicken Stir-Fry

Prep time: 15 minutes / Cook time: 15 minutes / Serves 2

- 1 (6-ounce / 170-g) chicken breast, cut into 1-inch cubes
- ½ medium zucchini, chopped
- ½ medium red bell pepper, seeded and chopped
- ¼ medium red onion, peeled and sliced
- 1 tablespoon coconut oil
- 1 teaspoon dried oregano
- ½ teaspoon garlic powder
- ¼ teaspoon dried thyme

1. Place all ingredients into a large mixing bowl

and toss until the coconut oil coats the meat and vegetables. Pour the contents of the bowl into the air fryer basket.
2. Adjust the temperature to 375°F (191°C) and air fry for 15 minutes.
3. Shake the basket halfway through the cooking time to redistribute the food. Serve immediately.

*Per Serving:calorie: 248 / fat: 11g / protein: 30g / carbs: 9g / sugars: 4g / fiber: 3g / sodium: 97mg*

## Tangy Barbecue Strawberry-Peach Chicken

Prep time: 20 minutes / Cook time: 40 minutes / Serves 4

- For the barbecue sauce
- 1 cup frozen peaches
- 1 cup frozen strawberries
- ¼ cup tomato purée
- ½ cup white vinegar
- 1 tablespoon yellow mustard
- 1 teaspoon mustard seeds
- 1 teaspoon turmeric
- 1 teaspoon sweet paprika
- 1 teaspoon garlic powder
- ½ teaspoon cayenne pepper
- ½ teaspoon onion powder
- ½ teaspoon freshly ground black pepper
- 1 teaspoon celery seeds
- For the chicken
- 4 boneless, skinless chicken thighs

1. To make the barbecue sauce 1. In a stockpot, combine the peaches, strawberries, tomato purée, vinegar, mustard, mustard seeds, turmeric, paprika, garlic powder, cayenne, onion powder, black pepper, and celery seeds. Cook over low heat for 15 minutes, or until the flavors come together.
2. Remove the sauce from the heat, and let cool for 5 minutes.
3. Transfer the sauce to a blender, and purée until smooth. To make the chicken 1. Preheat the oven to 350°F.
2. Put the chicken in a medium bowl. Coat well with ½ cup of barbecue sauce.
3. Place the chicken on a rimmed baking sheet.
4. Place the baking sheet on the middle rack of the oven, and bake for about 20 minutes (depending on the thickness of thighs), or until the juices run clear.
5. Brush the chicken with additional sauce, return to the oven, and broil on high for 3 to 5 minutes, or until a light crust forms.
6. Serve.

*Per Serving:calorie: 389 / fat: 8g / protein: 63g / carbs: 13g / sugars: 7g / fiber: 3g / sodium: 175mg*

## Tantalizing Jerked Chicken

Prep time: 10 minutes / Cook time: 20 minutes / Serves 4

- 4 (5 ounces) boneless, skinless chicken breasts
- ½ sweet onion, cut into chunks
- 2 habanero chile peppers, halved lengthwise, seeded
- ¼ cup freshly squeezed lime juice
- 2 tablespoons extra-virgin olive oil
- 1 tablespoon minced garlic
- 1 tablespoon ground allspice
- 2 teaspoons chopped fresh thyme
- 1 teaspoon freshly ground black pepper
- ½ teaspoon ground nutmeg
- ¼ teaspoon ground cinnamon
- 2 cups fresh greens (such as arugula or spinach)
- 1 cup halved cherry tomatoes

1. Place two chicken breasts in each of two large resealable plastic bags. Set them aside.
2. Place the onion, habaneros, lime juice, olive oil, garlic, allspice, thyme, black pepper, nutmeg, and cinnamon in a food processor and pulse until very well blended.
3. Pour half the marinade into each bag with the chicken breasts. Squeeze out as much air as possible, seal the bags, and place them in the refrigerator for 4 hours.
4. Preheat a barbecue to medium-high heat.
5. Let the chicken sit at room temperature for 15 minutes and then grill, turning at least once, until cooked through, about 15 minutes total.
6. Let the chicken rest for about 5 minutes before serving. Divide the greens and tomatoes among four serving plates, and top with the chicken.

*Per Serving:calorie: 268 / fat: 10g / protein: 33g / carbs: 9g / sugars: 4g / fiber: 2g / sodium: 74mg*

## Chicken Legs with Leeks

Prep time: 30 minutes / Cook time: 18 minutes / Serves 6
- 2 leeks, sliced
- 2 large-sized tomatoes, chopped
- 3 cloves garlic, minced
- ½ teaspoon dried oregano
- 6 chicken legs, boneless and skinless
- ½ teaspoon smoked cayenne pepper
- 2 tablespoons olive oil
- A freshly ground nutmeg

1. In a mixing dish, thoroughly combine all ingredients, minus the leeks. Place in the refrigerator and let it marinate overnight.
2. Lay the leeks onto the bottom of the air fryer basket. Top with the chicken legs.
3. Roast chicken legs at 375ºF (191ºC) for 18 minutes, turning halfway through. Serve with hoisin sauce.

*Per Serving:calorie: 271 / fat: 12g / protein: 33g / carbs: 9g / sugars: 4g / fiber: 2g / sodium: 263mg*

## Cast Iron Hot Chicken

Prep time: 10 minutes / Cook time: 40 minutes / Serves 4
- 2 boneless, skinless chicken breasts
- Juice of 2 limes
- 2 garlic cloves, minced
- 1 medium yellow onion, chopped
- 1½ teaspoons cayenne pepper
- 1 teaspoon smoked paprika

1. Preheat the oven to 375°F.
2. In a shallow bowl, massage the chicken all over with the lime juice, garlic, onion, cayenne, and paprika.
3. In a cast iron skillet, place the chicken in one even layer.
4. Transfer the skillet to the oven and cook for 35 to 40 minutes, or until cooked through.
5. Remove the chicken from the oven, and let rest for 5 minutes.
6. Divide each breast into two portions. Serve.

*Per Serving:calorie: 286 / fat: 4g / protein: 31g / carbs: 6g / sugars: 2g / fiber: 1g / sodium: 64mg*

## Fiber-Full Chicken Tostadas

Prep time: 15 minutes / Cook time: 10 minutes / Serves 4
- 1 tablespoon (9 g) chili powder
- ½ tablespoon (5 g) onion powder
- 1 tablespoon (9 g) paprika
- 1 teaspoon garlic powder
- 1 teaspoon ground cumin
- 1 teaspoon dried oregano
- ¼ teaspoon black pepper
- ¼ teaspoon sea salt
- 2 tablespoons (30 ml) cooking oil of choice
- 1 pound (454 g) boneless, skinless chicken breast, cut into 1 to 1½-inch (2. 5 to 3. 8 cm) strips
- 8 corn tostada shells
- 1 (15½ ounces [439 g]) can low-sodium pinto beans, undrained
- 1 cup (30 g) baby arugula leaves, coarsely chopped
- 1 large avocado, peeled and sliced to the desired thickness
- 4 tablespoons (32 g) crumbled queso fresco cheese
- Jalapeño slices (optional)
- Chopped onion (optional)
- Diced tomatoes (optional)

1. In a small bowl, mix together the chili powder, onion powder, paprika, garlic powder, cumin, oregano, black pepper, and sea salt. Add the cooking oil and mix it with the seasonings to make a marinade.
2. Place the chicken strips in a large ziptop plastic bag, then add the marinade. Seal the bag and shake it to coat the chicken with the marinade. (If time

permits, marinate the chicken for 30 to 60 minutes.)

3. Heat a large skillet over medium-high heat. Add the chicken strips and cook them for 4 to 5 minutes. Flip the chicken strips and cook them for 3 to 4 minutes, until they are cooked through and no longer pink. Set the skillet aside.

4. Line up the tostada shells on a serving tray. Place the pinto beans in a medium bowl and mash them to the desired consistency. Spread the beans on top of each tostada. Top each tostada with an equal amount of arugula, avocado slices, cheese, chicken and any desired additional toppings, then serve.

*Per Serving:calorie: 547 / fat: 27g / protein: 40g / carbs: 12g / sugars: 1g / fiber: 12g / sodium: 738mg*

## Lemony Chicken Thighs

Prep time: 15 minutes / Cook time: 15 minutes / Serves 3 to 5

- 1 cup low-sodium chicken bone broth
- 5 frozen bone-in chicken thighs
- 1 small onion, diced
- 5 to 6 cloves garlic, diced
- Juice of 1 lemon
- 2 tablespoons margarine, melted
- ½ teaspoon salt
- ¼ teaspoon black pepper
- 1 teaspoon True Lemon Lemon Pepper seasoning
- 1 teaspoon parsley flakes
- ¼ teaspoon oregano
- Rind of 1 lemon

1. Add the chicken bone broth into the inner pot of the Instant Pot.
2. Add the chicken thighs.
3. Add the onion and garlic.
4. Pour the fresh lemon juice in with the melted margarine.
5. Add the seasonings.
6. Lock the lid, make sure the vent is at sealing, then press the Poultry button. Set to 15 minutes.
7. When cook time is up, let the pressure naturally release for 3 to 5 minutes, then manually release the rest.
8. You can place these under the broiler for 2 to 3 minutes to brown.
9. Plate up and pour some of the sauce over top with fresh grated lemon rind.

*Per Serving:calories: 329 / fat: 24g / protein: 26g / carbs: 3g / sugars: 1g / fiber: 0g / sodium: 407mg*

## Ginger Turmeric Chicken Thighs

Prep time: 5 minutes / Cook time: 25 minutes / Serves 4

- 4 (4 ounces / 113 g) boneless, skin-on chicken thighs
- 2 tablespoons coconut oil, melted
- ½ teaspoon ground turmeric
- ½ teaspoon salt
- ½ teaspoon garlic powder
- ½ teaspoon ground ginger
- ¼ teaspoon ground black pepper

1. Place chicken thighs in a large bowl and drizzle with coconut oil. Sprinkle with remaining ingredients and toss to coat both sides of thighs.
2. Place thighs skin side up into ungreased air fryer basket. Adjust the temperature to 400°F (204°C) and air fry for 25 minutes. After 10 minutes, turn thighs. When 5 minutes remain, flip thighs once more. Chicken will be done when skin is golden brown and the internal temperature is at least 165°F (74°C). Serve warm.

*Per Serving:calorie: 233 / fat: 19g / protein: 13g / carbs: 1g / sugars: 0g / fiber: 0g / sodium: 340mg*

## Turkey Bolognese with Chickpea Pasta

Prep time: 5 minutes / Cook time: 25 minutes / Serves 4

- 1 onion, coarsely chopped
- 1 large carrot, coarsely chopped
- 2 celery stalks, coarsely chopped
- 1 tablespoon extra-virgin olive oil
- 1 pound ground turkey
- ½ cup milk
- ¾ cup red or white wine
- 1 (28-ounce) can diced tomatoes
- 10 ounces cooked chickpea pasta

1. Place the onion, carrots, and celery in a food processor and pulse until finely chopped.
2. Heat the extra-virgin olive oil in a Dutch oven or medium skillet over medium-high heat. Sauté the chopped vegetables for 3 to 5 minutes, or until softened. Add the ground turkey, breaking the poultry into smaller pieces, and cook for 5 minutes.
3. Add the milk and wine and cook until the liquid is nearly evaporated (turn up the heat to high to quicken the process).
4. Add the tomatoes and bring the sauce to a simmer. Reduce the heat to low and simmer for 10 to 15 minutes.
5. Meanwhile, cook the pasta according to the package instructions and set aside.
6. Serve the sauce with the cooked chickpea pasta.
7. Store any leftovers in an airtight container in the refrigerator for 3 to 4 days.

*Per Serving:calorie: 419 / fat: 15g / protein: 31g / carbs: 34g / sugars: 8g / fiber: 11g / sodium: 150mg*

# Chapter 4 Beef, Pork, and Lamb

## Traditional Beef Stroganoff

Prep time: 10 minutes / Cook time: 30 minutes / Serves 4

- 1 teaspoon extra-virgin olive oil
- 1 pound top sirloin, cut into thin strips
- 1 cup sliced button mushrooms
- ½ sweet onion, finely chopped
- 1 teaspoon minced garlic
- 1 tablespoon whole-wheat flour
- ½ cup low-sodium beef broth
- ¼ cup dry sherry
- ½ cup fat-free sour cream
- 1 tablespoon chopped fresh parsley
- Sea salt
- Freshly ground black pepper

1. Place a large skillet over medium-high heat and add the oil.
2. Sauté the beef until browned, about 10 minutes, then remove the beef with a slotted spoon to a plate and set it aside.
3. Add the mushrooms, onion, and garlic to the skillet and sauté until lightly browned, about 5 minutes.
4. Whisk in the flour and then whisk in the beef broth and sherry.
5. Return the sirloin to the skillet and bring the mixture to a boil.
6. Reduce the heat to low and simmer until the beef is tender, about 10 minutes.
7. Stir in the sour cream and parsley. Season with salt and pepper.

*Per Serving:calorie: 320 / fat: 18g / protein: 26g / carbs: 13g / sugars: 3g / fiber: 1g / sodium: 111mg*

## Bacon-Wrapped Vegetable Kebabs

Prep time: 10 minutes / Cook time: 10 to 12 minutes / Serves 4

- 4 ounces (113 g) mushrooms, sliced
- 1 small zucchini, sliced
- 12 grape tomatoes
- 4 ounces (113 g) sliced bacon, halved
- Avocado oil spray
- Sea salt and freshly ground black pepper, to taste

1. Stack 3 mushroom slices, 1 zucchini slice, and 1 grape tomato. Wrap a bacon strip around the vegetables and thread them onto a skewer. Repeat with the remaining vegetables and bacon. Spray with oil and sprinkle with salt and pepper.
2. Set the air fryer to 400°F (204°C). Place the skewers in the air fryer basket in a single layer, working in batches if necessary, and air fry for 5 minutes. Flip the skewers and cook for 5 to 7 minutes more, until the bacon is crispy and the vegetables are tender.
3. Serve warm.

*Per Serving:calorie: 140 / fat: 11g / protein: 5g / carbs: 5g / sugars: 4g / fiber: 1g / sodium: 139mg*

## Open-Faced Pulled Pork

Prep time: 15 minutes / Cook time: 1 hour 35minutes / Serves 2

- 2 tablespoons hoisin sauce
- 2 tablespoons tomato paste
- 2 tablespoons rice vinegar
- 1 tablespoon minced fresh ginger
- 2 teaspoons minced garlic
- 1 teaspoon chile-garlic sauce
- ¾ pound pork shoulder, trimmed of any visible fat, cut into 2-inch-square cubes
- 4 large romaine lettuce leaves

1. Preheat the oven to 300°F.
2. In a medium ovenproof pot with a tight-fitting lid, stir together the hoisin sauce, tomato paste, rice vinegar, ginger, garlic, and chile-garlic sauce.
3. Add the pork. Toss to coat.
4. Place the pot over medium heat. Bring to a simmer. Cover and carefully transfer the ovenproof pot to the preheated oven. Cook for 90 minutes.
5. Check the meat for doneness by inserting a fork into one of the chunks. If it goes in easily and the pork falls apart, the meat is done. If not, cook for another 30 minutes or so, until the meat passes the fork test.
6. Using a coarse strainer, strain the cooked pork into a fat separator. Shred the meat. Set aside. If you don't have a fat separator, remove the meat from the sauce and set aside. Let the sauce cool until any fat has risen to the top. With a spoon, remove as much fat as possible or use paper towels to blot it off.
7. In a small saucepan set over high heat, pour the defatted sauce. Bring to a boil, stirring frequently to prevent scorching. Cook for 2 to 3 minutes, or until thickened.
8. Add the shredded meat. Toss to coat with the sauce. Cook for 1 minute to reheat the meat.
9. Spoon equal amounts of pork into the romaine lettuce leaves and enjoy!

*Per Serving:calorie: 289 / fat: 11g / protein: 33g / carbs: 13g / sugars: 7g / fiber: 1g / sodium: 391mg*

## Red Wine Pot Roast with Winter Vegetables

Prep time: 10 minutes / Cook time: 1 hour 35 minutes / Serves 6

- One 3-pound boneless beef chuck roast or bottom round roast (see Note)
- 2 teaspoons fine sea salt
- 1 teaspoon freshly ground black pepper
- 1 tablespoon cold-pressed avocado oil
- 4 large shallots, quartered
- 4 garlic cloves, minced
- 1 cup dry red wine
- 2 tablespoons Dijon mustard
- 2 teaspoons chopped fresh rosemary
- 1 pound parsnips or turnips, cut into ½-inch pieces
- 1 pound carrots, cut into ½-inch pieces
- 4 celery stalks, cut into ½-inch pieces

1. Put the beef onto a plate, pat it dry with paper towels, and then season all over with the salt and pepper.
2. Select the Sauté setting on the Instant Pot and heat the oil for 2 minutes. Using tongs, lower the roast into the pot and sear for about 4 minutes, until browned on the first side. Flip the roast and sear for about 4 minutes more, until browned on the second side. Return the roast to the plate.
3. Add the shallots to the pot and sauté for about 2 minutes, until they begin to soften. Add the garlic and sauté for about 1 minute more. Stir in the wine, mustard, and rosemary, using a wooden spoon to nudge any browned bits from the bottom of the pot. Return the roast to the pot, then spoon some of the cooking liquid over the top.
4. Secure the lid and set the Pressure Release to Sealing. Press the Cancel button to reset the cooking program, then select the Meat/Stew setting and set the cooking time for 1 hour 5 minutes at high pressure. (The pot will take about 5 minutes to come up to pressure before the cooking program begins. )
5. When the cooking program ends, let the pressure release naturally for at least 15 minutes, then move the Pressure Release to Venting to release any remaining steam. Open the pot and, using tongs, carefully transfer the pot roast to a cutting board. Tent with aluminum foil to keep warm.
6. Add the parsnips, carrots, and celery to the pot.
7. Secure the lid and set the Pressure Release to Sealing. Press the Cancel button to reset the cooking program, then select the Pressure Cook or Manual setting and set the cooking time for 3 minutes at low pressure. (The pot will take about 10 minutes to come up to pressure before the cooking program begins. )
8. When the cooking program ends, perform a quick pressure release by moving the Pressure Release to Venting. Open the pot and, using a slotted spoon, transfer the vegetables to a serving dish. Wearing heat-resistant mitts, lift out the inner pot and pour the cooking liquid into a gravy boat or other serving vessel with a spout. (If you like, use a fat separator to remove the fat from the liquid before serving. )
9. If the roast was tied, snip the string and discard. Carve the roast against the grain into ½-inch-thick slices and arrange them on the dish with the vegetables. Pour some cooking liquid over the roast and serve, passing the remaining cooking liquid on the side.

*Per Serving:calorie: 448 / fat: 25g / protein: 26g / carbs: 26g / sugars: 7g / fiber: 6g / sodium: 945mg*

## Creole Braised Sirloin

Prep time: 15 minutes / Cook time: 40 minutes / Serves 4

- 1 pound beef round sirloin tip, cut into 4 strips
- ¼ teaspoon freshly ground black pepper
- 2 cups store-bought low-sodium chicken broth, divided
- 1 medium onion, chopped
- 1 celery stalk, coarsely chopped
- 1 medium green bell pepper, coarsely chopped
- 2 garlic cloves, minced
- 4 medium tomatoes, coarsely chopped
- 1 bunch mustard greens including stems, coarsely chopped
- 1 tablespoon Creole seasoning
- ¼ teaspoon red pepper flakes
- 2 bay leaves

1. Preheat the oven to 450°F.
2. Massage the beef all over with black pepper.
3. In a Dutch oven, bring 1 cup of broth to a simmer over medium heat.
4. Add the onion, celery, bell pepper, and garlic and cook, stirring often, for 5 minutes, or until the vegetables are softened.
5. Add the tomatoes, mustard greens, Creole seasoning, and red pepper flakes and cook for 3 to 5 minutes, or until the greens are wilted.
6. Add the bay leaves, beef, and remaining 1 cup of broth.
7. Cover the pot, transfer to the oven, and cook for 30 minutes, or until the juices run clear when you pierce the beef.
8. Remove the beef from the oven, and let rest for 5 to 7 minutes. Discard the bay leaves.
9. Thinly slice the beef and serve.

*Per Serving:calorie: 215 / fat: 6g / protein: 29g / carbs: 11g / sugars: 5g / fiber: 3g / sodium: 121mg*

## Beef and Pepper Fajita Bowls

Prep time: 10 minutes / Cook time: 15 minutes / Serves 4

- 4 tablespoons extra-virgin olive oil, divided
- 1 head cauliflower, riced
- 1 pound sirloin steak, cut into ¼-inch-thick strips
- 1 red bell pepper, seeded and sliced
- 1 onion, thinly sliced
- 2 garlic cloves, minced
- Juice of 2 limes
- 1 teaspoon chili powder

1. In a large skillet over medium-high heat, heat 2 tablespoons of olive oil until it shimmers. Add the cauliflower. Cook, stirring occasionally, until it softens, about 3 minutes. Set aside.
2. Wipe out the skillet with a paper towel. Add the remaining 2 tablespoons of oil to the skillet, and heat it on medium-high until it shimmers. Add the steak and cook, stirring occasionally, until it browns, about 3 minutes. Use a slotted spoon to remove the steak from the oil in the pan and set aside.
3. Add the bell pepper and onion to the pan. Cook, stirring occasionally, until they start to brown, about 5 minutes.
4. Add the garlic and cook, stirring constantly, for 30 seconds.
5. Return the beef along with any juices that have collected and the cauliflower to the pan. Add the lime juice and chili powder. Cook, stirring, until everything is warmed through, 2 to 3 minutes.

*Per Serving:calorie: 390 / fat: 27g / protein: 27g / carbs: 12g / sugars: 5g / fiber: 4g / sodium: 126mg*

## Pork Tacos

Prep time: 30 minutes / Cook time: 10 minutes / Serves 2

- 8 ounces boneless skinless pork tenderloin, thinly sliced, ¼-inch thick, across the grain
- Pinch salt
- ⅓ cup ancho chile sauce
- 2 tablespoons chipotle purée (see Recipe Tip)
- ¼ cup freshly squeezed lime juice
- 2 (6-inch) soft low-carb corn tortillas, such as La Tortilla
- 4 tablespoons diced tomatoes, divided
- 1 cup shredded lettuce, divided
- ½ avocado, sliced
- 4 tablespoons salsa, divided

1. Sprinkle the pork slices with salt. Set aside.
2. In a small bowl, stir together the ancho chile sauce, chipotle purée, and lime juice. Reserve 3 tablespoons of the marinade. Set aside.
3. In a large sealable plastic bag, add the pork. Pour the remaining marinade over it. Seal the bag,

removing as much air as possible. Marinate the meat for 20 minutes to 1 hour at room temperature, or refrigerate for several hours. Turn the meat twice while it marinates.

4. Place a small nonstick skillet over medium heat. Have a large piece of aluminum foil nearby.
5. Working with one tortilla at a time, heat both sides in the skillet until they puff slightly. As they are done, stack the tortillas on the foil. When they are all heated, wrap the tortillas in the foil.
6. Preheat the broiler.
7. Adjust the rack so it is 4 inches from the heating element.
8. Remove the pork slices from the marinade. Discard the marinade. Place the pork on a rack set over a sheet pan.
9. Place the pan in the oven. Broil for 3 to 4 minutes, or until the edges of the pork begin to brown. Remove from the oven. Turn and brush the pork with the reserved marinade. Broil the second side for 3 minutes, or until the pork is just barely pink inside.
10. Place the foil packet with the tortillas in the oven to warm while the pork finishes cooking.
11. To serve, pile each tortilla with a few slices of pork. Top each with about 2 tablespoons of diced tomato, ½ cup of shredded lettuce, half of the avocado slices, and about 2 tablespoons of salsa.

*Per Serving:calorie: 328 / fat: 13g / protein: 30g / carbs: 25g / sugars: 5g / fiber: 7g / sodium: 563mg*

## Pork Chops Pomodoro

Prep time: 0 minutes / Cook time: 30 minutes / Serves 6

- 2 pounds boneless pork loin chops, each about 5⅓ ounces and ½ inch thick
- ¾ teaspoon fine sea salt
- ½ teaspoon freshly ground black pepper
- 2 tablespoons extra-virgin olive oil
- 2 garlic cloves, chopped
- ½ cup low-sodium chicken broth or vegetable broth
- ½ teaspoon Italian seasoning
- 1 tablespoon capers, drained
- 2 cups cherry tomatoes
- 2 tablespoons chopped fresh basil or flat-leaf parsley
- Spiralized zucchini noodles, cooked cauliflower "rice," or cooked whole-grain pasta for serving
- Lemon wedges for serving

1. Pat the pork chops dry with paper towels, then season them all over with the salt and pepper.
2. Select the Sauté setting on the Instant Pot and heat 1 tablespoon of the oil for 2 minutes. Swirl the oil to coat the bottom of the pot. Using tongs, add half of the pork chops in a single layer and

sear for about 3 minutes, until lightly browned on the first side. Flip the chops and sear for about 3 minutes more, until lightly browned on the second side. Transfer the chops to a plate. Repeat with the remaining 1 tablespoon oil and pork chops.

3. Add the garlic to the pot and sauté for about 1 minute, until bubbling but not browned. Stir in the broth, Italian seasoning, and capers, using a wooden spoon to nudge any browned bits from the bottom of the pot and working quickly so not too much liquid evaporates. Using the tongs, transfer the pork chops to the pot. Add the tomatoes in an even layer on top of the chops.

4. Secure the lid and set the Pressure Release to Sealing. Press the Cancel button to reset the cooking program, then select the Pressure Cook or Manual setting and set the cooking time for 10 minutes at high pressure. (The pot will take about 5 minutes to come up to pressure before the cooking program begins. )

5. When the cooking program ends, let the pressure release naturally for at least 10 minutes, then move the Pressure Release to Venting to release any remaining steam. Open the pot and, using the tongs, transfer the pork chops to a serving dish.

6. Spoon the tomatoes and some of the cooking liquid on top of the pork chops. Sprinkle with the basil and serve right away, with zucchini noodles and lemon wedges on the side.

*Per Serving:calorie: 265 / fat: 13g / protein: 31g / carbs: 3g / sugars: 2g / fiber: 1g / sodium: 460mg*

## Parmesan-Crusted Pork Chops

Prep time: 5 minutes / Cook time: 12 minutes / Serves 4

- 1 large egg
- ½ cup grated Parmesan cheese
- 4 (4-ounce / 113-g) boneless pork chops
- ½ teaspoon salt
- ¼ teaspoon ground black pepper

1. Whisk egg in a medium bowl and place Parmesan in a separate medium bowl.
2. Sprinkle pork chops on both sides with salt and pepper. Dip each pork chop into egg, then press both sides into Parmesan.
3. Place pork chops into ungreased air fryer basket. Adjust the temperature to 400°F (204°C) and air fry for 12 minutes, turning chops halfway through cooking. Pork chops will be golden and have an internal temperature of at least 145°F (63°C) when done. Serve warm.

*Per Serving:calorie: 265 / fat: 13g / protein: 32g / carbs: 3g / sugars: 0g / fiber: 0g / sodium: 674mg*

## Butterflied Beef Eye Roast

Prep time: 10 minutes / Cook time: 40 minutes / Serves 12

- 3 pounds lean beef eye roast
- 3 tablespoons extra-virgin olive oil
- ¼ cup water
- ½ cup red wine vinegar
- 3 garlic cloves, minced
- ½ teaspoon crushed red pepper
- 1 tablespoon chopped fresh thyme

1. Slice the roast down the middle, open it, and lay it flat in a shallow baking dish.
2. In a small bowl, combine the remaining ingredients, and pour the mixture over the roast. Cover, and let the meat marinate in the refrigerator for at least 12 hours, or up to 24 hours. Turn the roast occasionally.
3. Set the oven to broil. Remove the roast from the marinade, discard the marinade, and place the roast on a rack in the broiler pan. Broil the roast 5 to 7 inches from the heat, turning occasionally, for 20 to 25 minutes or until desired degree of doneness.
4. Remove from the oven, cover with foil, and let stand for 15 to 20 minutes before carving. Transfer to a serving platter, spoon any juices over the top, and serve.

*Per Serving:calorie: 191 / fat: 10g / protein: 24g / carbs: 0g / sugars: 0g / fiber: 0g / sodium: 98mg*

## Mexican-Style Shredded Beef

Prep time: 5 minutes / Cook time: 35 minutes / Serves 6

- 1 (2-pound / 907-g) beef chuck roast, cut into 2-inch cubes
- 1 teaspoon salt
- ½ teaspoon ground black pepper
- ½ cup no-sugar-added chipotle sauce

1. In a large bowl, sprinkle beef cubes with salt and pepper and toss to coat. Place beef into ungreased air fryer basket. Adjust the temperature to 400°F (204°C) and air fry for 30 minutes, shaking the basket halfway through cooking. Beef will be done when internal temperature is at least 160°F (71°C).
2. Place cooked beef into a large bowl and shred with two forks. Pour in chipotle sauce and toss to coat.
3. Return beef to air fryer basket for an additional 5 minutes at 400°F (204°C) to crisp with sauce. Serve warm.

*Per Serving:calorie: 295 / fat: 16g / protein: 31g / carbs: 3g / sugars: 2g / fiber: 0g / sodium: 449mg*

## Spice-Rubbed Pork Loin

Prep time: 5 minutes / Cook time: 20 minutes / Serves 6

- 1 teaspoon paprika
- ½ teaspoon ground cumin
- ½ teaspoon chili powder
- ½ teaspoon garlic powder
- 2 tablespoons coconut oil
- 1 (1½ pounds / 680 g) boneless pork loin
- ½ teaspoon salt
- ¼ teaspoon ground black pepper

1. In a small bowl, mix paprika, cumin, chili powder, and garlic powder.
2. Drizzle coconut oil over pork. Sprinkle pork loin with salt and pepper, then rub spice mixture evenly on all sides.
3. Place pork loin into ungreased air fryer basket. Adjust the temperature to 400°F (204°C) and air fry for 20 minutes, turning pork halfway through cooking. Pork loin will be browned and have an internal temperature of at least 145°F (63°C) when done. Serve warm.

*Per Serving:calorie: 199 / fat: 11g / protein: 22g / carbs: 1g / sugars: 0g / fiber: 0g / sodium: 239mg*

## Broiled Dijon Burgers

Prep time: 25 minutes / Cook time: 10 minutes / Makes 6 burgers

- ¼ cup fat-free egg product or 2 egg whites
- 2 tablespoons fat-free (skim) milk
- 2 teaspoons Dijon mustard or horseradish sauce
- ¼ teaspoon salt
- ⅛ teaspoon pepper
- 1 cup soft bread crumbs (about 2 slices bread)
- 1 small onion, finely chopped (⅓ cup)
- 1 pound extra-lean (at least 90%) ground beef
- 6 whole-grain burger buns, split, toasted

1. Set oven control to broil. Spray broiler pan rack with cooking spray.
2. In medium bowl, mix egg product, milk, mustard, salt and pepper. Stir in bread crumbs and onion. Stir in beef. Shape mixture into 6 patties, each about ½ inch thick. Place patties on rack in broiler pan.
3. Broil with tops of patties about 5 inches from heat 6 minutes. Turn; broil until meat thermometer inserted in center of patties reads 160°F, 4 to 6 minutes longer. Serve patties in buns.

*Per Serving:calories: 250 / fat: 8g / protein: 22g / carbs: 23g / sugars: 5g / fiber: 3g / sodium: 450mg*

## Bavarian Beef

Prep time: 35 minutes / Cook time: 1 hour 15 minutes / Serves 8

- 1 tablespoon canola oil
- 3-pound boneless beef chuck roast, trimmed of fat
- 3 cups sliced carrots
- 3 cups sliced onions
- 2 large kosher dill pickles, chopped
- 1 cup sliced celery
- ½ cup dry red wine or beef broth
- ⅓ cup German-style mustard
- 2 teaspoons coarsely ground black pepper
- 2 bay leaves
- ¼ teaspoon ground cloves
- 1 cup water
- ⅓ cup flour

1. Press Sauté on the Instant Pot and add in the oil. Brown roast on both sides for about 5 minutes. Press Cancel.
2. Add all of the remaining ingredients, except for the flour, to the Instant Pot.
3. Secure the lid and make sure the vent is set to sealing. Press Manual and set the time to 1 hour and 15 minutes. Let the pressure release naturally.
4. Remove meat and vegetables to large platter. Cover to keep warm.
5. Remove 1 cup of the liquid from the Instant Pot and mix with the flour. Press Sauté on the Instant Pot and add the flour/broth mixture back in, whisking. Cook until the broth is smooth and thickened.
6. Serve over noodles or spaetzle.

*Per Serving:calories: 251 / fat: 8g / protein: 26g / carbs: 17g / sugars: 7g / fiber: 4g / sodium: 525mg*

## Herb-Crusted Lamb Chops

Prep time: 10 minutes / Cook time: 5 minutes / Serves 2

- 1 large egg
- 2 cloves garlic, minced
- ¼ cup pork dust
- ¼ cup powdered Parmesan cheese
- 1 tablespoon chopped fresh oregano leaves
- 1 tablespoon chopped fresh rosemary leaves
- 1 teaspoon chopped fresh thyme leaves
- ½ teaspoon ground black pepper
- 4 (1-inch-thick) lamb chops
- For Garnish/Serving (Optional):
- Sprigs of fresh oregano
- Sprigs of fresh rosemary
- Sprigs of fresh thyme
- Lavender flowers
- Lemon slices

1. Spray the air fryer basket with avocado oil. Preheat the air fryer to 400°F (204°C).

2. Beat the egg in a shallow bowl, add the garlic, and stir well to combine. In another shallow bowl, mix together the pork dust, Parmesan, herbs, and pepper.
3. One at a time, dip the lamb chops into the egg mixture, shake off the excess egg, and then dredge them in the Parmesan mixture. Use your hands to coat the chops well in the Parmesan mixture and form a nice crust on all sides; if necessary, dip the chops again in both the egg and the Parmesan mixture.
4. Place the lamb chops in the air fryer basket, leaving space between them, and air fry for 5 minutes, or until the internal temperature reaches 145°F (63°C) for medium doneness. Allow to rest for 10 minutes before serving.
5. Garnish with sprigs of oregano, rosemary, and thyme, and lavender flowers, if desired. Serve with lemon slices, if desired.
6. Best served fresh. Store leftovers in an airtight container in the fridge for up to 4 days. Serve chilled over a salad, or reheat in a 350°F (177°C) air fryer for 3 minutes, or until heated through.

*Per Serving:calorie: 360 / fat: 21g / protein: 36g / carbs: 8g / sugars: 1g / fiber: 1g / sodium: 420mg*

## Sage-Parmesan Pork Chops

Prep time: 30 minutes / Cook time: 25 minutes / Serves 2
• Extra-virgin olive oil cooking spray
• 2 tablespoons coconut flour
• ¼ teaspoon salt
• Pinch freshly ground black pepper
• ¼ cup almond meal
• ½ cup finely ground flaxseed meal
• ½ cup soy Parmesan cheese
• 1½ teaspoons rubbed sage
• ½ teaspoon grated lemon zest
• 2 (4-ounce) boneless pork chops
• 1 large egg, lightly beaten
• 1 tablespoon extra-virgin olive oil

1. Preheat the oven to 425°F.
2. Lightly coat a medium baking dish with cooking spray.
3. In a shallow dish, mix together the coconut flour, salt, and pepper.
4. In a second shallow dish, stir together the almond meal, flaxseed meal, soy Parmesan cheese, sage, and lemon zest.
5. Gently press one pork chop into the coconut flour mixture to coat. Shake off any excess. Dip into the beaten egg. Press into the almond meal mixture. Gently toss between your hands so any coating that hasn't stuck can fall away. Place the coated chop on a plate. Repeat the process with the

remaining pork chop and coating ingredients.
6. In a large skillet set over medium heat, heat the olive oil.
7. Add the coated chops. Cook for about 4 minutes per side, or until browned. Transfer to the prepared baking dish. Place the dish in the preheated oven. Bake for 10 to 15 minutes, or until the juices run clear and an instant-read thermometer inserted into the middle of the pork reads 160°F.

*Per Serving:calorie: 520 / fat: 31g / protein: 45g / carbs: 14g / sugars: 1g / fiber: 6g / sodium: 403mg*

## Open-Faced Philly Cheesesteak Sandwiches

Prep time: 5 minutes / Cook time: 25 minutes / Serves 4
• Avocado oil cooking spray
• 1 cup chopped yellow onion
• 1 green bell pepper, chopped
• 12 ounces 93% lean ground beef
• Pinch salt
• ¾ teaspoon freshly ground black pepper
• 4 slices provolone or Swiss cheese
• 4 English muffins, 100% whole-wheat

1. Heat a large skillet over medium-low heat. When hot, coat the cooking surface with cooking spray, and arrange the onion and pepper in an even layer. Cook for 8 to 10 minutes, stirring every 3 to 4 minutes.
2. Push the vegetables to one side of the skillet and add the beef, breaking it into large chunks. Cook for 7 to 9 minutes, until a crisp crust forms on the bottom of the meat.
3. Season the beef with the salt and pepper, then flip the beef over and break it down into smaller chunks.
4. Stir the vegetables and the beef together, then top with the cheese and cook for 2 minutes.
5. Meanwhile, split each muffin in half, if necessary, then toast the muffins in a toaster.
6. Place one-eighth of the filling on each muffin half.

*Per Serving:calorie: 373 / fat: 13g / protein: 33g / carbs: 33g / sugars: 8g / fiber: 6g / sodium: 303mg*

## Pork Carnitas

Prep time: 10 minutes / Cook time: 20 minutes / Serves 8
• 1 teaspoon kosher salt
• 2 teaspoons chili powder
• 2 teaspoons dried oregano
• ½ teaspoon freshly ground black pepper
• 1 (2½-pound) pork sirloin roast or boneless pork butt, cut into 1½-inch cubes
• 2 tablespoons avocado oil, divided
• 3 garlic cloves, minced
• Juice and zest of 1 large orange
• Juice and zest of 1 medium lime

- 6-inch gluten-free corn tortillas, warmed, for serving (optional)
- Chopped avocado, for serving (optional)
- Roasted Tomatillo Salsa or salsa verde, for serving (optional)
- Shredded cheddar cheese, for serving (optional)

1. In a large bowl or gallon-size zip-top bag, combine the salt, chili powder, oregano, and pepper. Add the pork cubes and toss to coat.
2. Set the electric pressure cooker to the Sauté/More setting. When the pot is hot, pour in 1 tablespoon of avocado oil.
3. Add half of the pork to the pot and sear until the pork is browned on all sides, about 5 minutes. Transfer the pork to a plate, add the remaining 1 tablespoon of avocado oil to the pot, and sear the remaining pork. Hit Cancel.
4. Return all of the pork to the pot and add the garlic, orange zest and juice, and lime zest and juice to the pot.
5. Close and lock the lid of the pressure cooker. Set the valve to sealing.
6. Cook on high pressure for 20 minutes.
7. When the cooking is complete, hit Cancel. Allow the pressure to release naturally for 15 minutes then quick release any remaining pressure.
8. Once the pin drops, unlock and remove the lid.
9. Using two forks, shred the meat right in the pot.
10. (Optional) For more authentic carnitas, spread the shredded meat on a broiler-safe sheet pan. Preheat the broiler with the rack 6 inches from the heating element. Broil the pork for about 5 minutes or until it begins to crisp. (Watch carefully so you don't let the pork burn. )
11. Place the pork in a serving bowl. Top with some of the juices from the pot. Serve with tortillas, avocado, salsa, and Cheddar cheese (if using).

*Per Serving:calorie: 218 / fat: 7g / protein: 33g / carbs: 4g / sugars: 2g / fiber: 1g / sodium: 400mg*

## Rosemary Lamb Chops

Prep time: 25 minutes / Cook time: 2 minutes / Serves 4
- 1½ pounds lamb chops (4 small chops)
- 1 teaspoon kosher salt
- Leaves from 1 (6-inch) rosemary sprig
- 2 tablespoons avocado oil
- 1 shallot, peeled and cut in quarters
- 1 tablespoon tomato paste
- 1 cup beef broth

1. Place the lamb chops on a cutting board. Press the salt and rosemary leaves into both sides of the chops. Let rest at room temperature for 15 to 30 minutes.
2. Set the electric pressure cooker to Sauté/More setting. When hot, add the avocado oil.

3. Brown the lamb chops, about 2 minutes per side. (If they don't all fit in a single layer, brown them in batches. )
4. Transfer the chops to a plate. In the pot, combine the shallot, tomato paste, and broth. Cook for about a minute, scraping up the brown bits from the bottom. Hit Cancel.
5. Add the chops and any accumulated juices back to the pot.
6. Close and lock the lid of the pressure cooker. Set the valve to sealing.
7. Cook on high pressure for 2 minutes.
8. When the cooking is complete, hit Cancel and quick release the pressure.
9. Once the pin drops, unlock and remove the lid.
10. Place the lamb chops on plates and serve immediately.

*Per Serving:calorie: 352 / fat: 20g / protein: 37g / carbs: 7g / sugars: 1g / fiber: 0g / sodium: 440mg*

## Beef Burgundy

Prep time: 30 minutes / Cook time: 30 minutes / Serves 6
- 2 tablespoons olive oil
- 2 pounds stewing meat, cubed, trimmed of fat
- 2½ tablespoons flour
- 5 medium onions, thinly sliced
- ½ pound fresh mushrooms, sliced
- 1 teaspoon salt
- ¼ teaspoon dried marjoram
- ¼ teaspoon dried thyme
- ⅛ teaspoon pepper
- ¾ cup beef broth
- 1½ cups burgundy

1. Press Sauté on the Instant pot and add in the olive oil.
2. Dredge meat in flour, then brown in batches in the Instant Pot. Set aside the meat. Sauté the onions and mushrooms in the remaining oil and drippings for about 3–4 minutes, then add the meat back in. Press Cancel.
3. Add the salt, marjoram, thyme, pepper, broth, and wine to the Instant Pot.
4. Secure the lid and make sure the vent is set to sealing. Press the Manual button and set to 30 minutes.
5. When cook time is up, let the pressure release naturally for 15 minutes, then perform a quick release.
6. Serve over cooked noodles.

*Per Serving:calories: 358 / fat: 11g / protein: 37g / carbs: 15g / sugars: 5g / fiber: 2g / sodium: 472mg*

## Homey Pot Roast

Prep time: 15 minutes / Cook time: 2 hour 15 minutes / Serves 6
- 1 pound boneless beef chuck roast

- 2 tablespoons Creole seasoning
- 2 cups store-bought low-sodium chicken broth, divided
- 1 large portobello mushroom, cut into 2-inch pieces
- 1 small onion, roughly chopped
- 3 celery stalks, roughly chopped
- 4 medium tomatoes, chopped
- 2 garlic cloves, minced
- 1 medium green pepper, roughly chopped
- 8 ounces steamer potatoes, skin on, halved
- 6 small parsnips, peeled and halved
- 2 large carrots, peeled and cut into 2-inch pieces
- 3 bay leaves
- Freshly ground black pepper
- Pinch cayenne pepper
- Pinch smoked paprika

1. Preheat the oven to 325°F.
2. Massage the roast all over with the Creole seasoning.
3. In a Dutch oven, bring ½ cup of broth to a simmer over medium heat.
4. Add the beef and cook on all sides, turning to avoid burning the meat, no more than about 2½ minutes per side, or until browned. Remove the beef from the pot and set aside.
5. Add the mushroom, onion, celery, tomatoes, garlic, and green pepper to pot, adding up to ½ cup of broth if needed to prevent blackening of the vegetables.
6. Reduce the heat to medium-low and cook, stirring continuously, for 5 to 7 minutes, or until the vegetables have softened.
7. Return the beef to the pot. Add the potatoes, parsnips, carrots, bay leaves, and remaining 1 cup of broth.
8. Season with the black pepper, cayenne, and paprika.
9. Cover the pot, transfer to the oven, and bake for 2 hours, or until the beef is juicy and falls apart easily. Discard the bay leaves.
10. Serve.

*Per Serving:calorie: 237 / fat: 5g / protein: 20g / carbs: 29g / sugars: 8g / fiber: 7g / sodium: 329mg*

## Easy Beef Curry

Prep time: 15 minutes / Cook time: 10 minutes / Serves 6
- 1 tablespoon extra-virgin olive oil
- 1 small onion, thinly sliced
- 2 teaspoons minced fresh ginger
- 3 garlic cloves, minced
- 2 teaspoons ground coriander
- 1 teaspoon ground cumin
- 1 jalapeño or serrano pepper, slit lengthwise but not all the way through
- ¼ teaspoon ground turmeric
- ¼ teaspoon salt
- 1 pound grass-fed sirloin tip steak, top round steak, or top sirloin steak, cut into bite-size pieces
- 2 tablespoons chopped fresh cilantro

1. In a large skillet, heat the oil over medium high.
2. Add the onion, and cook for 3 to 5 minutes until browned and softened. Add the ginger and garlic, stirring continuously until fragrant, about 30 seconds.
3. In a small bowl, mix the coriander, cumin, jalapeño, turmeric, and salt. Add the spice mixture to the skillet and stir continuously for 1 minute. Deglaze the skillet with about ¼ cup of water.
4. Add the beef and stir continuously for about 5 minutes until well-browned yet still medium rare. Remove the jalapeño. Serve topped with the cilantro.

*Per Serving:calories: 140 / fat: 7g / protein: 18g / carbs: 3g / sugars: 1g / fiber: 1g / sodium: 141mg*

## Creole Steak

Prep time: 5 minutes / Cook time: 1 hour 40 minutes / Serves 4
- 2 teaspoons extra-virgin olive oil
- ¼ cup chopped onion
- ¼ cup chopped green bell pepper
- 1 cup canned crushed tomatoes
- ½ teaspoon chili powder
- ¼ teaspoon celery seed
- 4 cloves garlic, finely chopped
- ¼ teaspoon salt
- 1 teaspoon cumin
- 1 pound lean boneless round steak

1. In a large skillet over medium heat, heat the oil. Add the onions and green pepper, and sauté until the onions are translucent (about 5 minutes).
2. Add the tomatoes, chili powder, celery seed, garlic, salt, and cumin; cover and let simmer over low heat for 20–25 minutes. This allows the flavors to blend.
3. Preheat the oven to 350 degrees. Trim all visible fat off the steak.
4. In a nonstick pan or a pan that has been sprayed with nonstick cooking spray, lightly brown the steak on each side. Transfer the steak to a 13-x-9-x-2-inch baking dish; pour the sauce over the steak, and cover.
5. Bake for 1¼ hours or until the steak is tender. Remove from the oven; slice the steak, and arrange on a serving platter. Spoon the sauce over the steak, and serve.

*Per Serving:calorie: 213 / fat: 10g / protein: 25g / carbs: 5g / sugars: 2g / fiber: 2g / sodium: 235mg*

## Mustard Herb Pork Tenderloin

Prep time: 5 minutes / Cook time: 20 minutes / Serves 6
- ¼ cup mayonnaise
- 2 tablespoons Dijon mustard

- ½ teaspoon dried thyme
- ¼ teaspoon dried rosemary
- 1 (1 pound / 454 g) pork tenderloin
- ½ teaspoon salt
- ¼ teaspoon ground black pepper

1. In a small bowl, mix mayonnaise, mustard, thyme, and rosemary. Brush tenderloin with mixture on all sides, then sprinkle with salt and pepper on all sides.
2. Place tenderloin into ungreased air fryer basket. Adjust the temperature to 400°F (204°C) and air fry for 20 minutes, turning tenderloin halfway through cooking. Tenderloin will be golden and have an internal temperature of at least 145°F (63°C) when done. Serve warm.

*Per Serving:calorie: 118 / fat: 5g / protein: 17g / carbs: 1g / sugars: 0g / fiber: 0g / sodium: 368mg*

## Steak with Bell Pepper

Prep time: 30 minutes / Cook time: 20 to 23 minutes / Serves 6

- ¼ cup avocado oil
- ¼ cup freshly squeezed lime juice
- 2 teaspoons minced garlic
- 1 tablespoon chili powder
- ½ teaspoon ground cumin
- Sea salt and freshly ground black pepper, to taste
- 1 pound (454 g) top sirloin steak or flank steak, thinly sliced against the grain
- 1 red bell pepper, cored, seeded, and cut into ½-inch slices
- 1 green bell pepper, cored, seeded, and cut into ½-inch slices
- 1 large onion, sliced

1. In a small bowl or blender, combine the avocado oil, lime juice, garlic, chili powder, cumin, and salt and pepper to taste.
2. Place the sliced steak in a zip-top bag or shallow dish. Place the bell peppers and onion in a separate zip-top bag or dish. Pour half the marinade over the steak and the other half over the vegetables. Seal both bags and let the steak and vegetables marinate in the refrigerator for at least 1 hour or up to 4 hours.
3. Line the air fryer basket with an air fryer liner or aluminum foil. Remove the vegetables from their bag or dish and shake off any excess marinade. Set the air fryer to 400°F (204°C). Place the vegetables in the air fryer basket and cook for 13 minutes.
4. Remove the steak from its bag or dish and shake off any excess marinade. Place the steak on top of the vegetables in the air fryer, and cook for 7 to 10 minutes or until an instant-read thermometer reads 120°F (49°C) for medium-rare (or cook to your desired doneness).

5. Serve with desired fixings, such as keto tortillas, lettuce, sour cream, avocado slices, shredded Cheddar cheese, and cilantro.

*Per Serving:calorie: 330 / fat: 24g / protein: 20g / carbs: 12g / sugars: 4g / fiber: 3g / sodium: 160mg*

## Grilled Steak and Vegetables

Prep time: 15 minutes / Cook time: 25 minutes / Serves 2

- Extra-virgin olive oil cooking spray
- 2 (8-ounce) sirloin steaks
- 2 medium pear-shaped tomatoes, halved lengthwise
- 1 medium zucchini, cut into chunks
- 1 medium yellow squash, cut into chunks
- 1 bell pepper (any color), cut into 1-inch pieces
- 2 tablespoons extra-virgin olive oil, divided
- 1 garlic clove, minced
- ¼ cup fresh basil, plus fresh sprigs, for garnish
- Pinch salt
- Freshly ground black pepper, to season

1. Preheat the grill (charcoal or gas).
2. Lightly coat a grill rack with cooking spray.
3. Place the steaks on the grill rack, about 4 to 6 inches above the heat—whether a solid bed of medium-hot coals or gas. Cook for about 15 minutes, turning as needed, until evenly browned on the outside and an instant-read thermometer inserted in the center registers 145°F for medium-rare.
4. While the steaks cook, place the tomatoes, zucchini, yellow squash, and bell pepper on the grill. Brush lightly with 1 tablespoon of olive oil. Grill for about 3 minutes, or until the vegetables are browned on the bottom. Turn them over. Continue to cook for about 3 minutes more, or until soft.
5. In a medium skillet with a heatproof handle set over medium-high heat, stir together the remaining 1 tablespoon of olive oil, garlic, and basil.
6. Transfer the grilled vegetables to the skillet. Stir to combine. Reduce the heat to low.
7. Serve each steak accompanied by half of the vegetables. Season with salt and pepper. Garnish with the basil sprigs.

*Per Serving:calorie: 631 / fat: 38g / protein: 52g / carbs: 18g / sugars: 8g / fiber: 5g / sodium: 239mg*

## Pork and Apple Skillet

Prep time: 10 minutes / Cook time: 20 minutes / Serves 4
- 1 pound ground pork
- 1 red onion, thinly sliced
- 2 apples, peeled, cored, and thinly sliced
- 2 cups shredded cabbage
- 1 teaspoon dried thyme
- 2 garlic cloves, minced

- ¼ cup apple cider vinegar
- 1 tablespoon Dijon mustard
- ½ teaspoon sea salt
- ⅛ teaspoon freshly ground black pepper

1. In a large skillet over medium-high heat, cook the ground pork, crumbling it with a spoon, until browned, about 5 minutes. Use a slotted spoon to transfer the pork to a plate.
2. Add the onion, apples, cabbage, and thyme to the fat in the pan. Cook, stirring occasionally, until the vegetables are soft, about 5 minutes.
3. Add the garlic and cook, stirring constantly, for 5 minutes.
4. Return the pork to the pan.
5. In a small bowl, whisk together the vinegar, mustard, salt, and pepper. Add to the pan. Bring to a simmer. Cook, stirring, until the sauce thickens, about 2 minutes.

*Per Serving:calorie: 218 / fat: 5g / protein: 25g / carbs: 20g / sugars: 12g / fiber: 4g / sodium: 425mg*

## Marjoram-Pepper Steaks

Prep time: 5 minutes / Cook time: 8 minutes / Serves 2
- 1 tablespoon freshly ground black pepper
- ¼ teaspoon dried marjoram
- 2 (6-ounce, 1-inch-thick) beef tenderloins
- 1 tablespoon extra-virgin olive oil
- ¼ cup low-sodium beef broth
- Fresh marjoram sprigs, for garnish

1. In a large bowl, mix together the pepper and marjoram.
2. Add the steaks. Coat both sides with the spice mixture.
3. In a skillet set over medium-high heat, heat the olive oil.
4. Add the steaks. Cook for 5 to 7 minutes, or until an instant-read thermometer inserted in the center registers 160°F (for medium). Remove from the skillet. Cover to keep warm.
5. Add the broth to the skillet. Increase the heat to high. Bring to a boil, scraping any browned bits from the bottom. Boil for about 1 minute, or until the liquid is reduced by half.
6. Spoon the broth sauce over the steaks. Garnish with marjoram sprigs and serve immediately.

*Per Serving:calorie: 339 / fat: 19g / protein: 38g / carbs: 2g / sugars: 0g / fiber: 1g / sodium: 209mg*

## Open-Faced Pub-Style Bison Burgers

Prep time: 10 minutes / Cook time: 15 minutes / Serves 4
- 2 tablespoons extra-virgin olive oil
- 1 onion, thinly sliced
- 1 pound ground bison

- 1 teaspoon sea salt, divided
- 1 cup blue cheese crumbles
- 4 slices sourdough bread
- 1 garlic clove, halved
- Pub Sauce

1. In a large skillet over medium-high heat, heat the olive oil until it shimmers. Add the onion. Cook, stirring, until it begins to brown, about 5 minutes.
2. Set the onion aside, and wipe out the skillet with a paper towel and return it to the stove at medium-high heat. Season the bison with the salt and form it into 4 patties. Brown the patties in the hot skillet until they reach an internal temperature of 140°F, about 5 minutes per side.
3. Sprinkle the blue cheese over the tops of the burgers and remove the skillet from the heat. Cover the skillet and allow the cheese to melt.
4. Meanwhile, toast the bread and then rub the garlic halves over the pieces of toast to flavor them.
5. To assemble, put a piece of toast on a plate. Top with onion slices, place a burger patty on top, and then spoon the sauce over the patty.

*Per Serving:calorie: 433 / fat: 25g / protein: 33g / carbs: 18g / sugars: 2g / fiber: 1g / sodium: 563mg*

## Bone-in Pork Chops

Prep time: 5 minutes / Cook time: 10 to 12 minutes / Serves 2
- 1 pound (454 g) bone-in pork chops
- 1 tablespoon avocado oil
- 1 teaspoon smoked paprika
- ½ teaspoon onion powder
- ¼ teaspoon cayenne pepper
- Sea salt and freshly ground black pepper, to taste

1. Brush the pork chops with the avocado oil. In a small dish, mix together the smoked paprika, onion powder, cayenne pepper, and salt and black pepper to taste. Sprinkle the seasonings over both sides of the pork chops.
2. Set the air fryer to 400°F (204°C). Place the chops in the air fryer basket in a single layer, working in batches if necessary. Air fry for 10 to 12 minutes, until an instant-read thermometer reads 145°F (63°C) at the chops' thickest point.
3. Remove the chops from the air fryer and allow them to rest for 5 minutes before serving.

*Per Serving:calorie: 429 / fat: 29g / protein: 39g / carbs: 1g / sugars: 0g / fiber: 0g / sodium: 82mg*

## Asian-Style Grilled Beef Salad

Prep time: 15 minutes / Cook time: 15 minutes / Serves 4
- For The Dressing
- ¼ cup freshly squeezed lime juice

- 1 tablespoon low-sodium tamari or gluten-free soy sauce
- 1 tablespoon extra-virgin olive oil
- 1 garlic clove, minced
- 1 teaspoon honey
- ¼ teaspoon red pepper flakes
- For The Salad
- 1 pound grass-fed flank steak
- ¼ teaspoon salt
- Pinch freshly ground black pepper
- 6 cups chopped leaf lettuce
- 1 cucumber, halved lengthwise and thinly cut into half moons
- ½ small red onion, sliced
- 1 carrot, cut into ribbons
- ¼ cup chopped fresh cilantro

1. In a small bowl, whisk together the lime juice, tamari, olive oil, garlic, honey, and red pepper flakes. Set aside. Make The Salad: 1. Season the beef on both sides with the salt and pepper.
2. Heat a skillet over high heat until hot. Cook the beef for 3 to 6 minutes per side, depending on preferred doneness. Set aside, tented with aluminum foil, for 10 minutes.
3. In a large bowl, toss the lettuce, cucumber, onion, carrot, and cilantro.
4. Slice the beef thinly against the grain and transfer to the salad bowl.
5. Drizzle with the dressing and toss. Serve.

*Per Serving:calories: 231 / fat: 10g / protein: 26g / carbs: 10g / sugars: 4g / fiber: 2g / sodium: 349mg*

## Slow Cooker Ropa Vieja

Prep time: 5 minutes / Cook time: 20 minutes / Serves 4

- ½ small yellow onion
- 1 red bell pepper
- 1 (14 ounces) can no-salt-added diced tomatoes
- 1 teaspoon dried oregano
- ½ teaspoon salt
- ½ teaspoon smoked paprika
- ½ teaspoon garlic powder
- 1 pound chuck beef roast, trimmed of visible fat
- 1 head cauliflower

1. Cut the onion and bell pepper into ½-inch-thick slices.
2. Place the onion, bell pepper, diced tomatoes with their juices, oregano, salt, paprika, and garlic powder in a slow cooker, then add the beef.
3. Place the head of cauliflower on top of the beef, and cook on low for 8 hours.
4. When fully cooked, the cauliflower will fall apart when scooped.

*Per Serving:calorie: 228 / fat: 7g / protein: 27g / carbs: 14g / sugars: 7g / fiber: 6g / sodium: 445mg*

## Homestyle Herb Meatballs

Prep time: 10 minutes / Cook time: 15 minutes / Serves 4

- ½ pound lean ground pork
- ½ pound lean ground beef
- 1 sweet onion, finely chopped
- ¼ cup bread crumbs
- 2 tablespoons chopped fresh basil
- 2 teaspoons minced garlic
- 1 egg
- Pinch sea salt
- Pinch freshly ground black pepper

1. Preheat the oven to 350°F.
2. Line a baking tray with parchment paper and set it aside.
3. In a large bowl, mix together the pork, beef, onion, bread crumbs, basil, garlic, egg, salt, and pepper until very well mixed.
4. Roll the meat mixture into 2-inch meatballs.
5. Transfer the meatballs to the baking sheet and bake until they are browned and cooked through, about 15 minutes.
6. Serve the meatballs with your favorite marinara sauce and some steamed green beans.

*Per Serving:calorie: 214 / fat: 7g / protein: 27g / carbs: 12g / sugars: 5g / fiber: 1g / sodium: 147mg*

## "Smothered" Steak

Prep time: 20 minutes / Cook time: 15 minutes / Serves 6

- 1 tablespoon olive oil
- ¼ teaspoon pepper
- ⅓ cup flour
- 1½-pound chuck, or round, steak, cut into strips, trimmed of fat
- 1 large onion, sliced
- 1 green pepper, sliced
- 14½-ounce can stewed tomatoes
- 4-ounce can mushrooms, drained
- 2 tablespoons soy sauce
- 10-ounce package frozen French-style green beans

1. Press Sauté and add the oil to the Instant Pot.
2. Mix together the flour and pepper in a small bowl. Place the steak pieces into the mixture in the bowl and coat each of them well.
3. Lightly brown each of the steak pieces in the Instant Pot, about 2 minutes on each side. Press Cancel when done.
4. Add the remaining ingredients to the Instant Pot and mix together gently.
5. Secure the lid and make sure vent is set to sealing. Press Manual and set for 15 minutes.
6. When cook time is up, let the pressure release naturally for 15 minutes, then perform a quick release.

*Per Serving:calories: 386 / fat: 24g / protein: 25g / carbs: 20g / sugars: 4g / fiber: 4g / sodium: 746mg*

## Ground Beef Tacos

Prep time: 0 minutes / Cook time: 25 minutes / Serves 6

- Filling
- 1 tablespoon cold-pressed avocado oil or other neutral oil
- 2 garlic cloves, minced
- 1 yellow onion, diced
- 1½ pounds 95 percent lean ground beef
- 2 tablespoons chili powder
- ½ cup low-sodium roasted beef bone broth
- Fine sea salt
- 1 tablespoon tomato paste
- Twelve 7-inch corn tortillas, warmed
- 1 cup chopped white onion
- 1 cup chopped tomatoes
- 2 tablespoons chopped fresh cilantro
- 1 large avocado, pitted, peeled, and sliced
- Hot sauce (such as Cholula or Tapatío) for serving

1. To make the filling: Select the Sauté setting on the Instant Pot and heat the oil and garlic for 2 minutes, until the garlic is bubbling but not browned. Add the yellow onion and sauté for about 3 minutes, until it begins to soften. Add the ground beef and sauté, using a wooden spoon or spatula to break up the meat as it cooks for about 3 minutes more; it's fine if some streaks of pink remain, the beef does not need to be cooked through. Stir in the chili powder, bone broth, and ½ teaspoon salt. Dollop the tomato paste on top. Do not stir it in.
2. Secure the lid and set the Pressure Release to Sealing. Press the Cancel button to reset the cooking program, then select the Pressure Cook or Manual setting and set the cooking time for 10 minutes at high pressure. (The pot will take about 5 minutes to come up to pressure before the cooking program begins. )
3. When the cooking program ends, you can either perform a quick pressure release by moving the Pressure Release to Venting, or you can let the pressure release naturally and leave the pot on the Keep Warm setting for up to 10 hours. Open the pot and give the meat a stir. Taste for seasoning and add more salt, if needed.
4. Using a slotted spoon, spoon the meat onto the tortillas. Top with the white onion, tomatoes, cilantro, and avocado and serve right away. Pass the hot sauce at the table.

*Per Serving:calories: 353 / fat: 13g / protein: 28g / carbs: 28g / sugars: 3g / fiber: 6g / sodium: 613mg*

## Roasted Pork Loin

Prep time: 5 minutes / Cook time: 40 minutes / Serves 4

- 1 pound pork loin
- 1 tablespoon extra-virgin olive oil, divided
- 2 teaspoons honey
- ¼ teaspoon freshly ground black pepper
- ½ teaspoon dried rosemary
- 2 small gold potatoes, chopped into 2-inch cubes
- 4 (6-inch) carrots, chopped into ½-inch rounds

1. Preheat the oven to 350ºF.
2. Rub the pork loin with ½ tablespoon of oil and the honey. Season with the pepper and rosemary.
3. In a medium bowl, toss the potatoes and carrots in the remaining ½ tablespoon of oil.
4. Place the pork and the vegetables on a baking sheet in a single layer. Cook for 40 minutes.
5. Remove the baking sheet from the oven and let the pork rest for at least 10 minutes before slicing. Divide the pork and vegetables into four equal portions.

*Per Serving:calorie: 281 / fat: 8g / protein: 28g / carbs: 24g / sugars: 6g / fiber: 4g / sodium: 103mg*

## Mango-Glazed Pork Tenderloin Roast

Prep time: 10 minutes / Cook time: 20 minutes / Serves 4

- 1 pound boneless pork tenderloin, trimmed of fat
- 1 teaspoon chopped fresh rosemary
- 1 teaspoon chopped fresh thyme
- ¼ teaspoon salt, divided
- ¼ teaspoon freshly ground black pepper, divided
- 1 teaspoon extra-virgin olive oil
- 1 tablespoon honey
- 2 tablespoons white wine vinegar
- 2 tablespoons dry cooking wine
- 1 tablespoon minced fresh ginger
- 1 cup diced mango

1. Preheat the oven to 400°F.
2. Season the tenderloin with the rosemary, thyme, ⅛ teaspoon of salt, and ⅛ teaspoon of pepper.
3. Heat the olive oil in an oven-safe skillet over medium-high heat, and sear the tenderloin until browned on all sides, about 5 minutes total.
4. Transfer the skillet to the oven and roast for 12 to 15 minutes until the pork is cooked through, the juices run clear, and the internal temperature reaches 145°F. Transfer to a cutting board to rest for 5 minutes.
5. In a small bowl, combine the honey, vinegar, cooking wine, and ginger. In to the same skillet, pour the honey mixture and simmer for 1 minute. Add the mango and toss to coat. Transfer to a blender and purée until smooth. Season with the remaining ⅛ teaspoon of salt and ⅛ teaspoon of

pepper.

6. Slice the pork into rounds and serve with the mango sauce.

*Per Serving:calories: 182 / fat: 4g / protein: 24 / carbs: 12g / sugars: 10g / fiber: 1g / sodium: 240mg*

## Chipotle Chili Pork Chops

Prep time: 5 minutes / Cook time: 20 minutes / Serves 4

- Juice and zest of 1 lime
- 1 tablespoon extra-virgin olive oil
- 1 tablespoon chipotle chili powder
- 2 teaspoons minced garlic
- 1 teaspoon ground cinnamon
- Pinch sea salt
- 4 (5-ounce) pork chops, about 1 inch thick
- Lime wedges, for garnish

1. Combine the lime juice and zest, oil, chipotle chili powder, garlic, cinnamon, and salt in a resealable plastic bag. Add the pork chops. Remove as much air as possible and seal the bag.
2. Marinate the chops in the refrigerator for at least 4 hours, and up to 24 hours, turning them several times.
3. Preheat the oven to 400°F and set a rack on a baking sheet. Let the chops rest at room temperature for 15 minutes, then arrange them on the rack and discard the remaining marinade.
4. Roast the chops until cooked through, turning once, about 10 minutes per side.
5. Serve with lime wedges.

*Per Serving:calorie: 224 / fat: 9g / protein: 32g / carbs: 4g / sugars: 0g / fiber: 2g / sodium: 140mg*

## Lamb Chops with Cherry Glaze

Prep time: 10 minutes / Cook time: 20 minutes / Serves 4

- 4 (4-ounce) lamb chops
- 1½ teaspoons chopped fresh rosemary
- ¼ teaspoon salt
- ¼ teaspoon freshly ground black pepper
- 1 cup frozen cherries, thawed
- ¼ cup dry red wine
- 2 tablespoons orange juice

- 1 teaspoon extra-virgin olive oil

1. Season the lamb chops with the rosemary, salt, and pepper.
2. In a small saucepan over medium-low heat, combine the cherries, red wine, and orange juice, and simmer, stirring regularly, until the sauce thickens, 8 to 10 minutes.
3. Heat a large skillet over medium-high heat. When the pan is hot, add the olive oil to lightly coat the bottom.
4. Cook the lamb chops for 3 to 4 minutes on each side until well-browned yet medium rare.
5. Serve, topped with the cherry glaze.

*Per Serving:calories: 356 / fat: 27g / protein: 20g / carbs: 6g / sugars: 4g / fiber: 1g / sodium: 199mg*

## Lime-Parsley Lamb Cutlets

Prep time: 10 minutes / Cook time: 10 minutes / Serves 4

- ¼ cup extra-virgin olive oil
- ¼ cup freshly squeezed lime juice
- 2 tablespoons lime zest
- 2 tablespoons chopped fresh parsley
- Pinch sea salt
- Pinch freshly ground black pepper
- 12 lamb cutlets (about 1½ pounds total)

1. In a medium bowl, whisk together the oil, lime juice, zest, parsley, salt, and pepper.
2. Transfer the marinade to a resealable plastic bag.
3. Add the cutlets to the bag and remove as much air as possible before sealing.
4. Marinate the lamb in the refrigerator for about 4 hours, turning the bag several times.
5. Preheat the oven to broil.
6. Remove the chops from the bag and arrange them on an aluminum foil–lined baking sheet. Discard the marinade.
7. Broil the chops for 4 minutes per side for medium doneness.
8. Let the chops rest for 5 minutes before serving.

*Per Serving:calorie: 333 / fat: 20g / protein: 36g / carbs: 20g / sugars: 0g / fiber: 0g / sodium: 182mg*

# Chapter 5 Fish and Seafood

## Sesame-Crusted Tuna Steak

Prep time: 5 minutes / Cook time: 8 minutes / Serves 2

- 2 (6 ounces / 170 g) tuna steaks
- 1 tablespoon coconut oil, melted
- ½ teaspoon garlic powder
- 2 teaspoons white sesame seeds
- 2 teaspoons black sesame seeds

1. Brush each tuna steak with coconut oil and sprinkle with garlic powder.
2. In a large bowl, mix sesame seeds and then press each tuna steak into them, covering the steak as completely as possible. Place tuna steaks into the air fryer basket.
3. Adjust the temperature to 400ºF (204ºC) and air fry for 8 minutes.
4. Flip the steaks halfway through the cooking time. Steaks will be well-done at 145ºF (63ºC) internal temperature. Serve warm.

*Per Serving:calorie: 290 / fat: 14g / protein: 36g / carbs: 2g / sugars: 0g / fiber: 1g / sodium: 160mg*

## Roasted Salmon with Salsa Verde

Prep time: 5 minutes / Cook time: 25 minutes / Serves 4

- Nonstick cooking spray
- 8 ounces tomatillos, husks removed
- ½ onion, quartered
- 1 jalapeño or serrano pepper, seeded
- 1 garlic clove, unpeeled
- 1 teaspoon extra-virgin olive oil
- ½ teaspoon salt, divided
- 4 (4-ounce) wild-caught salmon fillets
- ¼ teaspoon freshly ground black pepper
- ¼ cup chopped fresh cilantro
- Juice of 1 lime

1. Preheat the oven to 425ºF. Spray a baking sheet with nonstick cooking spray.
2. In a large bowl, toss the tomatillos, onion, jalapeño, garlic, olive oil, and ¼ teaspoon of salt to coat. Arrange in a single layer on the prepared baking sheet, and roast for about 10 minutes until just softened. Transfer to a dish or plate and set aside.
3. Arrange the salmon fillets skin-side down on the same baking sheet, and season with the remaining ¼ teaspoon of salt and the pepper. Bake for 12 to 15 minutes until the fish is firm and flakes easily.
4. Meanwhile, peel the roasted garlic and place it and the roasted vegetables in a blender or food processor. Add a scant ¼ cup of water to the jar, and process until smooth.

5. Add the cilantro and lime juice and process until smooth. Serve the salmon topped with the salsa verde.

*Per Serving:calories: 199 / fat: 9g / protein: 23g / carbs: 6g / sugars: 3g / fiber: 2g / sodium: 295mg*

## Peppercorn-Crusted Baked Salmon

Prep time: 5 minutes / Cook time: 20 minutes / Serves 4

- Nonstick cooking spray
- ½ teaspoon freshly ground black pepper
- ¼ teaspoon salt
- Zest and juice of ½ lemon
- ¼ teaspoon dried thyme
- 1 pound salmon fillet

1. Preheat the oven to 425ºF. Spray a baking sheet with nonstick cooking spray.
2. In a small bowl, combine the pepper, salt, lemon zest and juice, and thyme. Stir to combine.
3. Place the salmon on the prepared baking sheet, skin-side down. Spread the seasoning mixture evenly over the fillet.
4. Bake for 15 to 20 minutes, depending on the thickness of the fillet, until the flesh flakes easily.

*Per Serving:calories: 163 / fat: 7g / protein: 23g / carbs: 1g / sugars: 0g / fiber: 0g / sodium: 167mg*

## Seafood Stew

Prep time: 20 minutes / Cook time: 30 minutes / Serves 6

- 1 tablespoon extra-virgin olive oil
- 1 sweet onion, chopped
- 2 teaspoons minced garlic
- 3 celery stalks, chopped
- 2 carrots, peeled and chopped
- 1 (28 ounces) can sodium-free diced tomatoes, undrained
- 3 cups low-sodium chicken broth
- ½ cup clam juice
- ¼ cup dry white wine
- 2 teaspoons chopped fresh basil
- 2 teaspoons chopped fresh oregano
- 2 (4 ounces) haddock fillets, cut into 1-inch chunks
- 1 pound mussels, scrubbed, debearded
- 8 ounces (16 to 20 count) shrimp, peeled, deveined, quartered
- Sea salt
- Freshly ground black pepper
- 2 tablespoons chopped fresh parsley

1. Place a large saucepan over medium-high heat and add the olive oil.

2. Sauté the onion and garlic until softened and translucent, about 3 minutes.
3. Stir in the celery and carrots and sauté for 4 minutes.
4. Stir in the tomatoes, chicken broth, clam juice, white wine, basil, and oregano.
5. Bring the sauce to a boil, then reduce the heat to low. Simmer for 15 minutes.
6. Add the fish and mussels, cover, and cook until the mussels open, about 5 minutes.
7. Discard any unopened mussels. Add the shrimp to the pan and cook until the shrimp are opaque, about 2 minutes.
8. Season with salt and pepper. Serve garnished with the chopped parsley.

*Per Serving:calories: 230 / fat: 6g / protein: 27g / carbs: 18g / sugars: 8g / fiber: 4g / sodium: 490mg*

## Greek Scampi

Prep time: 10 minutes / Cook time: 5 minutes / Serves 2
- 2 garlic cloves, minced
- 2 tablespoons extra-virgin olive oil
- ½ pound shrimp, peeled, deveined, and thoroughly rinsed
- 1 cup diced tomatoes
- ½ cup nonfat ricotta cheese
- 6 Kalamata olives
- Juice of ½ lemon
- 2 teaspoons chopped fresh dill, or ¾ teaspoon dried
- Dash salt
- Dash freshly ground black pepper
- Lemon wedges, for garnish

1. In a large skillet set over medium heat, sauté the garlic in the olive oil for 30 seconds.
2. Add the shrimp. Cook for 1 minute.
3. Add the tomatoes, ricotta cheese, olives, lemon juice, and dill. Reduce the heat to low. Simmer for 5 to 10 minutes, stirring so the shrimp cook on both sides. When the shrimp are pink and the tomatoes and ricotta have made a sauce, the dish is ready.
4. Sprinkle with salt and pepper.
5. Serve immediately, garnished with lemon wedges.

*Per Serving:calories: 345 / fat: 21g / protein: 31g / carbs: 11g / sugars: 3g / fiber: 2g / sodium: 406mg*

## Halibut Supreme

Prep time: 10 minutes / Cook time: 25 minutes / Serves 6
- Nonstick cooking spray
- 1½ pound halibut steaks
- 1 cup sliced mushrooms
- 1 tablespoon extra-virgin olive oil
- 1 small onion, finely chopped

- 3 tablespoons white wine
- ¾ cup water
- ⅛ teaspoon freshly ground black pepper
- ¼ teaspoon salt
- ¼ cup toasted almond slivers
- 1 tablespoon chopped fresh parsley

1. Preheat the oven to 325 degrees. Coat a 13-x-9-x-2-inch baking dish with cooking spray, and place the halibut steaks in a baking dish.
2. Add the remaining ingredients except the almonds and parsley, and bake at 325 degrees, basting frequently, for 25 minutes until the fish flakes easily with a fork.
3. Remove from the oven, and top the halibut steaks with the toasted almond slivers. Garnish with parsley.

*Per Serving:calories: 267 / fat: 20g / protein: 18g / carbs: 3g / sugars: 1g / fiber: 1g / sodium: 190mg*

## Walnut-Crusted Halibut with Pear Salad

Prep time: 10 minutes / Cook time: 10 minutes / Serves 4
- For the halibut
- ¾ cup finely chopped toasted walnuts
- 2 tablespoons bread crumbs
- ¼ cup chopped fresh parsley
- 2 tablespoons chopped fresh chives
- 4 (6 to 8 ounces) halibut fillets
- Kosher salt
- Freshly ground black pepper
- 1 tablespoon extra-virgin olive oil
- For the salad
- 6 cups packed mixed greens
- 1 pear, thinly sliced
- ¼ cup chopped fresh parsley
- ¼ cup chopped fresh chives
- Zest and juice of 1 lemon
- Extra-virgin olive oil, for the dressing
- Kosher salt
- Freshly ground black pepper

1. To make the halibut 1. Preheat the broiler. Line a baking sheet with parchment paper.
2. In a small bowl, combine the walnuts, bread crumbs, parsley, and chives.
3. Pat the halibut fillets dry, season them with salt and pepper and rub ½ tablespoon of extra-virgin olive oil on each fillet. Place the fillets on the prepared baking sheet. Sprinkle the walnut mixture evenly on top of each fillet and press slightly, so the topping will stick.
4. Broil the fish until the crust is golden and the fish is fully cooked, 5 to 8 minutes. To make the salad 5. Meanwhile, in a large bowl, toss the greens, pear, parsley, chives, and zest until well combined. Drizzle the salad with the lemon juice and a bit of

extra-virgin olive oil to taste. Season with salt and pepper to taste.

6. Evenly divide the salad among four plates and top with the fish. Serve.
7. Store any leftovers in an airtight container in the refrigerator for up to 2 days.

*Per Serving:calories: 551 / fat: 43g / protein: 31g / carbs: 13g / sugars: 4g / fiber: 5g / sodium: 196mg*

## Creamy Cod with Asparagus

Prep time: 5 minutes / Cook time: 15 minutes / Serves 4

- ½ cup uncooked brown rice or quinoa
- 4 (4-ounce) cod fillets
- ¼ teaspoon salt
- ¼ teaspoon freshly ground black pepper
- ½ teaspoon garlic powder, divided
- 24 asparagus spears
- Avocado oil cooking spray
- 1 cup half-and-half

1. Cook the rice according to the package instructions.
2. Meanwhile, season both sides of the cod fillets with the salt, pepper, and ¼ teaspoon of garlic powder.
3. Cut the bottom 1½ inches from the asparagus.
4. Heat a large pan over medium-low heat. When hot, coat the cooking surface with cooking spray, and arrange the cod and asparagus in a single layer.
5. Cover and cook for 8 minutes.
6. Add the half-and-half and the remaining ¼ teaspoon of garlic powder and stir. Increase the heat to high and simmer for 2 minutes.
7. Divide the rice, cod, and asparagus into four equal portions.

*Per Serving:calories: 219 / fat: 2g / protein: 24g / carbs: 24g / sugars: 4g / fiber: 1g / sodium: 267mg*

## Quinoa Pilaf with Salmon and Asparagus

Prep time: 30 minutes / Cook time: 15 minutes / Serves 4

- 1 cup uncooked quinoa
- 6 cups water
- 1 vegetable bouillon cube
- 1 pound salmon fillets
- 2 teaspoons butter or margarine
- 20 stalks fresh asparagus, cut diagonally into 2-inch pieces (2 cups)
- 4 medium green onions, sliced (¼ cup)
- 1 cup frozen sweet peas (from 1 pound bag), thawed
- ½ cup halved grape tomatoes
- ½ cup vegetable or chicken broth
- 1 teaspoon lemon-pepper seasoning
- 2 teaspoons chopped fresh or ½ teaspoon dried dill weed

1. Rinse quinoa thoroughly by placing in a fine-mesh strainer and holding under cold running water until water runs clear; drain well.
2. In 2-quart saucepan, heat 2 cups of the water to boiling over high heat. Add quinoa; reduce heat to low. Cover; simmer 10 to 12 minutes or until water is absorbed.
3. Meanwhile, in 12-inch skillet, heat remaining 4 cups water and the bouillon cube to boiling over high heat. Add salmon, skin side up; reduce heat to low. Cover; simmer 10 to 12 minutes or until fish flakes easily with fork. Transfer with slotted spoon to plate; let cool. Discard water. Remove skin from salmon; break into large pieces.
4. Meanwhile, rinse and dry skillet. Melt butter in skillet over medium heat. Add asparagus; cook 5 minutes, stirring frequently. Stir in onions; cook 1 minute, stirring frequently. Stir in peas, tomatoes and broth; cook 1 minute.
5. Gently stir quinoa, salmon, lemon-pepper seasoning and dill weed into asparagus mixture. Cover; cook about 2 minutes or until hot.

*Per Serving:calories: 380 / fat: 12g / protein: 32g / carbs: 37g / sugars: 7g / fiber: 6g / sodium: 600mg*

## Broiled Sole with Mustard Sauce

Prep time: 5 minutes / Cook time: 20 minutes / Serves 6

- Nonstick cooking spray
- 1½ pound fresh sole filets
- 3 tablespoons low-fat mayonnaise
- 2 tablespoons Dijon mustard
- 2 tablespoons chopped parsley
- ⅛ teaspoon freshly ground black pepper
- 1 large lemon, cut into wedges

1. Preheat broiler. Coat a baking sheet with nonstick cooking spray. Arrange the filets so they don't overlap.
2. In a small bowl, combine the mayonnaise, mustard, parsley, and pepper, and mix thoroughly. Spread the mixture evenly over the filets. Broil 3–4 inches from the heat for 4 minutes until the fish flakes easily with a fork.
3. Arrange the filets on a serving platter, garnish with lemon wedges, and serve.

*Per Serving:calories: 104 / fat: 4g / protein: 14g / carbs: 3g / sugars: 1g / fiber: 1g / sodium: 402mg*

## Friday Night Fish Fry

Prep time: 10 minutes / Cook time: 10 minutes / Serves 4

- 1 large egg
- ½ cup powdered Parmesan cheese (about 1½ ounces / 43 g)

- 1 teaspoon smoked paprika
- ¼ teaspoon celery salt
- ¼ teaspoon ground black pepper
- 4 (4-ounce / 113-g) cod fillets
- Chopped fresh oregano or parsley, for garnish (optional)
- Lemon slices, for serving (optional)

1. Spray the air fryer basket with avocado oil. Preheat the air fryer to 400ºF (204ºC).
2. Crack the egg in a shallow bowl and beat it lightly with a fork. Combine the Parmesan cheese, paprika, celery salt, and pepper in a separate shallow bowl.
3. One at a time, dip the fillets into the egg, then dredge them in the Parmesan mixture. Using your hands, press the Parmesan onto the fillets to form a nice crust. As you finish, place the fish in the air fryer basket.
4. Air fry the fish in the air fryer for 10 minutes, or until it is cooked through and flakes easily with a fork. Garnish with fresh oregano or parsley and serve with lemon slices, if desired.
5. Store leftovers in an airtight container in the refrigerator for up to 3 days. Reheat in a preheated 400ºF (204ºC) air fryer for 5 minutes, or until warmed through.

*Per Serving:calorie: 300 / fat: 12g / protein: 40g / carbs: 6g / sugars: 1g / fiber: 0g / sodium: 800mg*

## Air Fryer Fish Fry

Prep time: 5 minutes / Cook time: 15 minutes / Serves 4

- 2 cups low-fat buttermilk
- ½ teaspoon garlic powder
- ½ teaspoon onion powder
- 4 (4 ounces) flounder fillets
- ½ cup plain yellow cornmeal
- ½ cup chickpea flour
- ¼ teaspoon cayenne pepper
- Freshly ground black pepper

1. In a large bowl, combine the buttermilk, garlic powder, and onion powder.
2. Add the flounder, turning until well coated, and set aside to marinate for 20 minutes.
3. In a shallow bowl, stir the cornmeal, chickpea flour, cayenne, and pepper together.
4. Dredge the fillets in the meal mixture, turning until well coated. Place in the basket of an air fryer.
5. Set the air fryer to 380°F, close, and cook for 12 minutes.

*Per Serving:calories: 266 / fat: 7g / protein: 27g / carbs: 24g / sugars: 8g / fiber: 2g / sodium: 569mg*

## Carrots

Prep time: 0 minutes / Cook time: 15 minutes / Serves 4

- 1 pound tilapia fillets
- 1 teaspoon lemon pepper seasoning
- ¼ teaspoon fine sea salt
- 2 tablespoons extra-virgin olive oil
- 2 garlic cloves, minced
- 1 small yellow onion, sliced
- ½ cup low-sodium vegetable broth
- 2 tablespoons fresh lemon juice
- 1 pound broccoli crowns, cut into bite-size florets
- 8 ounces carrots, cut into ¼-inch thick rounds

1. Sprinkle the tilapia fillets all over with the lemon pepper seasoning and salt.
2. Select the Sauté setting on the Instant Pot and heat the oil and garlic for 2 minutes, until the garlic is bubbling but not browned. Add the onion and sauté for about 3 minutes more, until it begins to soften.
3. Pour in the broth and lemon juice, then use a wooden spoon to nudge any browned bits from the bottom of the pot. Using tongs, add the fish fillets to the pot in a single layer; it's fine if they overlap slightly. Place the broccoli and carrots on top.
4. Secure the lid and set the Pressure Release to Sealing. Press the Cancel button to reset the cooking program, then select the Pressure Cook or Manual setting and set the cooking time for 1 minute at low pressure. (The pot will take about 10 minutes to come up to pressure before the cooking program begins. )
5. When the cooking program ends, let the pressure release naturally for 10 minutes (don't open the pot before the 10 minutes are up, even if the float valve has gone down), then move the Pressure Release to Venting to release any remaining steam. Open the pot. Use a fish spatula to transfer the vegetables and fillets to plates. Serve right away.

*Per Serving:calories: 243 / fat: 9g / protein: 28g / carbs: 15g / sugars: 4g / fiber: 5g / sodium: 348mg*

## Salmon with Brussels Sprouts

Prep time: 5 minutes / Cook time: 20 minutes / Serves 4

- 2 tablespoons unsalted butter, divided
- 20 Brussels sprouts, halved lengthwise
- 4 (4-ounce) skinless salmon fillets
- ½ teaspoon salt
- ¼ teaspoon garlic powder

1. Heat a medium skillet over medium-low heat. When hot, melt 1 tablespoon of butter in the skillet, then add the Brussels sprouts cut-side down. Cook for 10 minutes.
2. Season both sides of the salmon fillets with the salt

and garlic powder.

3. Heat another medium skillet over medium-low heat. When hot, melt the remaining 1 tablespoon of butter in the skillet, then add the salmon. Cover and cook for 6 to 8 minutes, or until the salmon is opaque and flakes easily with a fork.
4. Meanwhile, flip the Brussels sprouts and cover. Cook for 10 minutes or until tender.
5. Divide the Brussels sprouts into four equal portions and add 1 salmon fillet to each portion.

*Per Serving:calories: 236 / fat: 11g / protein: 27g / carbs: 9g / sugars: 2g / fiber: 4g / sodium: 400mg*

## Bacon-Wrapped Scallops

Prep time: 5 minutes / Cook time: 10 minutes / Serves 4

- 8 (1-ounce / 28-g) sea scallops, cleaned and patted dry
- 8 slices sugar-free bacon
- ¼ teaspoon salt
- ¼ teaspoon ground black pepper

1. Wrap each scallop in 1 slice bacon and secure with a toothpick. Sprinkle with salt and pepper.
2. Place scallops into ungreased air fryer basket. Adjust the temperature to 360ºF (182ºC) and air fry for 10 minutes. Scallops will be opaque and firm, and have an internal temperature of 135ºF (57ºC) when done. Serve warm.

*Per Serving:calories: 251 / fat: 21g / protein: 13g / carbs: 2g / sugars: 0g / fiber: 0g / sodium: 612mg*

## Lemon-Pepper Salmon with Roasted Broccoli

Prep time: 5 minutes / Cook time: 20 minutes / Serves 4

- 4 (6 ounces [170 g]) salmon fillets
- Cooking oil spray, as needed
- Juice of 1 medium lemon (see Tips)
- ½ teaspoon black pepper
- ¼ teaspoon garlic salt or ¼ teaspoon sea salt mixed with ¼ teaspoon garlic powder
- 1 pound (454 g) broccoli florets
- ¼ teaspoon sea salt
- ¼ teaspoon garlic powder

1. Preheat the oven to 400°F (204°C). Line two large baking sheets with parchment paper.
2. Place the salmon on the first prepared baking sheet, making sure the fillets are evenly spaced. Spray the salmon with the cooking oil spray. Drizzle the lemon juice over each of the salmon fillets, then sprinkle the black pepper and garlic salt over each fillet.
3. Spread the broccoli out evenly on the second prepared baking sheet and spray the broccoli with cooking oil spray. Sprinkle the sea salt and garlic powder over the broccoli.

4. Place both baking sheets in the oven. Bake the salmon for 10 to 12 minutes, until it is light brown, depending on your preferred doneness and the thickness of the fillets. Bake the broccoli for 12 minutes, until the edges are slightly crispy. Serve the salmon and broccoli immediately.

*Per Serving:calorie: 353 / fat: 19g / protein: 37g / carbs: 9g / sugars: 2g / fiber: 3g / sodium: 406mg*

## Tuna Poke with Riced Broccoli

Prep time: 15 minutes / Cook time: 5 minutes / Serves 2

- For the tuna poke
- ½ pound sushi-grade tuna (see tip), cut into ½-inch cubes
- 2 tablespoons soy sauce or tamari
- 1 tablespoon rice vinegar
- 1 teaspoon sesame oil
- For the bowl
- ½ tablespoon extra-virgin olive oil
- 1 small head broccoli, grated
- 1 cup thawed (if frozen) edamame
- 1 medium carrot, julienned
- 1 cucumber, diced
- 2 scallions, both white and green parts, thinly sliced
- Optional toppings
- Avocado slices
- Shaved radish
- Toasted sesame seeds
- Pickled ginger

1. To make the tuna poke 1. In a medium bowl, toss together the tuna, soy sauce, rice vinegar, and sesame oil.
2. Set aside. To make the bowl
3. Heat the oil in a large skillet over medium heat and sauté the broccoli until tender, 2 to 3 minutes. Remove the skillet from the heat and allow the broccoli to cool.
4. Assemble two bowls by placing riced broccoli as the base. Top each bowl with the tuna poke, edamame, carrot, and cucumber. Drizzle the remaining juices from the tuna marinade over the bowls and garnish with sliced scallions.
5. Store any leftovers in an airtight container in the refrigerator for up to 2 days.

*Per Serving:calories: 454 / fat: 18g / protein: 43g / carbs: 34g / sugars: 13g / fiber: 13g / sodium: 412mg*

## Scallops and Asparagus Skillet

Prep time: 10 minutes / Cook time: 15 minutes / Serves 4

- 3 teaspoons extra-virgin olive oil, divided
- 1 pound asparagus, trimmed and cut into 2-inch segments
- 1 tablespoon butter

- 1 pound sea scallops
- ¼ cup dry white wine
- Juice of 1 lemon
- 2 garlic cloves, minced
- ¼ teaspoon freshly ground black pepper

1. In a large skillet, heat 1½ teaspoons of oil over medium heat.
2. Add the asparagus and sauté for 5 to 6 minutes until just tender, stirring regularly. Remove from the skillet and cover with aluminum foil to keep warm.
3. Add the remaining 1½ teaspoons of oil and the butter to the skillet. When the butter is melted and sizzling, place the scallops in a single layer in the skillet. Cook for about 3 minutes on one side until nicely browned. Use tongs to gently loosen and flip the scallops, and cook on the other side for another 3 minutes until browned and cooked through. Remove and cover with foil to keep warm.
4. In the same skillet, combine the wine, lemon juice, garlic, and pepper. Bring to a simmer for 1 to 2 minutes, stirring to mix in any browned pieces left in the pan.
5. Return the asparagus and the cooked scallops to the skillet to coat with the sauce. Serve warm.

*Per Serving:calories: 252 / fat: 7g / protein: 26g / carbs: 15g / sugars: 3g / fiber: 2g / sodium: 493mg*

## Salmon Florentine

Prep time: 10 minutes / Cook time: 30 minutes / Serves 4
- 1 teaspoon extra-virgin olive oil
- ½ sweet onion, finely chopped
- 1 teaspoon minced garlic
- 3 cups baby spinach
- 1 cup kale, tough stems removed, torn into 3-inch pieces
- Sea salt
- Freshly ground black pepper
- 4 (5-ounce) salmon fillets
- Lemon wedges, for serving

1. Preheat the oven to 350°F.
2. Place a large skillet over medium-high heat and add the oil.
3. Sauté the onion and garlic until softened and translucent, about 3 minutes.
4. Add the spinach and kale and sauté until the greens wilt, about 5 minutes.
5. Remove the skillet from the heat and season the greens with salt and pepper.
6. Place the salmon fillets so they are nestled in the greens and partially covered by them. Bake the salmon until it is opaque, about 20 minutes.
7. Serve immediately with a squeeze of fresh lemon.

*Per Serving:calories: 211 / fat: 8g / protein: 30g / carbs: 5g / sugars: 2g / fiber: 1g / sodium: 129mg*

## Tarragon Cod in a Packet

Prep time: 10 minutes / Cook time: 20 minutes / Serves 2
- 1 tablespoon extra-virgin olive oil, divided
- 1 small zucchini, thinly sliced
- 1 cup sliced fresh mushrooms
- 2 (6-ounce) cod fillets, rinsed
- ½ red onion, thinly sliced
- Juice of 1 lemon
- ¼ cup low-sodium vegetable broth
- 1 teaspoon dried tarragon
- Dash salt
- Dash freshly ground black pepper
- 1 (6. 5-ounce) jar marinated quartered artichoke hearts, drained
- 6 black olives, halved and pitted

1. Preheat the oven to 450°F.
2. Fold 2 (12-by-24-inch) aluminum foil sheets in half widthwise into 2 (12-by-12-inch) squares.
3. Brush ½ teaspoon of olive oil in the center of each foil square.
4. In the middle of each square, layer, in this order, half of the zucchini slices, ½ cup of mushrooms, 1 cod fillet, and half of the onion slices.
5. Sprinkle each packet with 1 of the remaining 2 teaspoons of olive oil, half of the lemon juice, 2 tablespoons of vegetable broth, and ½ teaspoon of tarragon. Season with salt and pepper.
6. Top with half of the artichokes and 6 black olive halves.
7. Fold and seal the foil into airtight packets. Place the packets in a baking dish and into the preheated oven. Bake for 20 minutes.
8. Carefully avoiding the steam that will be released, open a packet and check that the fish is cooked. It should be opaque and flake easily. To test for doneness, poke the tines of a fork into the thickest portion of the fish at a 45-degree angle. Gently twist the fork and pull up some of the fish. If the fish resists flaking, return it to the oven for another 2 minutes then test again. Fish cooks very quickly, so be careful not to overcook it.
9. With a spatula, lift the fish and vegetables onto individual serving plates. Pour any liquid left in the foil over each serving.
10. Enjoy!

*Per Serving:calories: 296 / fat: 10g / protein: 35g / carbs: 19g / sugars: 5g / fiber: 10g / sodium: 428mg*

## Teriyaki Salmon

Prep time: 30 minutes / Cook time: 12 minutes / Serves 4
- 4 (6-ounce / 170-g) salmon fillets

- ½ cup soy sauce
- ¼ cup packed light brown sugar
- 2 teaspoons rice vinegar
- 1 teaspoon minced garlic
- ¼ teaspoon ground ginger
- 2 teaspoons olive oil
- ½ teaspoon salt
- ¼ teaspoon freshly ground black pepper
- Oil, for spraying

1. Place the salmon in a small pan, skin-side up.
2. In a small bowl, whisk together the soy sauce, brown sugar, rice vinegar, garlic, ginger, olive oil, salt, and black pepper.
3. Pour the mixture over the salmon and marinate for about 30 minutes.
4. Line the air fryer basket with parchment and spray lightly with oil. Place the salmon in the prepared basket, skin-side down. You may need to work in batches, depending on the size of your air fryer.
5. Air fry at 400°F (204°C) for 6 minutes, brush the salmon with more marinade, and cook for another 6 minutes, or until the internal temperature reaches 145°F (63°C). Serve immediately.

*Per Serving:calories: 319 / fat: 14g / protein: 37g / carbs: 8g / sugars: 6g / fiber: 1g / sodium: 762mg*

## Tuna Steaks with Olive Tapenade

Prep time: 10 minutes / Cook time: 10 minutes / Serves 4
- 4 (6-ounce / 170-g) ahi tuna steaks
- 1 tablespoon olive oil
- Salt and freshly ground black pepper, to taste
- ½ lemon, sliced into 4 wedges
- Olive Tapenade:
- ½ cup pitted kalamata olives
- 1 tablespoon olive oil
- 1 tablespoon chopped fresh parsley
- 1 clove garlic
- 2 teaspoons red wine vinegar
- 1 teaspoon capers, drained

1. Preheat the air fryer to 400°F (204°C).
2. Drizzle the tuna steaks with the olive oil and sprinkle with salt and black pepper. Arrange the tuna steaks in a single layer in the air fryer basket. Pausing to turn the steaks halfway through the cooking time, air fry for 10 minutes until the fish is firm.
3. To make the tapenade: In a food processor fitted with a metal blade, combine the olives, olive oil, parsley, garlic, vinegar, and capers. Pulse until the mixture is finely chopped, pausing to scrape down the sides of the bowl if necessary. Spoon the tapenade over the top of the tuna steaks and serve with lemon wedges.

*Per Serving:calorie: 300 / fat: 15g / protein: 35g / carbs: 5g / sugars: 1g / fiber: 2g / sodium: 600mg*

## Salade Niçoise with Oil-Packed Tuna

Prep time: 5 minutes / Cook time: 20 minutes / Serves 4
- 8 ounces small red potatoes, quartered
- 8 ounces green beans, trimmed
- 4 large eggs
- french vinaigrette
- 2 tablespoons extra-virgin olive oil
- 2 tablespoons cold-pressed avocado oil
- 2 tablespoons white wine vinegar
- 1 tablespoon water
- 1 teaspoon Dijon mustard
- ½ teaspoon dried oregano
- ¼ teaspoon fine sea salt
- 1 tablespoon minced shallot
- 2 hearts romaine lettuce, leaves separated and torn into bite-size pieces
- ½ cup grape tomatoes, halved
- ¼ cup pitted Niçoise or Greek olives
- One 7 ounces can oil-packed tuna, drained and flaked
- Freshly ground black pepper
- 1 tablespoon chopped fresh flat-leaf parsley

1. Pour 1 cup water into the Instant Pot and place a steamer basket into the pot. Add the potatoes, green beans, and eggs to the basket.
2. Secure the lid and set the Pressure Release to Sealing. Select the Steam setting and set the cooking time for 3 minutes at high pressure. (The pot will take about 15 minutes to come up to pressure before the cooking program begins. )
3. To make the vinaigrette: While the vegetables and eggs are steaming, in a small jar or other small container with a tight-fitting lid, combine the olive oil, avocado oil, vinegar, water, mustard, oregano, salt, and shallot and shake vigorously to emulsify. Set aside.
4. Prepare an ice bath.
5. When the cooking program ends, perform a quick release by moving the Pressure Release to Venting. Open the pot and, wearing heat-resistant mitts, lift out the steamer basket. Using tongs, transfer the eggs and green beans to the ice bath, leaving the potatoes in the steamer basket.
6. While the eggs and green beans are cooling, divide the lettuce, tomatoes, olives, and tuna among four shallow individual bowls. Drain the eggs and green beans. Peel and halve the eggs lengthwise, then arrange them on the salads along with the green beans and potatoes.
7. Spoon the vinaigrette over the salads and sprinkle with the pepper and parsley. Serve right away.

*Per Serving:calories: 367 / fat: 23g / protein: 20g / carbs: 23g / sugars: 7g / fiber: 4g / sodium: 268mg*

## Catfish with Corn and Pepper Relish

Prep time: 10 minutes / Cook time: 10 minutes / Serves 4

- 3 tablespoons extra-virgin olive oil, divided
- 4 (5-ounce) catfish fillets
- ¼ teaspoon salt
- ¼ teaspoon freshly ground black pepper
- 1 (15-ounce) can low-sodium black beans, drained and rinsed
- 1 cup frozen corn
- 1 medium red bell pepper, diced
- 1 tablespoon apple cider vinegar
- 3 tablespoons chopped scallions

1. Use 1½ tablespoons of oil to coat both sides of the catfish fillets, then season the fillets with the salt and pepper.
2. Heat a small saucepan over medium-high heat. Put the remaining 1½ tablespoons of oil, beans, corn, bell pepper, and vinegar in the pan and stir. Cover and cook for 5 minutes.
3. Place the catfish fillets on top of the relish mixture and cover. Cook for 5 to 7 minutes.
4. Serve each catfish fillet with one-quarter of the relish and top with the scallions.

*Per Serving:calories: 379 / fat: 15g / protein: 32g / carbs: 31g / sugars: 2g / fiber: 10g / sodium: 366mg*

## Tuna Steak

Prep time: 10 minutes / Cook time: 12 minutes / Serves 4

- 1 pound (454 g) tuna steaks, boneless and cubed
- 1 tablespoon mustard
- 1 tablespoon avocado oil
- 1 tablespoon apple cider vinegar

1. Mix avocado oil with mustard and apple cider vinegar.
2. Then brush tuna steaks with mustard mixture and put in the air fryer basket.
3. Cook the fish at 360ºF (182ºC) for 6 minutes per side.

*Per Serving:calories: 197 / fat: 9g / protein: 27g / carbs: 0g / fiber: 0g / sodium: 87mg*

## Baked Monkfish

Prep time: 20 minutes / Cook time: 12 minutes / Serves 2

- 2 teaspoons olive oil
- 1 cup celery, sliced
- 2 bell peppers, sliced
- 1 teaspoon dried thyme
- ½ teaspoon dried marjoram
- ½ teaspoon dried rosemary
- 2 monkfish fillets

- 1 tablespoon coconut aminos
- 2 tablespoons lime juice
- Coarse salt and ground black pepper, to taste
- 1 teaspoon cayenne pepper
- ½ cup Kalamata olives, pitted and sliced

1. In a nonstick skillet, heat the olive oil for 1 minute. Once hot, sauté the celery and peppers until tender, about 4 minutes. Sprinkle with thyme, marjoram, and rosemary and set aside.
2. Toss the fish fillets with the coconut aminos, lime juice, salt, black pepper, and cayenne pepper. Place the fish fillets in the lightly greased air fryer basket and bake at 390ºF (199ºC) for 8 minutes.
3. Turn them over, add the olives, and cook an additional 4 minutes. Serve with the sautéed vegetables on the side. Bon appétit!

*Per Serving:calories: 263 / fat: 11g / protein: 27g / carbs: 13g / fiber: 5g / sodium: 332mg*

## Lemon Pepper Salmon

Prep time: 5 minutes / Cook time: 20 minutes / Serves 4

- Avocado oil cooking spray
- 20 Brussels sprouts, halved lengthwise
- 4 (4-ounce) skinless salmon fillets
- ½ teaspoon garlic powder
- ½ teaspoon freshly ground black pepper
- ¼ teaspoon salt
- 2 teaspoons freshly squeezed lemon juice

1. Heat a large skillet over medium-low heat. When hot, coat the cooking surface with cooking spray, and put the Brussels sprouts cut-side down in the skillet. Cover and cook for 5 minutes.
2. Meanwhile, season both sides of the salmon with the garlic powder, pepper, and salt.
3. Flip the Brussels sprouts, and move them to one side of the skillet. Add the salmon and cook, uncovered, for 4 to 6 minutes.
4. Check the Brussels sprouts. When they are tender, remove them from the skillet and set them aside.
5. Flip the salmon fillets. Cook for 4 to 6 more minutes, or until the salmon is opaque and flakes easily with a fork. Remove the salmon from the skillet, and let it rest for 5 minutes.
6. Divide the Brussels sprouts into four equal portions and add 1 salmon fillet to each portion. Sprinkle the lemon juice on top and serve.

*Per Serving:calories: 163 / fat: 7g / protein: 23g / carbs: 1g / sugars: 0g / fiber: 0g / sodium: 167mg*

## Spicy Citrus Sole

Prep time: 10 minutes / Cook time: 10 minutes / Serves 4

- 1 teaspoon chili powder
- 1 teaspoon garlic powder

- ½ teaspoon lime zest
- ½ teaspoon lemon zest
- ¼ teaspoon freshly ground black pepper
- ¼ teaspoon smoked paprika
- Pinch sea salt
- 4 (6-ounce) sole fillets, patted dry
- 1 tablespoon extra-virgin olive oil
- 2 teaspoons freshly squeezed lime juice

1. Preheat the oven to 450°F.
2. Line a baking sheet with aluminum foil and set it aside.
3. In a small bowl, stir together the chili powder, garlic powder, lime zest, lemon zest, pepper, paprika, and salt until well mixed.
4. Pat the fish fillets dry with paper towels, place them on the baking sheet, and rub them lightly all over with the spice mixture.
5. Drizzle the olive oil and lime juice on the top of the fish.
6. Bake until the fish flakes when pressed lightly with a fork, about 8 minutes. Serve immediately.

*Per Serving:calories: 155 / fat: 7g / protein: 21g / carbs: 1g / sugars: 0g / fiber: 1g / sodium: 524mg*

## Grilled Rosemary Swordfish

Prep time: 5 minutes / Cook time: 15 minutes / Serves 4
- 2 scallions, thinly sliced
- 2 tablespoons extra-virgin olive oil
- 2 tablespoons white wine vinegar
- 1 teaspoon fresh rosemary, finely chopped
- 4 swordfish steaks (1 pound total)

1. In a small bowl, combine the scallions, olive oil, vinegar, and rosemary. Pour over the swordfish steaks. Let the steaks marinate for 30 minutes.
2. Remove the steaks from the marinade, and grill for 5–7 minutes per side, brushing with marinade. Transfer to a serving platter, and serve.

*Per Serving:calories: 225 / fat: 14g / protein: 22g / carbs: 0g / sugars: 0g / fiber: 0g / sodium: 92mg*

## Apple Cider Mussels

Prep time: 10 minutes / Cook time: 2 minutes / Serves 5
- 2 pounds (907 g) mussels, cleaned, peeled
- 1 teaspoon onion powder
- 1 teaspoon ground cumin
- 1 tablespoon avocado oil
- ¼ cup apple cider vinegar

1. Mix mussels with onion powder, ground cumin, avocado oil, and apple cider vinegar.
2. Put the mussels in the air fryer and cook at 395°F (202°C) for 2 minutes.

*Per Serving:calorie: 200 / fat: 6g / protein: 24g / carbs: 8g / sugars: 0g / fiber: 1g / sodium: 300mg*

## Herb-Crusted Halibut

Prep time: 10 minutes / Cook time: 20 minutes / Serves 4
- 4 (5-ounce) halibut fillets
- Extra-virgin olive oil, for brushing
- ½ cup coarsely ground unsalted pistachios
- 1 tablespoon chopped fresh parsley
- 1 teaspoon chopped fresh thyme
- 1 teaspoon chopped fresh basil
- Pinch sea salt
- Pinch freshly ground black pepper

1. Preheat the oven to 350°F.
2. Line a baking sheet with parchment paper.
3. Pat the halibut fillets dry with a paper towel and place them on the baking sheet.
4. Brush the halibut generously with olive oil.
5. In a small bowl, stir together the pistachios, parsley, thyme, basil, salt, and pepper.
6. Spoon the nut and herb mixture evenly on the fish, spreading it out so the tops of the fillets are covered.
7. Bake the halibut until it flakes when pressed with a fork, about 20 minutes.
8. Serve immediately.

*Per Serving:calories: 351 / fat: 27g / protein: 24g / carbs: 4g / sugars: 1g / fiber: 2g / sodium: 214mg*

## Sole Piccata

Prep time: 10 minutes / Cook time: 20 minutes / Serves 4
- 1 teaspoon extra-virgin olive oil
- 4 (5-ounce) sole fillets, patted dry
- 3 tablespoons butter
- 2 teaspoons minced garlic
- 2 tablespoons all-purpose flour
- 2 cups low-sodium chicken broth
- Juice and zest of ½ lemon
- 2 tablespoons capers

1. Place a large skillet over medium-high heat and add the olive oil.
2. Pat the sole fillets dry with paper towels then pan-sear them until the fish flakes easily when tested with a fork, about 4 minutes on each side. Transfer the fish to a plate and set it aside.
3. Return the skillet to the stove and add the butter.
4. Sauté the garlic until translucent, about 3 minutes.
5. Whisk in the flour to make a thick paste and cook, stirring constantly, until the mixture is golden brown, about 2 minutes.
6. Whisk in the chicken broth, lemon juice, and lemon zest.
7. Cook until the sauce has thickened, about 4 minutes.
8. Stir in the capers and serve the sauce over the fish.

*Per Serving:calories: 224 / fat: 13g / protein: 21g / carbs: 6g / sugars: 0g / fiber: 1g / sodium: 558mg*

## Baked Salmon with Lemon Sauce

Prep time: 10 minutes / Cook time: 15 minutes / Serves 4

- 4 (5-ounce) salmon fillets
- Sea salt
- Freshly ground black pepper
- 1 tablespoon extra-virgin olive oil
- ½ cup low-sodium vegetable broth
- Juice and zest of 1 lemon
- 1 teaspoon chopped fresh thyme
- ½ cup fat-free sour cream
- 1 teaspoon honey
- 1 tablespoon chopped fresh chives

1. Preheat the oven to 400°F.
2. Season the salmon lightly on both sides with salt and pepper.
3. Place a large ovenproof skillet over medium-high heat and add the olive oil.
4. Sear the salmon fillets on both sides until golden, about 3 minutes per side.
5. Transfer the salmon to a baking dish and bake until it is just cooked through, about 10 minutes.
6. While the salmon is baking, whisk together the vegetable broth, lemon juice, zest, and thyme in a small saucepan over medium-high heat until the liquid reduces by about one-quarter, about 5 minutes.
7. Whisk in the sour cream and honey.
8. Stir in the chives and serve the sauce over the salmon.

*Per Serving:calories: 243 / fat: 10g / protein: 30g / carbs: 8g / sugars: 2g / fiber: 1g / sodium: 216mg*

## Roasted Tilapia and Vegetables

Prep time: 15 minutes / Cook time: 20 minutes / Serves 4

- ½ pound fresh asparagus spears, trimmed, halved
- 2 small zucchini, halved lengthwise, cut into ½-inch pieces
- 1 red bell pepper, cut into ½-inch strips
- 1 large onion, cut into ½-inch wedges
- 1 tablespoon olive oil
- 2 teaspoons Montreal steak seasoning
- 4 tilapia fillets (about 1½ pounds)
- 2 teaspoons butter or margarine, melted
- ½ teaspoon paprika

1. Heat oven to 450°F. In large bowl, toss asparagus, zucchini, bell pepper, onion and oil. Sprinkle with 1 teaspoon of the steak seasoning; toss to coat. Spread vegetables in ungreased 15x10x1-inch pan. Place on lower oven rack; roast 5 minutes.
2. Meanwhile, spray 13x9-inch (3-quart) glass baking dish with cooking spray. Pat tilapia fillets dry with paper towels. Brush with butter; sprinkle with remaining 1 teaspoon steak seasoning and the

paprika. Place in baking dish.
3. Place baking dish on middle oven rack. Roast fish and vegetables 17 to 18 minutes longer or until fish flakes easily with fork and vegetables are tender.

*Per Serving:calories: 250 / fat: 8g / protein: 35g / carbs: 10g / sugars: 5g / fiber: 3g / sodium: 160mg*

## Tomato Tuna Melts

Prep time: 5 minutes / Cook time: 5 minutes / Serves 2

- 1 (5-ounce) can chunk light tuna packed in water, drained
- 2 tablespoons plain nonfat Greek yogurt
- 2 teaspoons freshly squeezed lemon juice
- 2 tablespoons finely chopped celery
- 1 tablespoon finely chopped red onion
- Pinch cayenne pepper
- 1 large tomato, cut into ¾-inch-thick rounds
- ½ cup shredded cheddar cheese

1. Preheat the broiler to high.
2. In a medium bowl, combine the tuna, yogurt, lemon juice, celery, red onion, and cayenne pepper. Stir well.
3. Arrange the tomato slices on a baking sheet. Top each with some tuna salad and cheddar cheese.
4. Broil for 3 to 4 minutes until the cheese is melted and bubbly. Serve.

*Per Serving:calories: 243 / fat: 10g / protein: 30g / carbs: 7g / sugars: 2g / fiber: 1g / sodium: 444mg*

## Pecan-Crusted Catfish

Prep time: 5 minutes / Cook time: 12 minutes / Serves 4

- ½ cup pecan meal
- 1 teaspoon fine sea salt
- ¼ teaspoon ground black pepper
- 4 (4 ounces / 113 g) catfish fillets
- For Garnish (Optional):
- Fresh oregano
- Pecan halves

1. Spray the air fryer basket with avocado oil. Preheat the air fryer to 375ºF (191ºC).
2. In a large bowl, mix the pecan meal, salt, and pepper. One at a time, dredge the catfish fillets in the mixture, coating them well. Use your hands to press the pecan meal into the fillets. Spray the fish with avocado oil and place them in the air fryer basket.
3. Air fry the coated catfish for 12 minutes, or until it flakes easily and is no longer translucent in the center, flipping halfway through.
4. Garnish with oregano sprigs and pecan halves, if desired.
5. Store leftovers in an airtight container in the fridge

for up to 3 days. Reheat in a preheated 350°F (177°C) air fryer for 4 minutes, or until heated through.

*Per Serving:calorie: 350 / fat: 28g / protein: 20g / carbs: 8g / sugars: 2g / fiber: 4g / sodium: 600mg*

## Scallops in Lemon-Butter Sauce

Prep time: 10 minutes / Cook time: 6 minutes / Serves 2

- 8 large dry sea scallops (about ¾ pound / 340 g)
- Salt and freshly ground black pepper, to taste
- 2 tablespoons olive oil
- 2 tablespoons unsalted butter, melted
- 2 tablespoons chopped flat-leaf parsley
- 1 tablespoon fresh lemon juice
- 2 teaspoons capers, drained and chopped
- 1 teaspoon grated lemon zest
- 1 clove garlic, minced

1. Preheat the air fryer to 400°F (204°C).
2. Use a paper towel to pat the scallops dry. Sprinkle lightly with salt and pepper. Brush with the olive oil. Arrange the scallops in a single layer in the air fryer basket. Pausing halfway through the cooking time to turn the scallops, air fry for about 6 minutes until firm and opaque.
3. Meanwhile, in a small bowl, combine the oil, butter, parsley, lemon juice, capers, lemon zest, and garlic. Drizzle over the scallops just before serving.

*Per Serving:calorie: 350 / fat: 22g / protein: 30g / carbs: 4g / sugars: 1g / fiber: 1g / sodium: 400mg*

## Grilled Scallop Kabobs

Prep time: 15 minutes / Cook time: 20 minutes / Serves 6

- 15 ounces pineapple chunks, packed in their own juice, undrained
- ¼ cup dry white wine
- ¼ cup light soy sauce
- 2 tablespoons minced fresh parsley
- 4 garlic cloves, minced
- ⅛ teaspoon freshly ground black pepper
- 1 pound scallops
- 18 large cherry tomatoes
- 1 large green bell pepper, cut into 1-inch squares
- 18 medium mushroom caps

1. Drain the pineapple, reserving the juice. In a shallow baking dish, combine the pineapple juice, wine, soy sauce, parsley, garlic, and pepper. Mix well.
2. Add the pineapple, scallops, tomatoes, green pepper, and mushrooms to the marinade. Marinate 30 minutes at room temperature, stirring occasionally.
3. Alternate pineapple, scallops, and vegetables on metal or wooden skewers (remember to soak wooden skewers in water before using).
4. Grill the kabobs over medium-hot coals about 4 to 5 inches from the heat, turning frequently, for 5 to 7 minutes.

*Per Serving:calories: 132 / fat: 1g / protein: 13g / carbs: 18g / sugars: 10g / fiber: 3g / sodium: 587mg*

## Lime Lobster Tails

Prep time: 10 minutes / Cook time: 6 minutes / Serves 4

- 4 lobster tails, peeled
- 2 tablespoons lime juice
- ½ teaspoon dried basil
- ½ teaspoon coconut oil, melted

1. Mix lobster tails with lime juice, dried basil, and coconut oil.
2. Put the lobster tails in the air fryer and cook at 380°F (193°C) for 6 minutes.

*Per Serving:calorie: 124 / fat: 1g / protein: 26g / carbs: 2g / sugars: 0g / fiber: 0g / sodium: 484mg*

# Chapter 6 Snacks and Appetizers

## Lemon Artichokes

Prep time: 5 minutes / Cook time: 5 to 15 minutes / Serves 4
- 4 artichokes
- 1 cup water
- 2 tablespoons lemon juice
- 1 teaspoon salt

1. Wash and trim artichokes by cutting off the stems flush with the bottoms of the artichokes and by cutting ¾–1 inch off the tops. Stand upright in the bottom of the inner pot of the Instant Pot.
2. Pour water, lemon juice, and salt over artichokes.
3. Secure the lid and make sure the vent is set to sealing. On Manual, set the Instant Pot for 15 minutes for large artichokes, 10 minutes for medium artichokes, or 5 minutes for small artichokes.
4. When cook time is up, perform a quick release by releasing the pressure manually.

*Per Serving:calories: 60 / fat: 0g / protein: 4g / carbs: 13g / sugars: 1g / fiber: 6g / sodium: 397mg*

## Vegetable Kabobs with Mustard Dip

Prep time: 35 minutes / Cook time: 10 minutes / Serves 9
- Dip
- ⅔ cup plain fat-free yogurt
- ⅓ cup fat-free sour cream
- 1 tablespoon finely chopped fresh parsley
- 1 teaspoon onion powder
- 1 teaspoon garlic salt
- 1 tablespoon Dijon mustard
- Kabobs
- 1 medium bell pepper, cut into 6 strips, then cut into thirds
- 1 medium zucchini, cut diagonally into ½-inch slices
- 1 package (8 ounces) fresh whole mushrooms
- 9 large cherry tomatoes
- 2 tablespoons olive or vegetable oil

1. In small bowl, mix dip ingredients. Cover; refrigerate at least 1 hour.
2. Heat gas or charcoal grill. On 5 (12-inch) metal skewers, thread vegetables so that one kind of vegetable is on the same skewer (use 2 skewers for mushrooms); leave space between each piece. Brush vegetables with oil.
3. Place skewers of bell pepper and zucchini on grill over medium heat. Cover grill; cook 2 minutes. Add skewers of mushrooms and tomatoes. Cover grill; cook 4 to 5 minutes, carefully turning every 2 minutes, until vegetables are tender. Transfer vegetables from skewers to serving plate. Serve with dip.

*Per Serving:calories: 60 / fat: 4g / protein: 2g / carbs: 6g / sugars: 3g / fiber: 1g / sodium: 180mg*

## Creamy Cheese Dip

Prep time: 5 minutes / Cook time: 5 minutes / Serves 40
- 1 cup plain fat-free yogurt, strained overnight in cheesecloth over a bowl set in the refrigerator
- 1 cup fat-free ricotta cheese
- 1 cup low-fat cottage cheese

1. Combine all the ingredients in a food processor; process until smooth. Place in a covered container, and refrigerate until ready to use (this cream cheese can be refrigerated for up to 1 week).

*Per Serving:calorie: 21 / fat: 1g / protein: 2g / carbs: 1g / sugars: 1g / fiber: 0g / sodium: 81mg*

## Lemon Cream Fruit Dip

Prep time: 5 minutes / Cook time: 0 minutes / Serves 4
- 1 cup (200 g) plain nonfat Greek yogurt
- ¼ cup (28 g) coconut flour 1 tablespoon (15 ml) pure maple syrup
- ½ teaspoon pure vanilla extract
- ½ teaspoon pure almond extract
- Zest of 1 medium lemon
- Juice of ½ medium lemon

1. In a medium bowl, whisk together the yogurt, coconut flour, maple syrup, vanilla, almond extract, lemon zest, and lemon juice. Serve the dip with fruit or crackers.

*Per Serving:calorie: 80 / fat: 1g / protein: 7g / carbs: 10g / sugars: 6g / fiber: 3g / sodium: 37mg*

## Instant Popcorn

Prep time: 1 minutes / Cook time: 5 minutes / Serves 5
- 2 tablespoons coconut oil
- ½ cup popcorn kernels
- ¼ cup margarine spread, melted, optional
- Sea salt to taste

1. Set the Instant Pot to Sauté.
2. Melt the coconut oil in the inner pot, then add the popcorn kernels and stir.
3. Press Adjust to bring the temperature up to high.
4. When the corn starts popping, secure the lid on the Instant Pot.
5. When you no longer hear popping, turn off the

Instant Pot, remove the lid, and pour the popcorn into a bowl.

6. Top with the optional melted margarine and season the popcorn with sea salt to your liking.

*Per Serving:calories: 161 / fat: 12g / protein: 1g / carbs: 13g / sugars: 0g / fiber: 3g / sodium: 89mg*

## Low-Sugar Blueberry Muffins

Prep time: 5 minutes / Cook time: 20 to 25 minutes / Makes 12 muffins

- 2 large eggs
- 1½ cups (144 g) almond flour
- 1 cup (80 g) gluten-free rolled oats
- ½ cup (120 ml) pure maple syrup
- ½ cup (120 ml) avocado oil
- 1 teaspoon baking powder
- 1 teaspoon ground cinnamon
- ½ teaspoon pure vanilla extract
- ½ teaspoon pure almond extract
- 1 cup (150 g) fresh or frozen blueberries

1. Preheat the oven to 350°F (177°C). Line a 12-well muffin pan with paper liners or spray the wells with cooking oil spray.
2. In a blender, combine the eggs, almond flour, oats, maple syrup, oil, baking powder, cinnamon, vanilla, and almond extract. Blend the ingredients on high for 20 to 30 seconds, until the mixture is homogeneous.
3. Transfer the batter to a large bowl and gently stir in the blueberries.
4. Divide the batter evenly among the muffin wells. Bake the muffins for 20 to 25 minutes, until a toothpick inserted in the middle comes out clean.
5. Let the muffins rest for 5 minutes, then transfer them to a cooling rack.

*Per Serving:calorie: 240 / fat: 18g / protein: 5g / carbs: 19g / sugars: 10g / fiber: 3g / sodium: 19mg*

## Spinach and Artichoke Dip

Prep time: 5 minutes / Cook time: 4 minutes / Serves 11

- 8 ounces low-fat cream cheese
- 10-ounce box frozen spinach
- ½ cup no-sodium chicken broth
- 14-ounce can artichoke hearts, drained
- ½ cup low-fat sour cream
- ½ cup low-fat mayo
- 3 cloves of garlic, minced
- 1 teaspoon onion powder
- 16 ounces reduced-fat shredded Parmesan cheese
- 8 ounces reduced-fat shredded mozzarella

1. Put all ingredients in the inner pot of the Instant Pot, except the Parmesan cheese and the mozzarella cheese.
2. Secure the lid and set vent to sealing. Place on Manual high pressure for 4 minutes.

3. Do a quick release of steam.
4. Immediately stir in the cheeses.

*Per Serving:calories: 288 / fat: 18g / protein: 19g / carbs: 15g / sugars: 3g / fiber: 3g / sodium: 1007mg*

## Ground Turkey Lettuce Cups

Prep time: 5 minutes / Cook time: 30 minutes / Serves 8

- 3 tablespoons water
- 2 tablespoons soy sauce, tamari, or coconut aminos
- 3 tablespoons fresh lime juice
- 2 teaspoons Sriracha, plus more for serving
- 2 tablespoons cold-pressed avocado oil
- 2 teaspoons toasted sesame oil
- 4 garlic cloves, minced
- 1-inch piece fresh ginger, peeled and minced
- 2 carrots, diced    • 2 celery stalks, diced
- 1 yellow onion, diced
- 2 pounds 93 percent lean ground turkey
- ½ teaspoon fine sea salt
- Two 8-ounce cans sliced water chestnuts, drained and chopped    • 1 tablespoon cornstarch
- 2 hearts romaine lettuce or 2 heads butter lettuce, leaves separated
- ½ cup roasted cashews (whole or halves and pieces), chopped
- 1 cup loosely packed fresh cilantro leaves

1. In a small bowl, combine the water, soy sauce, 2 tablespoons of the lime juice, and the Sriracha and mix well. Set aside.
2. Select the Sauté setting on the Instant Pot and heat the avocado oil, sesame oil, garlic, and ginger for 2 minutes, until the garlic is bubbling but not browned. Add the carrots, celery, and onion and sauté for about 3 minutes, until the onion begins to soften.
3. Add the turkey and salt and sauté, using a wooden spoon or spatula to break up the meat as it cooks, for about 5 minutes, until cooked through and no streaks of pink remain. Add the water chestnuts and soy sauce mixture and stir to combine, working quickly so not too much steam escapes.
4. Secure the lid and set the Pressure Release to Sealing. Press the Cancel button to reset the cooking program, then select the Pressure Cook or Manual setting and set the cooking time for 5 minutes at high pressure. (The pot will take about 10 minutes to come up to pressure before the cooking program begins. )
5. When the cooking program ends, perform a quick pressure release by moving the Pressure Release to Venting, or let the pressure release naturally. Open the pot.
6. In a small bowl, stir together the remaining 1 tablespoon lime juice and the cornstarch, add the mixture to the pot, and stir to combine. Press the Cancel button to reset the cooking program, then

select the Sauté setting. Let the mixture come to a boil and thicken, stirring often, for about 2 minutes, then press the Cancel button to turn off the pot.

7. Spoon the turkey mixture onto the lettuce leaves and sprinkle the cashews and cilantro on top. Serve right away, with additional Sriracha at the table.

*Per Serving:calories: 127 / fat: 7g / protein: 6g / carbs: 10g / sugars: 2g / fiber: 3g / sodium: 392mg*

## Creamy Jalapeño Chicken Dip

Prep time: 5 minutes / Cook time: 12 minutes / Serves 10

- 1 pound boneless chicken breast
- 8 ounces low-fat cream cheese
- 3 jalapeños, seeded and sliced  • ½ cup water
- 8 ounces reduced-fat shredded cheddar cheese
- ¾ cup low-fat sour cream

1. Place the chicken, cream cheese, jalapeños, and water in the inner pot of the Instant Pot.
2. Secure the lid so it's locked and turn the vent to sealing.
3. Press Manual and set the Instant Pot for 12 minutes on high pressure.
4. When cooking time is up, turn off Instant Pot, do a quick release of the remaining pressure, then remove lid.
5. Shred the chicken between 2 forks, either in the pot or on a cutting board, then place back in the inner pot.
6. Stir in the shredded cheese and sour cream.

*Per Serving:calories: 238 / fat: 13g / protein: 24g / carbs: 7g / sugars: 5g / fiber: 1g / sodium: 273mg*

## Creamy Spinach Dip

Prep time: 13 minutes / Cook time: 5 minutes / Serves 11

- 8 ounces low-fat cream cheese
- 1 cup low-fat sour cream
- ½ cup finely chopped onion
- ½ cup no-sodium vegetable broth
- 5 cloves garlic, minced  • ½ teaspoon salt
- ¼ teaspoon black pepper • 10 ounces frozen spinach
- 12 ounces reduced-fat shredded Monterey Jack cheese
- 12 ounces reduced-fat shredded Parmesan cheese

1. Add cream cheese, sour cream, onion, vegetable broth, garlic, salt, pepper, and spinach to the inner pot of the Instant Pot.
2. Secure lid, make sure vent is set to sealing, and set to the Bean/Chili setting on high pressure for 5 minutes.
3. When done, do a manual release.
4. Add the cheeses and mix well until creamy and well combined.

*Per Serving:calorie: 274 / fat: 18g / protein: 19g / carbs: 10g / sugars: 3g / fiber: 1g / sodium: 948mg*

## Roasted Carrot and Chickpea Dip

Prep time: 10 minutes / Cook time: 15 minutes / Makes 4 cups

- 4 medium carrots, quartered lengthwise
- ¼ cup plus 2 teaspoons extra-virgin olive oil, divided
- Pinch kosher salt
- Pinch freshly ground black pepper
- 1 (15-ounce) can chickpeas, drained and rinsed
- 1 garlic clove, minced  • 1 red chile (optional)
- Zest and juice of 1 lemon
- 2 tablespoons tahini  • 1 tablespoon harissa
- ½ teaspoon ground cumin
- ¼ teaspoon ground coriander
- Pomegranate arils (seeds) (optional)
- Cilantro, chopped (optional)

1. Preheat the oven to 425°F. Line a baking sheet with parchment paper.
2. In a medium bowl, toss the carrots with 2 teaspoons of extra-virgin olive oil, the salt, and the pepper. Spread them in a single layer on the prepared baking sheet and roast until tender, about 15 minutes. Turn the carrots over halfway through.
3. Meanwhile, place the chickpeas, garlic, chile, lemon zest and juice, tahini, harissa, cumin, and coriander in a food processor. Set aside. Add the carrots to the processor when they are cooked. Pulse until the mixture is coarse. Scrape the bowl down, then turn the processor back on while you drizzle the remaining ¼ cup of extra-virgin olive oil through the feed tube of the machine. Adjust the seasonings as desired. If it's too thick, add water to thin.
4. Top with pomegranate seeds and chopped cilantro (if using,) and Serve with cut vegetables.
5. Store any leftovers in an airtight container in the refrigerator for up to 4 days.

*Per Serving:calorie: 141 / fat: 10g / protein: 3g / carbs: 12g / sugars: 3g / fiber: 3g / sodium: 93mg*

## Baked Scallops

Prep time: 5 minutes / Cook time: 10 minutes / Serves 4

- 12 ounces fresh bay or dry sea scallops
- 1½ teaspoons salt-free pickling spices
- ½ cup cider vinegar  • ¼ cup water
- 1 tablespoon finely chopped onion
- 1 red bell pepper, cut into thin strips
- 1 head butter lettuce, rinsed and dried
- ⅓ cup sesame seeds, toasted

1. Preheat the oven to 350 degrees. Wash the scallops in cool water, and cut any scallops that are too big in half.
2. Spread the scallops out in a large baking dish (be careful not to overlap them). In a small bowl, combine the spices, cider vinegar, water, onion, and pepper; pour the mixture over the scallops. Season with salt, if desired.
3. Cover the baking dish and bake for 7 minutes. Remove from the oven, and allow the scallops to chill in the refrigerator (leave them in the cooking

liquid/vegetable mixture).

4. Just before serving, place the lettuce leaves on individual plates or a platter, and place the scallops and vegetables over the top. Sprinkle with sesame seeds before serving.

*Per Serving:calorie: 159 / fat: 8g / protein: 14g / carbs: 7g / sugars: 2g / fiber: 3g / sodium: 344mg*

## Crab-Filled Mushrooms

Prep time: 5 minutes / Cook time: 25 minutes / Serves 10

- 20 large fresh mushroom caps
- 6 ounces canned crabmeat, rinsed, drained, and flaked
- ½ cup crushed whole-wheat crackers
- 2 tablespoons chopped fresh parsley
- 2 tablespoons finely chopped green onion
- ⅛ teaspoon freshly ground black pepper
- ¼ cup chopped pimiento
- 3 tablespoons extra-virgin olive oil
- 10 tablespoons wheat germ

1. Preheat the oven to 350 degrees. Clean the mushrooms by dusting off any dirt on the cap with a mushroom brush or paper towel; remove the stems.
2. In a small mixing bowl, combine the crabmeat, crackers, parsley, onion, and pepper.
3. Place the mushroom caps in a 13-x-9-x-2-inch baking dish, crown side down. Stuff some of the crabmeat filling into each cap. Place a little pimiento on top of the filling.
4. Drizzle the olive oil over the caps and sprinkle each cap with ½ tablespoon wheat germ. Bake for 15–17 minutes. Transfer to a serving platter, and serve hot.

*Per Serving:calorie: 113 / fat: 6g / protein: 7g / carbs: 9g / sugars: 1g / fiber: 2g / sodium: 77mg*

## Cucumber Roll-Ups

Prep time: 5 minutes / Cook time: 0 minutes / Serves 2 to 4

- 2 (6-inch) gluten-free wraps
- 2 tablespoons cream cheese
- 1 medium cucumber, cut into long strips
- 2 tablespoons fresh mint

1. Place the wraps on your work surface and spread them evenly with the cream cheese. Top with the cucumber and mint.
2. Roll the wraps up from one side to the other, kind of like a burrito. Slice into 1-inch bites or keep whole.
3. Serve.
4. Store any leftovers in an airtight container in the refrigerator for 1 to 2 days.

*Per Serving:calorie: 70 / fat: 1g / protein: 4g / carbs: 12g / sugars: 3g / fiber: 2g / sodium: 183mg*

## Fresh Dill Dip

Prep time: 5 minutes / Cook time: 5 minutes / Serves 6

- 1 cup plain fat-free yogurt

- ¼ teaspoon salt
- ¼ teaspoon freshly ground black pepper
- ¼ cup minced parsley
- 2 tablespoons finely chopped fresh chives
- 1 tablespoon finely chopped fresh dill
- 1 tablespoon apple cider vinegar

1. In a small bowl, combine all the ingredients. Chill for 2 to 4 hours. Serve with fresh cut vegetables.

*Per Serving:calorie: 20 / fat: 0g / protein: 2g / carbs: 3g / sugars: 2g / fiber: 0g / sodium: 120mg*

## Chilled Shrimp

Prep time: 5 minutes / Cook time: 5 minutes / Serves 20

- 5 pounds jumbo shrimp, unshelled
- ¼ cup plus 2 tablespoons extra-virgin olive oil, divided
- 4 medium lemons, thinly sliced
- 3 tablespoons minced garlic
- 3 medium red onions, thinly sliced
- ½ cup minced parsley
- Parsley sprigs (for garnish)

1. Preheat the oven to 400 degrees. Peel, and devein shrimp, leaving the tails intact.
2. Arrange the shrimp on a baking sheet and brush with 2 tablespoons of the olive oil. Bake the shrimp for 3 minutes or until they turn bright pink.
3. Place the lemon slices in a large bowl. Add the remaining ¼ cup of olive oil, garlic, onions, and minced parsley. Add the shrimp and toss vigorously to coat. Cover, and let marinate, refrigerated, for 6–8 hours.
4. Just before serving, arrange the shrimp on a serving platter. Garnish with parsley sprigs and some of the red onions and lemons from the bowl.

*Per Serving:calorie: 127 / fat: 3g / protein: 23g / carbs: 2g / sugars: 0g / fiber: 0g / sodium: 136mg*

## Turkey Rollups with Veggie Cream Cheese

Prep time: 10 minutes / Cook time: 0 minutes / Serves 2

- ¼ cup cream cheese, at room temperature
- 2 tablespoons finely chopped red onion
- 2 tablespoons finely chopped red bell pepper
- 1 tablespoon chopped fresh chives
- 1 teaspoon Dijon mustard
- 1 garlic clove, minced • ¼ teaspoon sea salt
- 6 slices deli turkey

1. In a small bowl, mix the cream cheese, red onion, bell pepper, chives, mustard, garlic, and salt.
2. Spread the mixture on the turkey slices and roll up.

*Per Serving:calorie: 146 / fat: 1g / protein: 24g / carbs: 8g / sugars: 6g / fiber: 1g / sodium: 572mg*

## Homemade Sun-Dried Tomato Salsa

Prep time: 5 minutes / Cook time: 0 minutes / Serves 4

- ½ (15 ounces [425 g]) can no-salt-added diced tomatoes, drained
- 6 tablespoons (20 g) julienned sun-dried tomatoes (see Tip)
- 1½ cups (330 g) canned artichoke hearts, drained
- 1 clove garlic
- ⅛ cup (3 g) fresh basil leaves
- 1 teaspoon balsamic vinegar
- 2 tablespoons (30 ml) olive oil
- Sea salt, as needed
- Black pepper, as needed

1. In a food processor or blender, combine the diced tomatoes, sun-dried tomatoes, artichoke hearts, garlic, basil, vinegar, oil, sea salt, and black pepper. Process or blend the ingredients to the desired consistency.

*Per Serving:calorie: 131 / fat: 7g / protein: 2g / carbs: 13g / sugars: 3g / fiber: 4g / sodium: 279mg*

## Lemony White Bean Puree

Prep time: 10 minutes / Cook time: 0 minutes / Makes 4 cups

- 1 (15-ounce) can white beans, drained and rinsed
- 1 small onion, coarsely chopped
- 1 garlic clove, minced
- Zest and juice of 1 lemon
- ½ teaspoon herbs de Provence
- 3 tablespoons extra-virgin olive oil, divided
- 1 tablespoon chopped fresh parsley

1. Place the beans, onion, garlic, lemon zest and juice, and herbs in a food processor and pulse until smooth. While the machine is running, slowly stream in 2 tablespoons of extra-virgin olive oil. If the mixture is too thick, add water very slowly until you've reached the desired consistency.
2. Transfer the puree to a medium serving bowl. Top with the remaining 1 tablespoon of extra-virgin olive oil and the parsley.
3. Serve with your favorite vegetable or flatbread of choice. Store any leftovers in an airtight container in the refrigerator for up to 4 days.

*Per Serving:calorie: 121 / fat: 5g / protein: 5g / carbs: 15g / sugars: 1g / fiber: 3g / sodium: 4mg*

## No-Bake Coconut and Cashew Energy Bars

Prep time: 5 minutes / Cook time: 0 minutes / Makes 12 energy bars

- 1 cup (110 g) raw cashews
- 1 cup (80 g) unsweetened shredded coconut
- ½ cup (120 g) unsweetened nut butter of choice
- 2 tablespoons (30 ml) pure maple syrup

1. Line an 8 x 8–inch (20 x 20–cm) baking pan with parchment paper.
2. In a large food processor, combine the cashews

and coconut. Pulse them for 15 to 20 seconds to form a powder.
3. Add the nut butter and maple syrup and process until a doughy paste is formed, scraping down the sides if needed.
4. Spread the dough into the prepared baking pan. Cover the dough with another sheet of parchment paper and press it flat.
5. Freeze the dough for 1 hour. Cut the dough into bars.

*Per Serving:calorie: 169 / fat: 14g / protein: 4g / carbs: 10g / sugars: 3g / fiber: 2g / sodium: 6mg*

## Peanut Butter Protein Bites

Prep time: 10 minutes / Cook time: 0 minutes / Makes 16 Balls

- ½ cup sugar-free peanut butter
- ¼ cup (1 scoop) sugar-free peanut butter powder or sugar-free protein powder
- 2 tablespoons unsweetened cocoa powder
- 2 tablespoons canned coconut milk (or more to adjust consistency)

1. In a bowl, mix all ingredients until well combined.
2. Roll into 16 balls. Refrigerate before serving.

*Per Serving:calorie: 59 / fat: 5g / protein: 3g / carbs: 2g / sugars: 1g / fiber: 1g / sodium: 4mg*

## Veggies with Cottage Cheese Ranch Dip

Prep time: 10 minutes / Cook time: 0 minutes / Serves 4

- 1 cup cottage cheese
- 2 tablespoons mayonnaise
- Juice of ½ lemon
- 2 tablespoons chopped fresh chives
- 2 tablespoons chopped fresh dill
- 2 scallions, white and green parts, finely chopped
- 1 garlic clove, minced
- ½ teaspoon sea salt
- 2 zucchinis, cut into sticks
- 8 cherry tomatoes

1. In a small bowl, mix the cottage cheese, mayonnaise, lemon juice, chives, dill, scallions, garlic, and salt.
2. Serve with the zucchini sticks and cherry tomatoes for dipping.

*Per Serving:calorie: 88 / fat: 3g / protein: 6g / carbs: 10g / sugars: 4g / fiber: 2g / sodium: 495mg*

## Guacamole with Jicama

Prep time: 5 minutes / Cook time: 0 minutes / Serves 4

- 1 avocado, cut into cubes
- Juice of ½ lime
- 2 tablespoons finely chopped red onion
- 2 tablespoons chopped fresh cilantro
- 1 garlic clove, minced
- ¼ teaspoon sea salt
- 1 cup sliced jicama

1. In a small bowl, combine the avocado, lime juice, onion, cilantro, garlic, and salt. Mash lightly with a fork.
2. Serve with the jicama for dipping.

*Per Serving:calorie: 97 / fat: 7g / protein: 1g / carbs: 8g / sugars: 1g / fiber: 5g / sodium: 151mg*

## Candied Pecans

Prep time: 5 minutes / Cook time: 20 minutes / Serves 10

- 4 cups raw pecans
- 1½ teaspoons liquid stevia
- ½ cup plus 1 tablespoon water, divided
- 1 teaspoon vanilla extract
- 1 teaspoon cinnamon
- ¼ teaspoon nutmeg
- ⅛ teaspoon ground ginger
- ⅛ teaspoon sea salt

1. Place the raw pecans, liquid stevia, 1 tablespoon water, vanilla, cinnamon, nutmeg, ground ginger, and sea salt into the inner pot of the Instant Pot.
2. Press the Sauté button on the Instant Pot and sauté the pecans and other ingredients until the pecans are soft.
3. Pour in the ½ cup water and secure the lid to the locked position. Set the vent to sealing.
4. Press Manual and set the Instant Pot for 15 minutes.
5. Preheat the oven to 350°F.
6. When cooking time is up, turn off the Instant Pot, then do a quick release.
7. Spread the pecans onto a greased, lined baking sheet.
8. Bake the pecans for 5 minutes or less in the oven, checking on them frequently so they do not burn.

*Per Serving:calories: 275 / fat: 28g / protein: 4g / carbs: 6g / sugars: 2g / fiber: 4g / sodium: 20mg*

## Monterey Jack Cheese Quiche Squares

Prep time: 10 minutes / Cook time: 15 minutes / Serves 12

- 4 egg whites
- 1 cup plus 2 tablespoons low-fat cottage cheese
- ¼ cup plus 2 tablespoons flour
- ¾ teaspoon baking powder
- 1 cup shredded reduced-fat Monterey Jack cheese
- ½ cup diced green chilies
- 1 red bell pepper, diced
- 1 cup lentils, cooked    • Parsley sprigs
- 1 tablespoon extra-virgin olive oil

1. Preheat the oven to 350 degrees.
2. In a medium bowl, beat the egg whites and cottage cheese for 2 minutes, until smooth.
3. Add the flour and baking powder, and beat until smooth. Stir in the cheese, green chilies, red pepper, and lentils.
4. Coat a 9-inch-square pan with the olive oil, and pour in the egg mixture. Bake for 30–35 minutes, until firm.

5. Remove the quiche from the oven, and allow to cool for 10 minutes (it will be easier to cut). Cut into 12 squares and transfer to a platter, garnish with parsley sprigs, and serve.

*Per Serving:calorie: 104 / fat: 6g / protein: 8g / carbs: 4g / sugars: 0g / fiber: 0g / sodium: 215mg*

## Hummus with Chickpeas and Tahini Sauce

Prep time: 10 minutes / Cook time: 55 minutes / Makes 4 cups

- 4 cups water    • 1 cup dried chickpeas
- 2½ teaspoons fine sea salt
- ½ cup tahini    • 3 tablespoons fresh lemon juice
- 1 garlic clove
- ¼ teaspoon ground cumin

1. Combine the water, chickpeas, and 1 teaspoon of the salt in the Instant Pot and stir to dissolve the salt.
2. Secure the lid and set the Pressure Release to Sealing. Select the Bean/Chili, Pressure Cook, or Manual setting and set the cooking time for 40 minutes at high pressure. (The pot will take about 15 minutes to come up to pressure before the cooking program begins. )
3. When the cooking program ends, let the pressure release naturally for 15 minutes, then move the Pressure Release to Venting to release any remaining steam.
4. Place a colander over a bowl. Open the pot and, wearing heat-resistant mitts, lift out the inner pot and drain the beans in the colander. Return the chickpeas to the inner pot and place it back in the Instant Pot housing on the Keep Warm setting. Reserve the cooking liquid.
5. In a blender or food processor, combine 1 cup of the cooking liquid, the tahini, lemon juice, garlic, cumin, and 1 teaspoon salt. Blend or process on high speed, stopping to scrape down the sides of the container as needed, for about 30 seconds, until smooth and a little fluffy. Scoop out and set aside ½ cup of this sauce for the topping.
6. Set aside ½ cup of the chickpeas for the topping. Add the remaining chickpeas to the tahini sauce in the blender or food processor along with ½ cup of the cooking liquid and the remaining ½ teaspoon salt. Blend or process on high speed, stopping to scrape down the sides of the container as needed, for about 1 minute, until very smooth.
7. Transfer the hummus to a shallow serving bowl. Spoon the reserved tahini mixture over the top, then sprinkle on the reserved chickpeas. The hummus will keep in an airtight container in the refrigerator for up to 3 days. Serve at room temperature or chilled.

*Per Serving:calories: 107 / fat: 5g / protein: 4g / carbs: 10g / sugars: 3g / fiber: 4g / sodium: 753mg*

## Ginger and Mint Dip with Fruit

Prep time: 20 minutes / Cook time: 0 minutes / Serves 6

- Dip
- 1¼ cups plain fat-free yogurt
- ¼ cup packed brown sugar
- 2 teaspoons chopped fresh mint leaves
- 2 teaspoons grated gingerroot
- ½ teaspoon grated lemon peel
- Fruit Skewers • 12 bamboo skewers (6 inch)
- 1 cup fresh raspberries
- 2 cups melon cubes (cantaloupe and/or honeydew)

1. In small bowl, mix dip ingredients with whisk until smooth. Cover; refrigerate at least 15 minutes to blend flavors.
2. On each skewer, alternately thread 3 raspberries and 2 melon cubes. Serve with dip.

*Per Serving:calories: 100 / fat: 0g / protein: 3g / carbs: 20g / sugars: 17g / fiber: 2g / sodium: 50mg*

## Kale Chip Nachos

Prep time: 10 minutes / Cook time: 20 minutes / Serves 2 to 4

- 1 bunch kale, torn into bite-size pieces
- 3 tablespoons extra-virgin olive oil, divided
- 2 teaspoons ground cumin, divided
- 1 large sweet potato, cut into ¼-inch-thick rounds
- 1 (15-ounce) can black beans, rinsed and drained
- ½ teaspoon ground coriander
- 1 teaspoon chili powder
- Optional Toppings • Avocado slices
- Salsa
- Jicama, sliced • Red onion, sliced
- Fresh cilantro • Fresh chiles, minced
- Fresh tomatoes, diced

1. Preheat the oven to 225°F. Line a baking sheet with parchment paper.
2. In a large bowl, toss the kale with 1 tablespoon of oil and 1 teaspoon of cumin. Use your hands to massage the kale and evenly distribute the oil.
3. Spread the kale in a single even layer on the prepared baking sheet. (You may need two lined baking sheets for this. ) Bake for 15 minutes, then flip and toss, and bake for another 5 to 10 minutes.
4. Meanwhile, heat 1 tablespoon of oil in a large skillet over medium-high heat. Arrange the sweet potato rounds in a single layer in the skillet, cover, and let them cook until they begin to brown on the bottom, about 3 minutes. Flip the potatoes over and cook for 3 to 5 minutes more.
5. Add the black beans to the skillet with the remaining 1 tablespoon of oil, remaining 1 teaspoon of cumin, the coriander, and chili powder. Cook for 3 minutes, then set aside and keep warm if the kale is not yet finished baking.

6. Serve on a platter, starting with the kale as a base, topped with sweet potatoes, black beans, and finally, any optional toppings.
7. Store any leftovers in an airtight container in the refrigerator for 3 to 4 days.

*Per Serving:calorie: 296 / fat: 14g / protein: 10g / carbs: 34g / sugars: 2g / fiber: 12g / sodium: 599mg*

## Southern Boiled Peanuts

Prep time: 5 minutes / Cook time: 1 hour 20 minutes / Makes 8 cups

- 1 pound raw jumbo peanuts in the shell
- 3 tablespoons fine sea salt

1. Remove the inner pot from the Instant Pot and add the peanuts to it. Cover the peanuts with water and use your hands to agitate them, loosening any dirt. Drain the peanuts in a colander, rinse out the pot, and return the peanuts to it. Return the inner pot to the Instant Pot housing.
2. Add the salt and 9 cups water to the pot and stir to dissolve the salt. Select a salad plate just small enough to fit inside the pot and set it on top of the peanuts to weight them down, submerging them all in the water.
3. Secure the lid and set the Pressure Release to Sealing. Select the Steam setting and set the cooking time for 1 hour at low pressure. (The pot will take about 20 minutes to come up to pressure before the cooking program begins. )
4. When the cooking program ends, let the pressure release naturally (this will take about 1 hour). Open the pot and, wearing heat-resistant mitts, remove the inner pot from the housing. Let the peanuts cool to room temperature in the brine (this will take about 1½ hours).
5. Serve at room temperature or chilled. Transfer the peanuts with their brine to an airtight container and refrigerate for up to 1 week.

*Per Serving:calories: 306 / fat: 17g / protein: 26g / carbs: 12g / sugars: 2g / fiber: 4g / sodium: 303mg*

## Baked Parmesan Crisps

Prep time: 5 minutes / Cook time: 5 minutes / Serves 2

- 1 cup grated Parmesan cheese

1. Preheat the oven to 400°F. Line a rimmed baking sheet with parchment paper.
2. Spread the Parmesan on the prepared baking sheet into 4 mounds, spreading each mound out so it is flat but not touching the others.
3. Bake until brown and crisp, 3 to 5 minutes.
4. Cool for 5 minutes. Use a spatula to remove to a plate to continue cooling.

*Per Serving:calorie: 226 / fat: 15g / protein: 21g / carbs: 2g / sugars: 0g / fiber: 0g / sodium: 32mg*

# Chapter 7 Vegetables and Sides

## Mashed Sweet Potatoes

Prep time: 10 minutes / Cook time: 20 minutes / Serves 6 to 8

- 2 medium sweet potatoes, cut into 1- to 2-inch cubes
- 4 medium carrots, cut into 1-inch cubes
- 6 garlic cloves, halved
- ¼ teaspoon kosher salt
- 2 tablespoons unsalted butter
- ⅓ cup unsweetened almond milk
- Freshly ground black pepper

1. Place the potatoes, carrots, garlic, and salt in a large stockpot and cover them with water by 1½ inches. Bring to a boil over high heat, reduce the heat to medium-high, and simmer for 10 to 15 minutes, until the vegetables become tender.
2. Drain the vegetables and return them to the pot. Add the butter and almond milk and mash until smooth with a potato masher. Season with pepper. Thin out with water or more milk to reach the desired consistency. Serve.
3. Store any leftovers in an airtight container in the refrigerator for up to 4 days.

*Per Serving:calories: 90 / fat: 3g / protein: 2g / carbs: 15g / sugars: 6g / fiber: 3g / sodium: 150mg*

## Spinach and Sweet Pepper Poppers

Prep time: 10 minutes / Cook time: 8 minutes / Makes 16 poppers

- 4 ounces (113 g) cream cheese, softened
- 1 cup chopped fresh spinach leaves
- ½ teaspoon garlic powder
- 8 mini sweet bell peppers, tops removed, seeded, and halved lengthwise

1. In a medium bowl, mix cream cheese, spinach, and garlic powder. Place 1 tablespoon mixture into each sweet pepper half and press down to smooth.
2. Place poppers into ungreased air fryer basket. Adjust the temperature to 400ºF (204ºC) and air fry for 8 minutes. Poppers will be done when cheese is browned on top and peppers are tender-crisp. Serve warm.

*Per Serving:calorie: 40 / fat: 3g / protein: 1g / carbs: 2g / sugars: 1g / fiber: 0g / sodium: 60mg*

## Cajun-Style Collards

Prep time: 10 minutes / Cook time: 20 minutes / Serves 4 to 6

- 2 tablespoons extra-virgin olive oil
- ½ large onion, chopped
- 1 pound collard greens, chopped
- 1 garlic clove, minced
- ½ teaspoon cayenne
- 3 cups low-sodium vegetable broth
- 2 tomatoes, diced

1. Heat the extra-virgin olive oil in a large stockpot over medium heat. Sauté the onion until slightly softened and translucent, about 2 minutes.
2. Add the collards, garlic, and cayenne and cook for 2 to 3 minutes. Add the vegetable broth, cover, and bring the mixture to a simmer.
3. Simmer until the greens are tender, about 15 minutes. Add the tomatoes, adjust the seasonings as desired, and serve.
4. Store any leftovers in an airtight container in the refrigerator for 3 to 4 days.

*Per Serving:calories: 122 / fat: 7g / protein: 5g / carbs: 14g / sugars: 7g / fiber: 5g / sodium: 103mg*

## Lemony Brussels Sprouts with Poppy Seeds

Prep time: 10 minutes / Cook time: 2 minutes / Serves 4

- 1 pound (454 g) Brussels sprouts
- 2 tablespoons avocado oil, divided
- 1 cup vegetable broth or chicken bone broth
- 1 tablespoon minced garlic
- ½ teaspoon kosher salt
- Freshly ground black pepper, to taste
- ½ medium lemon
- ½ tablespoon poppy seeds

1. Trim the Brussels sprouts by cutting off the stem ends and removing any loose outer leaves. Cut each in half lengthwise (through the stem).
2. Set the electric pressure cooker to the Sauté/More setting. When the pot is hot, pour in 1 tablespoon of the avocado oil.
3. Add half of the Brussels sprouts to the pot, cut-side down, and let them brown for 3 to 5 minutes without disturbing. Transfer to a bowl and add the remaining tablespoon of avocado oil and the remaining Brussels sprouts to the pot. Hit Cancel and return all of the Brussels sprouts to the pot.
4. Add the broth, garlic, salt, and a few grinds of pepper. Stir to distribute the seasonings.
5. Close and lock the lid of the pressure cooker. Set the valve to sealing.
6. Cook on high pressure for 2 minutes.
7. While the Brussels sprouts are cooking, zest the

lemon, then cut it into quarters.

8. When the cooking is complete, hit Cancel and quick release the pressure.
9. Once the pin drops, unlock and remove the lid.
10. Using a slotted spoon, transfer the Brussels sprouts to a serving bowl. Toss with the lemon zest, a squeeze of lemon juice, and the poppy seeds. Serve immediately.

*Per Serving:calories: 125 / fat: 8g / protein: 4g / carbs: 13g / sugars: 3g / fiber: 5g / sodium: 504mg*

## Smashed Cucumber Salad

Prep time: 10 minutes / Cook time: 0 minutes / Serves 4 to 6

- 2 pounds mini cucumbers (English or Persian), unpeeled
- ½ teaspoon kosher salt
- 1 tablespoon extra-virgin olive oil
- ¾ teaspoon ground cumin
- ¼ teaspoon turmeric
- Juice of 1 lime
- ½ cup cilantro leaves

1. Cut the cucumbers crosswise into 4-inch pieces and again in half lengthwise.
2. On a work surface, place one cucumber, flesh-side down. Place the side of the knife blade on the cucumber and carefully smash down lightly with your hand. Alternatively, put in a plastic bag, seal, and smash with a rolling pin or similar tool. Be careful not to break the bag. The skin of the cucumber should crack and flesh will break away. Repeat with all the cucumbers and cut the smashed pieces on a bias into bite-size pieces.
3. Transfer the cucumber pieces to a strainer and toss them with the salt. Allow the cucumbers to rest for at least 15 minutes.
4. Meanwhile, prepare the dressing by whisking together the extra-virgin olive oil, cumin, turmeric, and lime juice in a small bowl.
5. When the cucumbers are ready, shake them to remove any excess liquid. Transfer the cucumbers to a large bowl with the dressing and cilantro and toss to combine. Serve.
6. Store any leftovers in an airtight container in the refrigerator for up to 2 days.

*Per Serving:calories: 55 / fat: 3g / protein: 1g / carbs: 8g / sugars: 3g / fiber: 1g / sodium: 238mg*

## Mushroom Cassoulets

Prep time: 5 minutes / Cook time: 30 minutes / Serves 6

- 1 pound mushrooms, sliced
- ½ cup lentils, cooked
- 1 medium onion, chopped
- 1 cup low-sodium chicken broth
- 1 sprig thyme
- 1 bay leaf
- Leaves from 1 celery stalk
- 2 tablespoons lemon juice
- ⅛ teaspoon freshly ground black pepper
- ½ cup wheat germ
- 2 tablespoons extra-virgin olive oil

1. Preheat the oven to 350 degrees.
2. In a saucepan, combine the mushrooms, lentils, onion, and chicken broth. Tie together the thyme, bay leaf, and celery leaves and add to the mushrooms.
3. Add the lemon juice and pepper, and bring to a boil. Boil until the liquid is reduced, about 10 minutes. Remove the bundle of herbs.
4. Divide the mushroom mixture equally into small ramekins. Mix the wheat germ and oil together, and sprinkle on top of each casserole.
5. Bake at 350 degrees for 20 minutes or until the tops are golden brown. Remove from the oven, and let cool slightly before serving. Add salt if desired.

*Per Serving:calories: 114 / fat: 6g / protein: 6g / carbs: 12g / sugars: 2g / fiber: 3g / sodium: 21mg*

## Callaloo Redux

Prep time: 15 minutes / Cook time: 25 minutes / Serves 6

- 3 cups store-bought low-sodium vegetable broth
- 1 (13½ ounces) can light coconut milk
- ¼ cup coconut cream
- 1 tablespoon unsalted non-hydrogenated plant-based butter
- 12 ounces okra, cut into 1-inch chunks
- 1 small onion, chopped
- ½ butternut squash, peeled, seeded, and cut into 4-inch chunks
- 1 bunch collard greens, stemmed and chopped
- 1 hot pepper (Scotch bonnet or habanero)

1. In an electric pressure cooker, combine the vegetable broth, coconut milk, coconut cream, and butter.
2. Layer the okra, onion, squash, collard greens, and whole hot pepper on top.
3. Close and lock the lid, and set the pressure valve to sealing.
4. Select the Manual/Pressure Cook setting, and cook for 20 minutes.
5. Once cooking is complete, quick-release the pressure. Carefully remove the lid.
6. Remove and discard the hot pepper. Carefully transfer the callaloo to a blender, and blend until smooth. Serve spooned over grits.

*Per Serving:calories: 258 / fat: 21g / protein: 5g / carbs: 17g / sugars: 8g / fiber: 5g / sodium: 88mg*

## Lemon-Garlic Mushrooms

Prep time: 10 minutes / Cook time: 10 to 15 minutes / Serves 6

- 12 ounces (340 g) sliced mushrooms
- 1 tablespoon avocado oil
- Sea salt and freshly ground black pepper, to taste
- 3 tablespoons unsalted butter
- 1 teaspoon minced garlic
- 1 teaspoon freshly squeezed lemon juice
- ½ teaspoon red pepper flakes
- 2 tablespoons chopped fresh parsley

1. Place the mushrooms in a medium bowl and toss with the oil. Season to taste with salt and pepper.
2. Place the mushrooms in a single layer in the air fryer basket. Set your air fryer to 375°F (191°C) and roast for 10 to 15 minutes, until the mushrooms are tender.
3. While the mushrooms cook, melt the butter in a small pot or skillet over medium-low heat. Stir in the garlic and cook for 30 seconds. Remove the pot from the heat and stir in the lemon juice and red pepper flakes.
4. Toss the mushrooms with the lemon-garlic butter and garnish with the parsley before serving.

*Per Serving:calorie: 90 / fat: 7g / protein: 2g / carbs: 6g / sugars: 2g / fiber: 2g / sodium: 70mg*

## Chinese Asparagus

Prep time: 5 minutes / Cook time: 5 minutes / Serves 4

- 1 pound asparagus
- ½ cup plus 1 tablespoon water, divided
- 1 tablespoon light soy sauce
- 1 tablespoon rice vinegar
- 2 teaspoons cornstarch
- 1 tablespoon canola oil
- 2 teaspoons grated fresh ginger
- 1 scallion, minced

1. Trim the tough ends off the asparagus. Cut the stalks diagonally into 2-inch pieces.
2. In a small bowl, combine the ½ cup water, soy sauce, and rice vinegar.
3. In a measuring cup, combine the cornstarch and 1 tablespoon water. Set aside.
4. Heat the oil in a wok or skillet. Add the ginger and scallions, and stir-fry for 30 seconds. Add the asparagus and stir-fry for a few seconds more. Add the broth mixture, and bring to a boil. Cover, and simmer for 3–5 minutes, until the asparagus is just tender.
5. Add the cornstarch mixture, and cook until thickened. Serve.

*Per Serving:calories: 73 / fat: 4g / protein: 3g / carbs: 7g / sugars: 3g / fiber: 3g / sodium: 64mg*

## Zucchini Sauté

Prep time: 5 minutes / Cook time: 10 minutes / Serves 4

- 1 tablespoon olive oil
- 1 medium red onion, finely chopped
- 3 medium zucchini (about 5–6 ounces each), cut into ¼-inch thick rounds
- ¼ teaspoon dried oregano
- ⅛ teaspoon salt
- ⅛ teaspoon freshly ground black pepper

1. In a large skillet over medium heat, heat the oil. Add the onion, and sauté until the onion is translucent but not browned.
2. Add the zucchini, cover, and simmer 3–4 minutes. Sprinkle with the oregano, salt, and pepper, and serve hot.

*Per Serving:calories: 43 / fat: 3g / protein: 1g / carbs: 3g / sugars: 1g / fiber: 1g / sodium: 79mg*

## Marinated Green Beans

Prep time: 10 minutes / Cook time: 10 minutes / Serves 3

- ½–¾ pound green beans, ends trimmed
- 1 tablespoon nutritional yeast
- 1 teaspoon Dijon mustard
- 1 tablespoon apple cider vinegar
- 2 teaspoons coconut nectar or pure maple syrup
- Rounded ¼ teaspoon sea salt
- Freshly ground black pepper to taste (optional)

1. Place a large pot of water over high heat, and bring to a boil. Add the green beans and cook for 2 to 3 minutes. Run the beans under cold water to stop the cooking process. Drain the beans and pat dry, if needed. In a large bowl, combine the yeast, mustard, vinegar, nectar or syrup, salt, and pepper (if using). Whisk until thoroughly combined. Add the green beans, and toss to coat thoroughly. Let sit for 30 minutes, then serve.

*Per Serving:calorie: 47 / fat: 0g / protein: 3g / carbs: 9g / sugars: 4g / fiber: 3g / sodium: 335mg*

## Roasted Lemon and Garlic Broccoli

Prep time: 10 minutes / Cook time: 25 minutes / Serves 8

- 2 large broccoli heads, cut into florets
- 3 garlic cloves, minced
- 2 tablespoons extra-virgin olive oil
- ¼ teaspoon salt
- ¼ teaspoon freshly ground black pepper
- 2 tablespoons freshly squeezed lemon juice

1. Preheat the oven to 425°F.
2. On a rimmed baking sheet, toss the broccoli, garlic, and olive oil. Season with the salt and pepper.
3. Roast, tossing occasionally, for 25 to 30 minutes

until tender and browned. Season with the lemon juice and serve.

*Per Serving:calories: 30 / fat: 2g / protein: 1g / carbs: 3g / sugars: 1g / fiber: 1g / sodium: 84mg*

## Zucchini Noodles with Lime-Basil Pesto

Prep time: 20 minutes / Cook time: 0 minutes / Serves 4

- 2 cups packed fresh basil leaves
- ½ cup pine nuts
- 2 teaspoons minced garlic
- Zest and juice of 1 lime
- Pinch sea salt
- Pinch freshly ground black pepper
- ¼ cup extra-virgin olive oil
- 4 green or yellow zucchini, rinsed, dried, and julienned or spiralized
- 1 tomato, diced

1. Place the basil, pine nuts, garlic, lime zest, lime juice, salt, and pepper in a food processor or a blender and pulse until very finely chopped.
2. While the machine is running, add the olive oil in a thin stream until a thick paste forms.
3. In a large bowl, combine the zucchini noodles and tomato. Add the pesto by the tablespoonful until you have the desired flavor. Serve the zucchini pasta immediately.
4. Store any leftover pesto in a sealed container in the refrigerator for up to 2 weeks.

*Per Serving:calories: 247 / fat: 25g / protein: 3g / carbs: 5g / sugars: 2g / fiber: 1g / sodium: 148mg*

## Not Slow-Cooked Collards

Prep time: 10 minutes / Cook time: 20 minutes / Serves 4

- 1 cup store-bought low-sodium vegetable broth, divided
- ½ onion, thinly sliced
- 2 garlic cloves, thinly sliced
- 1 large bunch collard greens including stems, roughly chopped
- 1 medium tomato, chopped
- 1 teaspoon ground cumin
- ½ teaspoon freshly ground black pepper

1. In a Dutch oven, bring ½ cup of broth to a simmer over medium heat.
2. Add the onion and garlic and cook for 3 to 5 minutes, or until translucent.
3. Add the collard greens, tomato, cumin, pepper, and the remaining ½ cup of broth, and gently stir.
4. Reduce the heat to low and cook, uncovered, for 15 minutes.

*Per Serving:calories: 27 / fat: 0g / protein: 1g / carbs: 5g / sugars: 3g / fiber: 1g / sodium: 53mg*

## Pico de Gallo Navy Beans

Prep time: 20 minutes / Cook time: 0 minutes / Serves 4

- 2½ cups cooked navy beans
- 1 tomato, diced
- ½ red bell pepper, seeded and chopped
- ¼ jalapeño pepper, chopped
- 1 scallion, white and green parts, chopped
- 1 teaspoon minced garlic
- 1 teaspoon ground cumin
- ½ teaspoon ground coriander
- ½ cup low-sodium feta cheese

1. Put the beans, tomato, bell pepper, jalapeño, scallion, garlic, cumin, and coriander in a medium bowl and stir until well mixed.
2. Top with the feta cheese and serve.

*Per Serving:calories: 218 / fat: 4g / protein: 14g / carbs: 33g / sugars: 2g / fiber: 13g / sodium: 6mg*

## Avocado Slaw

Prep time: 15 minutes / Cook time: 0 minutes / Serves 4 to 6

- 1 avocado
- ⅓ cup water
- 3 tablespoons apple cider vinegar
- 1 tablespoon Dijon mustard
- 4 cups packed shredded cabbage (red, green, or mixed)
- 2 cups shredded carrot
- Kosher salt
- Freshly ground black pepper

1. Place the avocado, water, vinegar, and mustard in a blender and puree until smooth. Add water if needed until you've reached a thin consistency, making the dressing easy to toss with the shredded vegetables.
2. In a large bowl, toss the cabbage and carrot with the dressing. Season to taste with salt and pepper and serve.
3. Store any leftovers in an airtight container in the refrigerator for up to 3 days.

*Per Serving:calories: 137 / fat: 8g / protein: 2g / carbs: 17g / sugars: 6g / fiber: 7g / sodium: 400mg*

## Green Beans with Garlic and Onion

Prep time: 5 minutes / Cook time: 12 minutes / Serves 8

- 1 pound fresh green beans, trimmed and cut into 2-inch pieces
- 1 tablespoon extra-virgin olive oil
- 1 small onion, chopped
- 1 large garlic clove, minced
- 1 tablespoon white vinegar
- ¼ cup Parmigiano-Reggiano cheese
- ⅛ teaspoon freshly ground black pepper

1. Steam the beans for 7 minutes or until just tender. Set aside.

2. In a skillet, heat the oil over low heat. Add the onion and garlic, and sauté for 4–5 minutes or until the onion is translucent.
3. Transfer the beans to a serving bowl, and add the onion mixture and vinegar, tossing well. Sprinkle with cheese and pepper, and serve.

*Per Serving:calories: 43 / fat: 3g / protein: 1g / carbs: 4g / sugars: 1g / fiber: 1g / sodium: 30mg*

## Peas with Mushrooms and Thyme

Prep time: 10 minutes / Cook time: 10 minutes / Serves 6

• 2 teaspoons olive, canola or soybean oil
• 1 medium onion, diced (½ cup)
• 1 cup sliced fresh mushrooms
• 1 bag (16 ounces) frozen sweet peas
• ¼ teaspoon coarse (kosher or sea) salt
• ⅛ teaspoon white pepper
• 1 teaspoon chopped fresh or ¼ teaspoon dried thyme leaves

1. In 10-inch skillet, heat oil over medium heat. Add onion and mushrooms; cook 3 minutes, stirring occasionally. Stir in peas. Cook 3 to 5 minutes, stirring occasionally, until vegetables are tender.
2. Sprinkle with salt, pepper and thyme. Serve immediately.

*Per Serving:calorie: 80 / fat: 1g / protein: 4g / carbs: 11g / sugars: 4g / fiber: 2g / sodium: 150mg*

## Crispy Green Beans

Prep time: 5 minutes / Cook time: 8 minutes / Serves 4

• 2 teaspoons olive oil
• ½ pound (227 g) fresh green beans, ends trimmed
• ¼ teaspoon salt
• ¼ teaspoon ground black pepper

1. In a large bowl, drizzle olive oil over green beans and sprinkle with salt and pepper.
2. Place green beans into ungreased air fryer basket. Adjust the temperature to 350ºF (177ºC) and set the timer for 8 minutes, shaking the basket two times during cooking. Green beans will be dark golden and crispy at the edges when done. Serve warm.

*Per Serving:calories: 30 / fat: 2g / protein: 1g / carbs: 3g / sugars: 2g / fiber: 2g / sodium: 148mg*

## Charred Miso Cabbage

Prep time: 5 minutes / Cook time: 20 minutes / Serves 4

• 3 tablespoons avocado oil
• 1 head green cabbage, cut into 8 wedges
• 3 tablespoons yellow or white miso
• 2 tablespoons rice wine vinegar
• 1 lime, cut into 8 wedges

1. Preheat the oven to 400°F. Line a baking sheet with parchment paper.
2. Heat the avocado oil in a large cast-iron pan or skillet over high heat. Arrange 2 or 3 cabbage wedges in the skillet and cook for about 3 minutes on each side until charred or lightly blackened. When they're seared on both sides, place the wedges on the baking sheet.
3. Repeat with the remaining wedges.
4. In a small bowl, mix the miso with the rice wine vinegar and brush it on the cabbage wedges evenly. Bake the wedges for 10 minutes.
5. When the wedges come out of the oven, squeeze the lime juice on them. Serve.
6. Store any leftovers in an airtight container in the refrigerator for 2 to 3 days.

*Per Serving:calories: 125 / fat: 11g / protein: 2g / carbs: 5g / sugars: 1g / fiber: 1g / sodium: 491mg*

## Roasted Beets, Carrots, and Parsnips

Prep time: 10 minutes / Cook time: 30 minutes / Serves 4

• 1 pound beets, peeled and quartered
• ½ pound carrots, peeled and cut into chunks
• ½ pound parsnips, peeled and cut into chunks
• 1 tablespoon extra-virgin olive oil
• 1 teaspoon apple cider vinegar
• Sea salt
• Freshly ground black pepper

1. Preheat the oven to 375°F. Line a baking tray with aluminum foil.
2. In a large bowl, toss the beets, carrots, and parsnips with the oil and vinegar until everything is well coated. Spread them out on the baking sheet.
3. Roast until the vegetables are tender and lightly caramelized, about 30 minutes.
4. Transfer the vegetables to a serving bowl, season with salt and pepper, and serve warm.

*Per Serving:calories: 122 / fat: 4g / protein: 4g / carbs: 21g / sugars: 6g / fiber: 9g / sodium: 592mg*

## "Honey" Mustard Sauce

Prep time: 5 minutes / Cook time: 0 minutes / Makes ½ cup

• ½ cup plain nonfat Greek yogurt
• 1 tablespoon apple cider vinegar
• 1 teaspoon dry mustard
• ¾ teaspoon garlic powder
• ⅛ teaspoon paprika
• 1 tablespoon granulated stevia

1. In a small bowl, whisk together the yogurt, apple cider vinegar, dry mustard, garlic powder, paprika, and stevia until smooth.
2. Refrigerate until needed.

*Per Serving:calories: 101 / fat: 0g / protein: 7g / carbs:*

*17g / sugars: 15g / fiber: 1g / sodium: 81mg*

## Zucchini Fritters

Prep time: 10 minutes / Cook time: 10 minutes / Serves 4

- 2 zucchini, grated (about 1 pound / 454 g)
- 1 teaspoon salt
- ¼ cup almond flour
- ¼ cup grated Parmesan cheese
- 1 large egg
- ¼ teaspoon dried thyme
- ¼ teaspoon ground turmeric
- ¼ teaspoon freshly ground black pepper
- 1 tablespoon olive oil
- ½ lemon, sliced into wedges

1. Preheat the air fryer to 400°F (204°C). Cut a piece of parchment paper to fit slightly smaller than the bottom of the air fryer.
2. Place the zucchini in a large colander and sprinkle with the salt. Let sit for 5 to 10 minutes. Squeeze as much liquid as you can from the zucchini and place in a large mixing bowl. Add the almond flour, Parmesan, egg, thyme, turmeric, and black pepper. Stir gently until thoroughly combined.
3. Shape the mixture into 8 patties and arrange on the parchment paper. Brush lightly with the olive oil. Pausing halfway through the cooking time to turn the patties, air fry for 10 minutes until golden brown. Serve warm with the lemon wedges.

*Per Serving:calorie: 140 / fat: 9g / protein: 8g / carbs: 9g / sugars: 3g / fiber: 3g / sodium: 520mg*

## Vegetable Medley

Prep time: 20 minutes / Cook time: 2 minutes / Serves 8

- 2 medium parsnips
- 4 medium carrots
- 1 turnip, about 4½ inches diameter
- 1 cup water
- 1 teaspoon salt
- 3 tablespoons sugar
- ½ teaspoon salt
- 2 tablespoons canola or olive oil

1. Clean and peel vegetables. Cut in 1-inch pieces.
2. Place the cup of water and 1 teaspoon salt into the Instant Pot's inner pot with the vegetables.
3. Secure the lid and make sure vent is set to sealing. Press Manual and set for 2 minutes.
4. When cook time is up, release the pressure manually and press Cancel. Drain the water from the inner pot.
5. Press Sauté and stir in sugar, oil, and salt. Cook until sugar is dissolved. Serve.

*Per Serving:calories: 63 / fat: 2g / protein: 1g / carbs: 12g / sugars: 6g / fiber: 2g / sodium: 327mg*

## Curry Roasted Cauliflower

Prep time: 10 minutes / Cook time: 20 minutes / Serves 4

- ¼ cup olive oil
- 2 teaspoons curry powder
- ½ teaspoon salt
- ¼ teaspoon freshly ground black pepper
- 1 head cauliflower, cut into bite-size florets
- ½ red onion, sliced
- 2 tablespoons freshly chopped parsley, for garnish (optional)

1. Preheat the air fryer to 400°F (204°C).
2. In a large bowl, combine the olive oil, curry powder, salt, and pepper. Add the cauliflower and onion. Toss gently until the vegetables are completely coated with the oil mixture. Transfer the vegetables to the basket of the air fryer.
3. Pausing about halfway through the cooking time to shake the basket, air fry for 20 minutes until the cauliflower is tender and beginning to brown. Top with the parsley, if desired, before serving.

*Per Serving:calories: 187 / fat: 17g / protein: 3g / carbs: 8g / sugars: 3g / fiber: 3g / sodium: 378mg*

## Vegetable-Stuffed Yellow Squash

Prep time: 10 minutes / Cook time: 30 minutes / Serves 6

- 6 small yellow squash
- 1 tomato, finely chopped
- ½ cup minced onion
- ¼ teaspoon salt
- ½ cup finely chopped green bell pepper
- ½ cup shredded 50 percent reduced-fat sharp cheddar
- ⅛ teaspoon freshly ground black pepper

1. Preheat the oven to 400 degrees.
2. Place the squash in a large pot of boiling water. Cover, reduce heat, and simmer for 5–7 minutes or until the squash is just tender. Drain, and allow to cool slightly.
3. Trim the stems from the squash, and cut in half lengthwise. Gently scoop out the pulp, leaving a firm shell. Drain, and chop the pulp.
4. In a large mixing bowl, combine the pulp and the remaining ingredients, blending well.
5. Place the squash shells in a 13-x-9-x-2-inch baking dish, gently spoon the vegetable mixture into the shells, and bake at 400 degrees for 15–20 minutes. Remove from the oven, and let cool slightly before serving.

*Per Serving:calories: 72 / fat: 4g / protein: 4g / carbs: 6g / sugars: 3g / fiber: 2g / sodium: 177mg*

## Dijon Roast Cabbage

Prep time: 10 minutes / Cook time: 10 minutes / Serves 4

- 1 small head cabbage, cored and sliced into 1-inch-thick slices
- 2 tablespoons olive oil, divided
- ½ teaspoon salt
- 1 tablespoon Dijon mustard
- 1 teaspoon apple cider vinegar
- 1 teaspoon granular erythritol

1. Drizzle each cabbage slice with 1 tablespoon

olive oil, then sprinkle with salt. Place slices into ungreased air fryer basket, working in batches if needed. Adjust the temperature to 350°F (177°C) and air fry for 10 minutes. Cabbage will be tender and edges will begin to brown when done.

2. In a small bowl, whisk remaining olive oil with mustard, vinegar, and erythritol. Drizzle over cabbage in a large serving dish. Serve warm.

*Per Serving:calories: 110 / fat: 7g / protein: 3g / carbs: 11g / sugars: 5g / fiber: 3g / sodium: 392mg*

## Spaghetti Squash with Sun-Dried Tomatoes

Prep time: 20 minutes / Cook time: 1hour / Serves 4

- 1 spaghetti squash, halved and seeded
- 3 teaspoons extra-virgin olive oil, divided
- ¼ sweet onion, chopped
- 1 teaspoon minced garlic
- 2 cups fresh spinach
- ¼ cup chopped sun-dried tomatoes
- ¼ cup roasted, shelled sunflower seeds
- Juice of ½ lemon
- Sea salt
- Freshly ground black pepper

1. Preheat the oven to 350°F. Line a baking sheet with parchment paper.
2. Place the squash on the baking sheet and brush the cut edges with 2 teaspoons of olive oil.
3. Bake the squash until it is tender and separates into strands with a fork, about 1 hour.
4. Let the squash cool for 5 minutes then use a fork to scrape out the strands from both halves of the squash. Cover the squash strands and set them aside.
5. Place a large skillet over medium-high heat and add the remaining 1 teaspoon of olive oil. Sauté the onion and garlic until softened and translucent, about 3 minutes.
6. Stir in the spinach and sun-dried tomatoes, and sauté until the spinach is wilted, about 4 minutes.
7. Remove the skillet from the heat and stir in the squash strands, sunflower seeds, and lemon juice.
8. Season with salt and pepper and serve warm.

*Per Serving:calories: 218 / fat: 10g / protein: 5g / carbs: 32g / sugars: 13g / fiber: 7g / sodium: 232mg*

## Caramelized Onions

Prep time: 10 minutes / Cook time: 35 minutes / Serves 8

- 4 tablespoons margarine
- 6 large Vidalia or other sweet onions, sliced into thin half rings
- 10-ounce can chicken, or vegetable, broth

1. Press Sauté on the Instant Pot. Add in the margarine and let melt.

2. Once the margarine is melted, stir in the onions and sauté for about 5 minutes. Pour in the broth and then press Cancel.
3. Secure the lid and make sure vent is set to sealing. Press Manual and set time for 20 minutes.
4. When cook time is up, release the pressure manually. Remove the lid and press Sauté. Stir the onion mixture for about 10 more minutes, allowing extra liquid to cook off.

*Per Serving:calorie: 123 / fat: 6g / protein: 2g / carbs: 15g / sugars: 10g / fiber: 3g / sodium: 325mg*

## Simple Bibimbap

Prep time: 15 minutes / Cook time: 15 minutes / Serves 2

- 4 teaspoons canola oil, divided
- 2½ cups cauliflower rice
- 2 cups fresh baby spinach
- 3 teaspoons low-sodium soy sauce or tamari, divided
- 8 ounces mushrooms, thinly sliced
- 2 large eggs
- 1 cup bean sprouts, rinsed
- 1 cup kimchi
- ½ cup shredded carrots

1. Heat 1 teaspoon of canola oil in a medium skillet and sauté the cauliflower rice, spinach, and 2 teaspoons of soy sauce until the greens are wilted, about 5 minutes. Put the vegetables in a small bowl and set aside.
2. Return the skillet to medium heat, add 2 teaspoons of vegetable oil and, when it's hot, add the mushrooms in a single layer and cook for 3 to 5 minutes, then stir and cook another 3 minutes or until mostly golden-brown in color. Put the mushrooms in a small bowl and toss them with the remaining 1 teaspoon of soy sauce.
3. Wipe out the skillet and heat the remaining 1 teaspoon of vegetable oil over low heat. Crack in the eggs and cook until the whites are set and the yolks begin to thicken but not harden, 4 to 5 minutes.
4. Assemble two bowls with cauliflower rice and spinach at the bottom. Then arrange each ingredient separately around the rim of the bowl: bean sprouts, mushrooms, kimchi, and shredded carrots, with the egg placed in the center, and serve.

*Per Serving:calories: 275 / fat: 16g / protein: 20g / carbs: 20g / sugars: 8g / fiber: 8g / sodium: 518mg*

## Roasted Peppers and Eggplant

Prep time: 5 minutes / Cook time: 20 minutes / Serves 2

- Extra-virgin olive oil cooking spray
- 1 small eggplant, halved and sliced
- 1 red bell pepper, cut into thick strips
- 1 yellow bell pepper, cut into thick strips

- 1 red onion, sliced
- 2 garlic cloves, quartered
- 1 tablespoon extra-virgin olive oil
- Salt, to season
- Freshly ground black pepper, to season
- ½ cup chopped fresh basil

1. Preheat the oven to 350°F.
2. Coat a nonstick baking dish with cooking spray.
3. To the prepared dish, add the eggplant, red bell pepper, yellow bell pepper, onion, and garlic. Drizzle with the olive oil. Toss to coat well. Spray any uncoated surfaces with cooking spray.
4. Place the dish in the preheated oven. Bake for 20 minutes, turning once halfway through cooking.
5. Transfer the vegetables to a serving dish. Season with salt and pepper.
6. Garnish with the basil and serve.

*Per Serving:calories: 185 / fat: 11g / protein: 4g / carbs: 23g / sugars: 12g / fiber: 10g / sodium: 651mg*

## Italian Wild Mushrooms

Prep time: 30 minutes / Cook time: 3 minutes / Serves 10
- 2 tablespoons canola oil
- 2 large onions, chopped
- 4 garlic cloves, minced
- 3 large red bell peppers, chopped
- 3 large green bell peppers, chopped
- 12 ounces package oyster mushrooms, cleaned and chopped
- 3 fresh bay leaves
- 10 fresh basil leaves, chopped
- 1 teaspoon salt
- 1½ teaspoons pepper
- 28 ounces can Italian plum tomatoes, crushed or chopped

1. Press Sauté on the Instant Pot and add in the oil. Once the oil is heated, add the onions, garlic, peppers, and mushroom to the oil. Sauté just until mushrooms begin to turn brown.
2. Add remaining ingredients. Stir well.
3. Secure the lid and make sure vent is set to sealing. Press Manual and set time for 3 minutes.
4. When cook time is up, release the pressure manually. Discard bay leaves.

*Per Serving:calories: 82 / fat: 3g / protein: 3g / carbs: 13g / sugars: 8g / fiber: 4g / sodium: 356mg*

## Nutmeg Green Beans

Prep time: 15 minutes / Cook time: 5 minutes / Serves 12
- 1 tablespoon butter
- 1½ pounds green beans, trimmed
- 1 teaspoon ground nutmeg     • Sea salt

1. Place a large skillet over medium heat and melt the butter.

2. Add the green beans and sauté, stirring often, until the beans are tender-crisp, about 5 minutes.
3. Stir in the nutmeg and season with salt.
4. Serve immediately.

*Per Serving:calories: 22 / fat: 1g / protein: 1g / carbs: 3g / sugars: 0g / fiber: 1g / sodium: 57mg*

## Broiled Asparagus

Prep time: 5 minutes / Cook time: 5 to 6 minutes / Serves 3
- 1 pound asparagus
- ¼ teaspoon sea salt
- 1 teaspoon lemon juice
- Lemon pepper (optional)

1. Set the oven or toaster oven to broil. Line a baking sheet with parchment paper.
2. Wash and trim the asparagus. (Use a knife or break off ends where they naturally snap. ) Pat the asparagus dry, and transfer to the prepared baking sheet. Sprinkle with the lemon juice, toss to coat, and then sprinkle with the salt. Broil for 5 to 6 minutes, or until the asparagus turns bright green. Remove, sprinkle with the lemon pepper (if using), and serve.

*Per Serving:calorie: 17 / fat: 0. 2g / protein: 2g / carbs: 3g / sugars: 1g / fiber: 2g / sodium: 206mg*

## Sweet Potato Crisps

Prep time: 10 minutes / Cook time: 30 minutes / Serves 3
- 1 pound sweet potatoes
- ½ tablespoon balsamic vinegar
- ½ tablespoon pure maple syrup
- Rounded ¼ teaspoon sea salt

1. Preheat the oven to 400°F. Line a large baking sheet with parchment paper.
2. Peel the sweet potatoes, then use the peeler to continue to make sweet potato peelings. (Alternatively, you can push peeled sweet potatoes through a food processor slicing blade. ) Transfer the peelings to a large mixing bowl and use your hands to toss with the vinegar and syrup, coating them as evenly as possible. Spread the peelings on the prepared baking sheet, spacing well. Sprinkle with the salt. Bake for 30 minutes, tossing once or twice. The pieces around the edges of the pan can get brown quickly, so move the chips around during baking. Turn off the oven and let the chips sit in the residual heat for 20 minutes, stir again, and let sit for another 15 to 20 minutes, until they crisp up. Remove, and snack!

*Per Serving:calorie: 94 / fat: 0g / protein: 2g / carbs: 22g / sugars: 8g / fiber: 3g / sodium: 326mg*

## Vegetable Curry

Prep time: 25 minutes / Cook time: 3 minutes / Serves 10
- 16-ounce package baby carrots

- 3 medium potatoes, unpeeled, cubed
- 1 pound fresh or frozen green beans, cut in 2-inch pieces
- 1 medium green pepper, chopped
- 1 medium onion, chopped
- 1–2 cloves garlic, minced
- 15-ounce can garbanzo beans, drained
- 28-ounce can crushed tomatoes
- 3 teaspoons curry powder
- 1½ teaspoons chicken bouillon granules
- 1¾ cups boiling water
- 3 tablespoons minute tapioca

1. Combine carrots, potatoes, green beans, pepper, onion, garlic, garbanzo beans, crushed tomatoes, and curry powder in the Instant Pot.
2. Dissolve bouillon in boiling water, then stir in tapicoa. Pour over the contents of the Instant Pot and stir.
3. Secure the lid and make sure vent is set to sealing. Press Manual and set for 3 minutes.
4. When cook time is up, manually release the pressure.

*Per Serving:calories: 166 / fat: 1g / protein: 6g / carbs: 35g / sugars: 10g / fiber: 8g / sodium: 436mg*

## Herb-Roasted Root Vegetables

Prep time: 15 minutes / Cook time: 45 to 55 minutes / Serves 6

- 2 medium turnips, peeled, cut into 1-inch pieces (3 cups)
- 2 medium parsnips, peeled, cut into ½-inch pieces (1½ cups)
- 1 medium red onion, cut into 1-inch wedges (1 cup)
- 1 cup ready-to-eat baby-cut carrots
- Cooking spray
- 2 teaspoons Italian seasoning
- ½ teaspoon coarse salt

1. Heat oven to 425°F. Spray 15x10x1-inch pan with cooking spray. Arrange vegetables in single layer in pan. Spray with cooking spray (2 or 3 seconds). Sprinkle with Italian seasoning and salt.
2. Bake uncovered 45 to 55 minutes, stirring once, until vegetables are tender.

*Per Serving:calorie: 70 / fat: 0g / protein: 1g / carbs: 15g / sugars: 7g / fiber: 4g / sodium: 260mg*

## Garlic Roasted Radishes

Prep time: 5 minutes / Cook time: 15 minutes / Serves 2 to 4

- 1 pound radishes, halved
- 1 tablespoon canola oil
- Pinch kosher salt
- 4 garlic cloves, thinly sliced
- ¼ cup chopped fresh dill

1. Preheat the oven to 425°F. Line a baking sheet with parchment paper.
2. In a medium bowl, toss the radishes with the canola oil and salt. Spread the vegetables on the prepared baking sheet and roast for 10 minutes. Remove the sheet from the oven, add the garlic, mix well, and return to the oven for 5 minutes.
3. Remove the radishes from the oven, adjust the seasoning as desired, and serve topped with dill on a serving plate or as a side dish.
4. Store any leftovers in an airtight container in the refrigerator for 3 to 4 days.

*Per Serving:calories: 75 / fat: 5g / protein: 1g / carbs: 8g / sugars: 4g / fiber: 3g / sodium: 420mg*

## Cheesy Broiled Tomatoes

Prep time: 5 minutes / Cook time: 10 minutes / Serves 2

- 2 large ripe tomatoes, halved widthwise
- ¼ cup nonfat ricotta cheese, divided
- ½ teaspoon dried basil, divided
- Salt, to season
- Freshly ground black pepper, to season

1. Preheat the broiler.
2. Top each tomato half with 1 tablespoon of ricotta cheese. Sprinkle with ⅛ teaspoon of basil. Season with salt and pepper.
3. On a broiler rack, place the tomatoes cut-side up. Place the rack into the preheated oven. Broil for 7 to 10 minutes.
4. Enjoy!

*Per Serving:calories: 49 / fat: 0g / protein: 4g / carbs: 9g / sugars: 5g / fiber: 3g / sodium: 658mg*

## Green Beans with Red Peppers

Prep time: 5 minutes / Cook time: 15 minutes / Serves 2

- 8 ounces fresh green beans, broken into 2-inch pieces
- 6 sun-dried tomatoes (not packed in oil), halved
- 1 medium red bell pepper, cut into ¼-inch strips
- 1 teaspoon extra-virgin olive oil
- Salt, to season
- Freshly ground black pepper, to season

1. In a 1-quart saucepan set over high heat, add the green beans to 1 inch of water. Bring to a boil. Boil for 5 minutes, uncovered.
2. Add the sun-dried tomatoes. Cover and boil 5 to 7 minutes more, or until the beans are crisp-tender, and the tomatoes have softened. Drain. Transfer to a serving bowl.
3. Add the red bell pepper and olive oil. Season with salt and pepper. Toss to coat.
4. Serve warm.

*Per Serving:calories: 82 / fat: 3g / protein: 3g / carbs: 13g / sugars: 6g / fiber: 4g / sodium: 601mg*

# Chapter 8 Vegetarian Mains

## Roasted Veggie Bowl

Prep time: 10 minutes / Cook time: 15 minutes / Serves 2

- 1 cup broccoli florets
- 1 cup quartered Brussels sprouts
- ½ cup cauliflower florets
- ¼ medium white onion, peeled and sliced ¼ inch thick
- ½ medium green bell pepper, seeded and sliced ¼ inch thick
- 1 tablespoon coconut oil
- 2 teaspoons chili powder
- ½ teaspoon garlic powder
- ½ teaspoon cumin

1. Toss all ingredients together in a large bowl until vegetables are fully coated with oil and seasoning.
2. Pour vegetables into the air fryer basket.
3. Adjust the temperature to 360ºF (182ºC) and roast for 15 minutes.
4. Shake two or three times during cooking. Serve warm.

*Per Serving:calories: 112 / fat: 8g / protein: 4g / carbs: 11g / sugars: 3g / fiber: 5g / sodium: 106mg*

## Caprese Eggplant Stacks

Prep time: 5 minutes / Cook time: 12 minutes / Serves 4

- 1 medium eggplant, cut into ¼-inch slices
- 2 large tomatoes, cut into ¼-inch slices
- 4 ounces (113 g) fresh Mozzarella, cut into ½-ounce / 14-g slices
- 2 tablespoons olive oil
- ¼ cup fresh basil, sliced

1. In a baking dish, place four slices of eggplant on the bottom. Place a slice of tomato on top of each eggplant round, then Mozzarella, then eggplant. Repeat as necessary.
2. Drizzle with olive oil. Cover dish with foil and place dish into the air fryer basket.
3. Adjust the temperature to 350ºF (177ºC) and bake for 12 minutes.
4. When done, eggplant will be tender. Garnish with fresh basil to serve.

*Per Serving:calories: 216 / fat: 16g / protein: 9g / carbs: 11g / sugars: 6g / fiber: 5g / sodium: 231mg*

## The Ultimate Veggie Burger

Prep time: 5 minutes / Cook time: 10 minutes / Serves 2

- ¾ cup shelled edamame
- ¾ cup frozen mixed vegetables, thawed
- 3 tablespoons hemp hearts
- 2 tablespoons quick-cook oatmeal
- ¼ teaspoon salt
- ¼ teaspoon onion powder
- ¼ teaspoon ground cumin
- 1 scallion, sliced
- 2 teaspoons chopped fresh cilantro
- 2 tablespoons coconut flour
- 2 large egg whites
- Extra-virgin olive oil cooking spray

1. In a food processor, combine the edamame, mixed vegetables, hemp hearts, oatmeal, salt, onion powder, cumin, scallion, cilantro, coconut flour, and egg whites. Pulse until blended, but not completely puréed. You want some texture.
2. Spray a nonstick skillet with cooking spray. Place it over medium-high heat.
3. Spoon half of the mixture into the pan. Using the back of a spoon, spread it out to form a patty. Repeat with the remaining half of the mixture.
4. Cook for 3 to 5 minutes, or until golden, and flip. Cook for about 3 minutes more, or until golden. Turn off the heat.
5. Transfer to serving plates and enjoy!

*Per Serving:calories: 154 / fat: 4g / protein: 13g / carbs: 19g / sugars: 4g / fiber: 7g / sodium: 467mg*

## Palak Tofu

Prep time: 5 minutes / Cook time: 40 minutes / Serves 4

- One 14-ounce package extra-firm tofu, drained
- 5 tablespoons cold-pressed avocado oil
- 1 yellow onion, diced
- 1-inch piece fresh ginger, peeled and minced
- 3 garlic cloves, minced
- 1 teaspoon fine sea salt
- ½ teaspoon freshly ground black pepper
- ¼ teaspoon cayenne pepper
- One 16-ounce bag frozen chopped spinach
- ⅓ cup water
- One 14½-ounce can fire-roasted diced tomatoes and their liquid
- ¼ cup coconut milk
- 2 teaspoons garam masala
- Cooked brown rice or cauliflower "rice" or whole-grain flatbread for serving

1. Cut the tofu crosswise into eight ½-inch-thick slices. Sandwich the slices between double layers of paper towels or a folded kitchen towel and press

firmly to wick away as much moisture as possible. Cut the slices into ½-inch cubes.

2. Select the Sauté setting on the Instant Pot and and heat 4 tablespoons of the oil for 2 minutes. Add the onion and sauté for about 10 minutes, until it begins to brown.

3. While the onion is cooking in the Instant Pot, in a large nonstick skillet over medium-high heat, warm the remaining 1 tablespoon oil. Add the tofu in a single layer and cook without stirring for about 3 minutes, until lightly browned.

4. Using a spatula, turn the cubes over and cook for about 3 minutes more, until browned on the other side. Remove from the heat and set aside.

5. Add the ginger and garlic to the onion in the Instant Pot and sauté for about 2 minutes, until the garlic is bubbling but not browned. Add the sautéed tofu, salt, black pepper, and cayenne and stir gently to combine, taking care not to break up the tofu. Add the spinach and stir gently. Pour in the water and then pour the tomatoes and their liquid over the top in an even layer. Do not stir them in.

6. Secure the lid and set the Pressure Release to Sealing. Press the Cancel button to reset the cooking program, then select the Manual or Pressure Cook setting and set the cooking time for 10 minutes at low pressure. (The pot will take about 15 minutes to come up to pressure before the cooking program begins. )

7. When the cooking program ends, let the pressure release naturally for 10 minutes, then move the Pressure Release to Venting to release any remaining steam. Open the pot, add the coconut milk and garam masala, and stir to combine.

8. Ladle the tofu onto plates or into bowls. Serve piping hot, with the "rice" alongside.

*Per Serving:calories: 345 / fat: 24g / protein: 14g / carbs: 18g / sugars: 5g / fiber: 6g / sodium: 777mg*

## Orange Tofu

Prep time: 10 minutes / Cook time: 20 minutes / Serves 4

- ⅓ cup freshly squeezed orange juice (zest orange first; see orange zest ingredient below)
- 1 tablespoon tamari
- 1 tablespoon tahini
- ½ tablespoon coconut nectar or pure maple syrup
- 2 tablespoons apple cider vinegar
- ½ tablespoon freshly grated ginger
- 1 large clove garlic, grated
- ½–1 teaspoon orange zest
- ¼ teaspoon sea salt
- Few pinches of crushed red-pepper flakes (optional)
- 1 package (12 ounces) extra-firm tofu, sliced into ¼"–½" thick squares and patted to remove excess moisture

1. Preheat the oven to 400°F.

2. In a small bowl, combine the orange juice, tamari, tahini, nectar or syrup, vinegar, ginger, garlic, orange zest, salt, and red-pepper flakes (if using). Whisk until well combined. Pour the sauce into an 8" x 12" baking dish. Add the tofu and turn to coat both sides. Bake for 20 minutes. Add salt to taste.

*Per Serving:calorie: 122 / fat: 7g / protein: 10g / carbs: 7g / sugars: 4g / fiber: 1g / sodium: 410mg*

## Chile Relleno Casserole with Salsa Salad

Prep time: 10 minutes / Cook time: 55 minutes / Serves 4

- Casserole
- ½ cup gluten-free flour (such as King Arthur)
- 1 teaspoon baking powder
- 6 large eggs
- ½ cup nondairy milk or whole milk
- Three 4 ounces cans fire-roasted diced green chiles, drained
- 1 cup nondairy cheese shreds or shredded mozzarella cheese
- Salad
- 1 head green leaf lettuce, shredded
- 2 Roma tomatoes, seeded and diced
- 1 green bell pepper, seeded and diced
- ½ small yellow onion, diced
- 1 jalapeño chile, seeded and diced (optional)
- 2 tablespoons chopped fresh cilantro
- 4 teaspoons extra-virgin olive oil
- 4 teaspoons fresh lime juice
- ⅛ teaspoon fine sea salt

1. To make the casserole: Pour 1 cup water into the Instant Pot. Butter a 7-cup round heatproof glass dish or coat with nonstick cooking spray and place the dish on a long-handled silicone steam rack. (If you don't have the long-handled rack, use the wire metal steam rack and a homemade sling)

2. In a medium bowl, whisk together the flour and baking powder. Add the eggs and milk and whisk until well blended, forming a batter. Stir in the chiles and ¾ cup of the cheese.

3. Pour the batter into the prepared dish and cover tightly with aluminum foil. Holding the handles of the steam rack, lower the dish into the Instant Pot.

4. Secure the lid and set the Pressure Release to Sealing. Select the Pressure Cook or Manual setting and set the cooking time for 40 minutes at high pressure. (The pot will take about 10 minutes to come up to pressure before the cooking program begins. )

5. When the cooking program ends, let the pressure release naturally for at least 10 minutes, then move the Pressure Release to Venting to release any remaining steam. Open the pot and, wearing

heat-resistant mitts, grasp the handles of the steam rack and lift it out of the pot. Uncover the dish, taking care not to get burned by the steam or to drip condensation onto the casserole. While the casserole is still piping hot, sprinkle the remaining ¼ cup cheese evenly on top. Let the cheese melt for 5 minutes.

6. To make the salad: While the cheese is melting, in a large bowl, combine the lettuce, tomatoes, bell pepper, onion, jalapeño (if using), cilantro, oil, lime juice, and salt. Toss until evenly combined.

7. Cut the casserole into wedges. Serve warm, with the salad on the side.

*Per Serving:calorie: 361 / fat: 22g / protein: 21g / carbs: 23g / sugars: 8g / fiber: 3g / sodium: 421mg*

## Asparagus, Sun-Dried Tomato, and Green Pea Sauté

Prep time: 10 minutes / Cook time: 10 minutes / Serves 2

• 6 packaged sun-dried tomatoes (not packed in oil)
• ½ cup boiling water
• 1 tablespoon extra-virgin olive oil
• 2 garlic cloves, minced
• ¾ pound fresh asparagus, trimmed and cut into 2-inch pieces
• ¼ cup chopped red bell pepper
• ½ cup sliced fresh button mushrooms
• ¼ cup reduced-sodium vegetable broth
• 2 tablespoons sliced almonds
• 1 large tomato, diced (about 1 cup)
• 1½ teaspoons dried tarragon
• ½ cup frozen peas
• Freshly ground black pepper, to season

1. In a small heatproof bowl, place the sun-dried tomatoes. Cover with the boiling water. Set aside.
2. In a large skillet or wok set over high heat, heat the olive oil.
3. Add the garlic. Swirl in the oil for a few seconds.
4. Toss in the asparagus, red bell pepper, and mushrooms. Stir-fry for 30 seconds.
5. Add the vegetable broth and almonds. Cover and steam for about 2 minutes. Uncover the skillet.
6. Add the tomato and tarragon. Cook for 2 to 3 minutes to reduce the liquid.
7. Drain and chop the sun-dried tomatoes. Add them and the peas to the skillet. Stir-fry for 3 to 4 minutes, or until the vegetables are crisp-tender and the liquid is reduced to a sauce.
8. Season with pepper and serve immediately.

*Per Serving:calories: 165 / fat: 8g / protein: 8g / carbs: 20g / sugars: 9g / fiber: 7g / sodium: 46mg*

## Chickpea and Tofu Bolognese

Prep time: 5 minutes / Cook time: 25 minutes / Serves 4

• 1 (3 to 4 pounds) spaghetti squash
• ½ teaspoon ground cumin
• 1 cup no-sugar-added spaghetti sauce
• 1 (15 ounces) can low-sodium chickpeas, drained and rinsed
• 6 ounces extra-firm tofu

1. Preheat the oven to 400°F.
2. Cut the squash in half lengthwise. Scoop out the seeds and discard.
3. Season both halves of the squash with the cumin, and place them on a baking sheet cut-side down. Roast for 25 minutes.
4. Meanwhile, heat a medium saucepan over low heat, and pour in the spaghetti sauce and chickpeas.
5. Press the tofu between two layers of paper towels, and gently squeeze out any excess water.
6. Crumble the tofu into the sauce and cook for 15 minutes.
7. Remove the squash from the oven, and comb through the flesh of each half with a fork to make thin strands.
8. Divide the "spaghetti" into four portions, and top each portion with one-quarter of the sauce.

*Per Serving:calories: 221 / fat: 6g / protein: 12g / carbs: 32g / sugars: 6g / fiber: 8g / sodium: 405mg*

## Black-Eyed Pea Sauté with Garlic and Olives

Prep time: 5 minutes / Cook time: 5 minutes / Serves 2

• 2 teaspoons extra-virgin olive oil
• 1 garlic clove, minced
• ½ red onion, chopped
• 1 cup cooked black-eyed peas; if canned, drain and rinse
• ½ teaspoon dried thyme
• ¼ cup water
• ¼ teaspoon salt
• ¼ teaspoon freshly ground black pepper
• 6 Kalamata olives, pitted and halved

1. In a medium saucepan set over medium heat, stir together the olive oil, garlic, and red onion. Cook for 2 minutes, continuing to stir.
2. Add the black-eyed peas and thyme. Cook for 1 minute.
3. Stir in the water, salt, pepper, and olives. Cook for 2 minutes more, or until heated through.

*Per Serving:calories: 140 / fat: 6g / protein: 5g / carbs: 18g / sugars: 8g / fiber: 5g / sodium: 426mg*

## Mushroom and Cauliflower Rice Risotto

Prep time: 5 minutes / Cook time: 10 minutes / Serves 4

• 1 teaspoon extra-virgin olive oil
• ½ cup chopped portobello mushrooms
• 4 cups cauliflower rice
• ¼ cup low-sodium vegetable broth

- ½ cup half-and-half
- 1 cup shredded Parmesan cheese

1. Heat the oil in a medium skillet over medium-low heat. When hot, put the mushrooms in the skillet and cook for 3 minutes, stirring once.
2. Add the cauliflower rice, broth, and half-and-half. Stir and cover. Increase to high heat and boil for 5 minutes.
3. Add the cheese. Stir to incorporate. Cook for 3 more minutes.

*Per Serving:calories: 159 / fat: 8g / protein: 10g / carbs: 12g / sugars: 4g / fiber: 2g / sodium: 531mg*

## Gingered Tofu and Greens

Prep time: 15 minutes / Cook time: 20 minutes / Serves 2
- For the marinade
- 2 tablespoons low-sodium soy sauce
- ¼ cup rice vinegar
- ⅓ cup water
- 1 tablespoon grated fresh ginger
- 1 tablespoon coconut flour
- 1 teaspoon granulated stevia
- 1 garlic clove, minced
- For the tofu and greens
- 8 ounces extra-firm tofu, drained, cut into 1-inch cubes
- 3 teaspoons extra-virgin olive oil, divided
- 1 tablespoon grated fresh ginger
- 2 cups coarsely shredded bok choy
- 2 cups coarsely shredded kale, thoroughly washed
- ½ cup fresh, or frozen, chopped green beans
- 1 tablespoon freshly squeezed lime juice
- 1 tablespoon chopped fresh cilantro
- 2 tablespoons hemp hearts

1. In a small bowl, whisk together the soy sauce, rice vinegar, water, ginger, coconut flour, stevia, and garlic until well combined.
2. Place a small saucepan set over high heat. Add the marinade. Bring to a boil. Cook for 1 minute. Remove from the heat. To make the tofu and greens
1. In a medium ovenproof pan, place the tofu in a single layer. Pour the marinade over. Drizzle with 1½ teaspoons of olive oil. Let sit for 5 minutes.
2. Preheat the broiler to high.
3. Place the pan under the broiler. Broil the tofu for 7 to 8 minutes, or until lightly browned. Using a spatula, turn the tofu over. Continue to broil for 7 to 8 minutes more, or until browned on this side.
4. In a large wok or skillet set over high heat, heat the remaining 1½ teaspoons of olive oil.
5. Stir in the ginger.
6. Add the bok choy, kale, and green beans. Cook for 2 to 3 minutes, stirring constantly, until the greens wilt.
7. Add the lime juice and cilantro. Remove from the heat.
8. Add the browned tofu with any remaining

marinade in the pan to the bok choy, kale, and green beans. Toss gently to combine.
9. Top with the hemp hearts and serve immediately.

*Per Serving:calories: 252 / fat: 14g / protein: 15g / carbs: 20g / sugars: 4g / fiber: 3g / sodium: 679mg*

## Quinoa–White Bean Loaf

Prep time: 15 minutes / Cook time: 1 hour / Serves 2
- Extra-virgin olive oil cooking spray
- 2 teaspoons extra-virgin olive oil
- 2 garlic cloves, minced
- ½ cup sliced fresh button mushrooms
- 6 ounces extra-firm tofu, crumbled
- Salt, to season
- Freshly ground black pepper, to season
- 1 (8-ounce) can cannellini beans, drained and rinsed
- 2 tablespoons coconut flour
- 1 tablespoon chia seeds
- ⅓ cup water
- ½ cup cooked quinoa
- ¼ cup chopped red onion
- ¼ cup chopped fresh parsley

1. Preheat the oven to 350°F.
2. Lightly coat 2 mini loaf pans with cooking spray. Set aside.
3. In a large skillet set over medium-high heat, heat the olive oil.
4. Add the garlic, mushrooms, and tofu. Season with salt and pepper.
5. Cook for 6 to 8 minutes, stirring occasionally, until the mushrooms and tofu are golden brown.
6. In a food processor, combine the cannellini beans, coconut flour, chia seeds, and water. Pulse until almost smooth.
7. In a large bowl, mix together the mushroom and tofu mixture, cannellini bean mixture, quinoa, red onion, and parsley. Season with salt and pepper.
8. Evenly divide the mixture between the 2 prepared loaf pans, gently pressing down and mounding the mixture in the middle.
9. Place the pans in the preheated oven. Bake for about 1 hour, or until firm and golden brown. Remove from the oven. Let rest for 10 minutes.
10. Slice and serve.

*Per Serving:calories: 193 / fat: 8g / protein: 12g / carbs: 20g / sugars: 4g / fiber: 4g / sodium: 366mg*

## Parmesan Artichokes

Prep time: 10 minutes / Cook time: 10 minutes / Serves 4
- 2 medium artichokes, trimmed and quartered, center removed
- 2 tablespoons coconut oil
- 1 large egg, beaten
- ½ cup grated vegetarian Parmesan cheese

- ¼ cup blanched finely ground almond flour
- ½ teaspoon crushed red pepper flakes

1. In a large bowl, toss artichokes in coconut oil and then dip each piece into the egg.
2. Mix the Parmesan and almond flour in a large bowl. Add artichoke pieces and toss to cover as completely as possible, sprinkle with pepper flakes. Place into the air fryer basket.
3. Adjust the temperature to 400°F (204°C) and air fry for 10 minutes.
4. Toss the basket two times during cooking. Serve warm.

*Per Serving:calories: 207 / fat: 13g / protein: 10g / carbs: 15g / sugars: 2g / fiber: 5g / sodium: 211mg*

## Tofu and Bean Chili

Prep time: 10 minutes / Cook time 30 minutes / Serves 4
- 1 (15 ounces) can low-sodium dark red kidney beans, drained and rinsed, divided
- 2 (15 ounces) cans no-salt-added diced tomatoes
- 1½ cups low-sodium vegetable broth
- ½ teaspoon chili powder
- ½ teaspoon ground cumin
- ½ teaspoon garlic powder
- ½ teaspoon dried oregano
- ¼ teaspoon onion powder
- ¼ teaspoon salt
- 8 ounces extra-firm tofu

1. In a small bowl, mash ⅓ of the beans with a fork.
2. Put the mashed beans, the remaining whole beans, and the diced tomatoes with their juices in a large stockpot.
3. Add the broth, chili powder, cumin, garlic powder, dried oregano, onion powder, and salt. Simmer over medium-high heat for 15 minutes.
4. Press the tofu between 3 or 4 layers of paper towels to squeeze out any excess moisture.
5. Crumble the tofu into the stockpot and stir. Simmer for another 10 to 15 minutes.

*Per Serving:calories: 207 / fat: 5g / protein: 15g / carbs: 31g / sugars: 11g / fiber: 12g / sodium: 376mg*

## Veggie Fajitas

Prep time: 10 minutes / Cook time: 15 minutes / Serves 4
- For The Guacamole
- 2 small avocados pitted and peeled
- 1 teaspoon freshly squeezed lime juice
- ¼ teaspoon salt
- 9 cherry tomatoes, halved
- For The Fajitas
- 1 red bell pepper
- 1 green bell pepper
- 1 small white onion
- Avocado oil cooking spray

- 1 cup canned low-sodium black beans, drained and rinsed
- ½ teaspoon ground cumin
- ¼ teaspoon chili powder
- ¼ teaspoon garlic powder
- 4 (6-inch) yellow corn tortillas

1. In a medium bowl, use a fork to mash the avocados with the lime juice and salt.
2. Gently stir in the cherry tomatoes. To Make The Fajitas 1. Cut the red bell pepper, green bell pepper, and onion into ½-inch slices.
2. Heat a large skillet over medium heat. When hot, coat the cooking surface with cooking spray. Put the peppers, onion, and beans into the skillet.
3. Add the cumin, chili powder, and garlic powder, and stir.
4. Cover and cook for 15 minutes, stirring halfway through.
5. Divide the fajita mixture equally between the tortillas, and top with guacamole and any preferred garnishes.

*Per Serving:calories: 269 / fat: 15g / protein: 8g / carbs: 30g / sugars: 5g / fiber: 11g / sodium: 175mg*

## Vegetable Burgers

Prep time: 10 minutes / Cook time: 12 minutes / Serves 4
- 8 ounces (227 g) cremini mushrooms
- 2 large egg yolks
- ½ medium zucchini, trimmed and chopped
- ¼ cup peeled and chopped yellow onion
- 1 clove garlic, peeled and finely minced
- ½ teaspoon salt
- ¼ teaspoon ground black pepper

1. Place all ingredients into a food processor and pulse twenty times until finely chopped and combined.
2. Separate mixture into four equal sections and press each into a burger shape. Place burgers into ungreased air fryer basket. Adjust the temperature to 375°F (191°C) and air fry for 12 minutes, turning burgers halfway through cooking. Burgers will be browned and firm when done.
3. Place burgers on a large plate and let cool 5 minutes before serving.

*Per Serving:calories: 77 / fat: 5g / protein: 3g / carbs: 6g / sugars: 2g / fiber: 1g / sodium: 309mg*

## Vegan Dal Makhani

Prep time: 0 minutes / Cook time: 55 minutes / Serves 6
- 1 cup dried kidney beans
- ⅓ cup urad dal or beluga or Puy lentils
- 4 cups water
- 1 teaspoon fine sea salt
- 1 tablespoon cold-pressed avocado oil

- 1 tablespoon cumin seeds
- 1-inch piece fresh ginger, peeled and minced
- 4 garlic cloves, minced
- 1 large yellow onion, diced
- 2 jalapeño chiles, seeded and diced
- 1 green bell pepper, seeded and diced
- 1 tablespoon garam masala
- 1 teaspoon ground turmeric
- ¼ teaspoon cayenne pepper (optional)
- One 15-ounce can fire-roasted diced tomatoes and liquid
- 2 tablespoons vegan buttery spread
- Cooked cauliflower "rice" for serving
- 2 tablespoons chopped fresh cilantro
- 6 tablespoons plain coconut yogurt

1. In a medium bowl, combine the kidney beans, urad dal, water, and salt and stir to dissolve the salt. Let soak for 12 hours.
2. Select the Sauté setting on the Instant Pot and heat the oil and cumin seeds for 3 minutes, until the seeds are bubbling, lightly toasted, and aromatic. Add the ginger and garlic and sauté for 1 minute, until bubbling and fragrant. Add the onion, jalapeños, and bell pepper and sauté for 5 minutes, until the onion begins to soften.
3. Add the garam masala, turmeric, cayenne (if using), and the soaked beans and their liquid and stir to mix. Pour the tomatoes and their liquid on top. Do not stir them in.
4. Secure the lid and set the Pressure Release to Sealing. Press the Cancel button to reset the cooking program, then select the Pressure Cook or Manual setting and set the cooking time for 30 minutes at high pressure. (The pot will take about 15 minutes to come up to pressure before the cooking program begins. )
5. When the cooking program ends, let the pressure release naturally for 30 minutes, then move the Pressure Release to Venting to release any remaining steam. Open the pot and stir to combine, then stir in the buttery spread. If you prefer a smoother texture, ladle 1½ cups of the dal into a blender and blend until smooth, about 30 seconds, then stir the blended mixture into the rest of the dal in the pot.
6. Spoon the cauliflower "rice" into bowls and ladle the dal on top. Sprinkle with the cilantro, top with a dollop of coconut yogurt, and serve.

*Per Serving:calorie: 245 / fat: 7g / protein: 11g / carbs: 37g / sugars: 4g / fiber: 10g / sodium: 518mg*

## Easy Cheesy Vegetable Frittata

Prep time: 10 minutes / Cook time: 15 minutes / Serves 2
- Extra-virgin olive oil cooking spray
- ½ cup sliced onion
- ½ cup sliced green bell pepper
- ½ cup sliced eggplant
- ½ cup frozen spinach
- ½ cup sliced fresh mushrooms
- 1 tablespoon chopped fresh basil
- Pinch freshly ground black pepper
- ½ cup liquid egg substitute
- ½ cup nonfat cottage cheese
- ¼ cup fat-free evaporated milk
- ¼ cup nonfat shredded Cheddar cheese

1. Coat an ovenproof 10-inch skillet with cooking spray. Place it over medium-low heat until hot.
2. Add the onion, green bell pepper, eggplant, spinach, and mushrooms. Sauté for 2 to 3 minutes, or until lightly browned.
3. Add the basil. Season with pepper. Stir to combine. Cook for 2 to 3 minutes more, or until the flavors blend. Remove from the heat.
4. Preheat the broiler.
5. In a blender, combine the egg substitute, cottage cheese, Cheddar cheese, and evaporated milk. Process until smooth. Pour the egg mixture over the vegetables in the skillet.
6. Return the skillet to medium-low heat. Cover and cook for about 5 minutes, or until the bottom sets and the top is still slightly wet.
7. Transfer the ovenproof skillet to the broiler. Broil for 2 to 3 minutes, or until the top is set.
8. Serve one-half of the frittata per person and enjoy!

*Per Serving:calories: 177 / fat: 7g / protein: 17g / carbs: 12g / sugars: 6g / fiber: 3g / sodium: 408mg*

## No-Tuna Lettuce Wraps

Prep time: 10 minutes / Cook time: 0 minutes / Serves 4
- 1 (15-ounce) can low-sodium chickpeas, drained and rinsed
- 1 celery stalk, thinly sliced
- 3 tablespoons honey mustard
- 2 tablespoons finely chopped red onion
- 2 tablespoons unsalted tahini
- 1 tablespoon capers, undrained
- 12 butter lettuce leaves

1. In a large bowl, mash the chickpeas.
2. Add the celery, honey mustard, onion, tahini, and capers, and mix well.
3. For each serving, place three lettuce leaves on a plate so they overlap, top with one-fourth of the chickpea filling, and roll up into a wrap. Repeat with the remaining lettuce leaves and filling.

*Per Serving:calories: 163 / fat: 8g / protein: 6g / carbs: 17g / sugars: 4g / fiber: 6g / sodium: 333mg*

## Chickpea-Spinach Curry

Prep time: 5 minutes / Cook time: 10 minutes / Serves 2

- 1 cup frozen chopped spinach, thawed
- 1 cup canned chickpeas, drained and rinsed
- ½ cup frozen green beans
- ½ cup frozen broccoli florets
- ½ cup no-salt-added canned chopped tomatoes, undrained
- 1 tablespoon curry powder
- 1 tablespoon granulated garlic
- Salt, to season
- Freshly ground black pepper, to season
- ½ cup chopped fresh parsley

1. In a medium saucepan set over high heat, stir together the spinach, chickpeas, green beans, broccoli, tomatoes and their juice, curry powder, and garlic. Season with salt and pepper. Bring to a fast boil. Reduce the heat to low. Cover and simmer for 10 minutes, or until heated through.
2. Top with the parsley, serve, and enjoy!

*Per Serving:calories: 203 / fat: 3g / protein: 13g / carbs: 35g / sugars: 7g / fiber: 13g / sodium: 375mg*

## Greek Stuffed Eggplant

Prep time: 15 minutes / Cook time: 20 minutes / Serves 2

- 1 large eggplant        • 2 tablespoons unsalted butter
- ¼ medium yellow onion, diced
- ¼ cup chopped artichoke hearts
- 1 cup fresh spinach
- 2 tablespoons diced red bell pepper
- ½ cup crumbled feta

1. Slice eggplant in half lengthwise and scoop out flesh, leaving enough inside for shell to remain intact. Take eggplant that was scooped out, chop it, and set aside.
2. In a medium skillet over medium heat, add butter and onion. Sauté until onions begin to soften, about 3 to 5 minutes. Add chopped eggplant, artichokes, spinach, and bell pepper. Continue cooking 5 minutes until peppers soften and spinach wilts. Remove from the heat and gently fold in the feta.
3. Place filling into each eggplant shell and place into the air fryer basket.
4. Adjust the temperature to 320ºF (160ºC) and air fry for 20 minutes.
5. Eggplant will be tender when done. Serve warm.

*Per Serving:calories: 259 / fat: 16g / protein: 10g / carbs: 22g / sugars: 12g / fiber: 10g / sodium: 386mg*

## Stuffed Portobellos

Prep time: 10 minutes / Cook time: 8 minutes / Serves 4

- 3 ounces (85 g) cream cheese, softened
- ½ medium zucchini, trimmed and chopped
- ¼ cup seeded and chopped red bell pepper
- 1½ cups chopped fresh spinach leaves
- 4 large portobello mushrooms, stems removed
- 2 tablespoons coconut oil, melted
- ½ teaspoon salt

1. In a medium bowl, mix cream cheese, zucchini, pepper, and spinach.
2. Drizzle mushrooms with coconut oil and sprinkle with salt. Scoop ¼ zucchini mixture into each mushroom.
3. Place mushrooms into ungreased air fryer basket. Adjust the temperature to 400ºF (204ºC) and air fry for 8 minutes. Portobellos will be tender and tops will be browned when done. Serve warm.

*Per Serving:calories: 154 / fat: 13g / protein: 4g / carbs: 6g / sugars: 3g / fiber: 2g / sodium: 355mg*

## Chickpea Coconut Curry

Prep time: 5 minutes / Cook time: 15 minutes / Serves 4

- 3 cups fresh or frozen cauliflower florets
- 2 cups unsweetened almond milk
- 1 (15 ounces) can coconut milk
- 1 (15 ounces) can low-sodium chickpeas, drained and rinsed        • 1 tablespoon curry powder
- ¼ teaspoon ground ginger
- ¼ teaspoon garlic powder
- ⅛ teaspoon onion powder        • ¼ teaspoon salt

1. In a large stockpot, combine the cauliflower, almond milk, coconut milk, chickpeas, curry, ginger, garlic powder, and onion powder. Stir and cover.
2. Cook over medium-high heat for 10 minutes.
3. Reduce the heat to low, stir, and cook for 5 minutes more, uncovered. Season with up to ¼ teaspoon salt.

*Per Serving:calories: 225 / fat: 7g / protein: 12g / carbs: 31g / sugars: 14g / fiber: 9g / sodium: 489mg*

## Italian Zucchini Boats

Prep time: 5 minutes / Cook time: 15 minutes / Serves 4

- 1 cup canned low-sodium chickpeas, drained and rinsed
- 1 cup no-sugar-added spaghetti sauce
- 2 zucchini
- ¼ cup shredded Parmesan cheese

1. Preheat the oven to 425ºF.
2. In a medium bowl, mix the chickpeas and spaghetti sauce together.
3. Cut the zucchini in half lengthwise, and scrape a spoon gently down the length of each half to remove the seeds.
4. Fill each zucchini half with the chickpea sauce, and top with one-quarter of the Parmesan cheese.
5. Place the zucchini halves on a baking sheet and roast in the oven for 15 minutes.

*Per Serving:calories: 120 / fat: 4g / protein: 7g / carbs: 14g / sugars: 5g / fiber: 4g / sodium: 441mg*

# Chapter 9 Salads

## Warm Barley and Squash Salad with Balsamic Vinaigrette

Prep time: 20 minutes / Cook time: 40 minutes / Serves 8

- 1 small butternut squash
- 3 teaspoons plus 2 tablespoons extra-virgin olive oil, divided
- 2 cups broccoli florets
- 1 cup pearl barley
- 1 cup toasted chopped walnuts
- 2 cups baby kale
- ½ red onion, sliced
- 2 tablespoons balsamic vinegar
- 2 garlic cloves, minced
- ½ teaspoon salt
- ¼ teaspoon freshly ground black pepper

1. Preheat the oven to 400°F. Line a baking sheet with parchment paper.
2. Peel and seed the squash, and cut it into dice. In a large bowl, toss the squash with 2 teaspoons of olive oil. Transfer to the prepared baking sheet and roast for 20 minutes.
3. While the squash is roasting, toss the broccoli in the same bowl with 1 teaspoon of olive oil. After 20 minutes, flip the squash and push it to one side of the baking sheet. Add the broccoli to the other side and continue to roast for 20 more minutes until tender.
4. While the veggies are roasting, in a medium pot, cover the barley with several inches of water. Bring to a boil, then reduce the heat, cover, and simmer for 30 minutes until tender. Drain and rinse.
5. Transfer the barley to a large bowl, and toss with the cooked squash and broccoli, walnuts, kale, and onion.
6. In a small bowl, mix the remaining 2 tablespoons of olive oil, balsamic vinegar, garlic, salt, and pepper. Toss the salad with the dressing and serve.

*Per Serving:calories: 274 / fat: 15g / protein: 6g / carbs: 32g / sugars: 3g / fiber: 7g / sodium: 144mg*

## Sesame Chicken-Almond Slaw

Prep time: 20 minutes / Cook time: 40 minutes / Serves 2

- For the dressing
- 1 tablespoon rice vinegar
- 1 teaspoon granulated stevia
- 2 teaspoons extra-virgin olive oil
- 1 teaspoon water
- ½ teaspoon sesame oil
- ¼ teaspoon reduced-sodium soy sauce
- Pinch salt
- Pinch freshly ground black pepper
- For the salad
- 8 ounces chicken breast, rinsed and drained
- 4 cups angel hair cabbage
- 1 cup shredded romaine lettuce
- 2 tablespoons sliced scallions
- 2 tablespoons toasted slivered almonds
- 2 teaspoons toasted sesame seeds

1. In a jar with a tight-fitting lid, add the rice vinegar, stevia, olive oil, water, sesame oil, soy sauce, salt, and pepper. Shake well to combine. Set aside.
2. Preheat the oven to 400°F.
3. To a medium baking dish, add the chicken. Place the dish in the preheated oven. Bake for 30 to 40 minutes, or until completely opaque and the temperature registers 165°F on an instant-read thermometer.
4. Remove from the oven. Slice into strips. Set aside.
5. In a large bowl, toss together the cabbage, romaine, scallions, almonds, sesame seeds, and chicken strips. Add the dressing. Toss again to coat the ingredients evenly.
6. Serve immediately.

*Per Serving:calorie: 318 / fat: 15g / protein: 31g / carbs: 17g / sugars: 8g / fiber: 6g / sodium: 125mg*

## Celery and Apple Salad with Cider Vinaigrette

Prep time: 20 minutes / Cook time: 0 minutes / Serves 4

- Dressing
- 2 tablespoons apple cider or apple juice
- 1 tablespoon cider vinegar
- 2 teaspoons canola oil
- 2 teaspoons finely chopped shallots
- ½ teaspoon Dijon mustard
- ½ teaspoon honey
- ½ teaspoon salt
- Salad
- 2 cups chopped romaine lettuce
- 2 cups diagonally sliced celery
- ½ medium apple, unpeeled, sliced very thin (about 1 cup)
- ⅓ cup sweetened dried cranberries
- 2 tablespoons chopped walnuts
- 2 tablespoons crumbled blue cheese

1. In small bowl, beat all dressing ingredients with whisk until blended; set aside.
2. In medium bowl, place lettuce, celery, apple and cranberries; toss with dressing. To serve, arrange salad on 4 plates. Sprinkle with walnuts and blue

cheese. Serve immediately.

*Per Serving:calorie: 130 / fat: 6g / protein: 2g / carbs: 17g / sugars: 13g / fiber: 3g / sodium: 410mg*

## Warm Sweet Potato and Black Bean Salad

Prep time: 5 minutes / Cook time: 35 minutes / Serves 2

- Extra-virgin olive oil cooking spray
- 1 large sweet potato, peeled and cubed
- 1 tablespoon extra-virgin olive oil
- 1 tablespoon balsamic vinegar
- 1 teaspoon dried rosemary
- ¼ teaspoon garlic powder
- ⅛ teaspoon salt
- ⅛ teaspoon freshly ground black pepper
- 1 cup canned black beans, drained and rinsed
- 2 tablespoons chopped chives

1. Preheat the oven to 450°F.
2. In a small baking dish coated with cooking spray, place the sweet potato cubes. Put the dish in the preheated oven. Bake for 20 to 35 minutes, uncovered, or until tender.
3. In a medium serving bowl, whisk together the olive oil, balsamic vinegar, rosemary, garlic powder, salt, and pepper.
4. Add the black beans and cooked sweet potato to the oil and herb mixture. Toss to coat.
5. Sprinkle with the chives.
6. Serve immediately and enjoy!

*Per Serving:calorie: 235 / fat: 7g / protein: 8g / carbs: 35g / sugars: 4g / fiber: 10g / sodium: 359mg*

## Zucchini, Carrot, and Fennel Salad

Prep time: 10 minutes / Cook time: 8 minutes / Serves ½ cup

- 2 medium carrots, peeled and julienned
- 1 medium zucchini, julienned
- ½ medium fennel bulb, core removed and julienned
- 1 tablespoon fresh orange juice
- 2 tablespoons Dijon mustard
- 3 tablespoons extra-virgin olive oil
- 1 teaspoon white wine vinegar
- ½ teaspoon dried thyme
- 1 tablespoon finely minced parsley
- ½ teaspoon salt
- ¼ teaspoon freshly ground black pepper
- ¼ cup chopped walnuts
- 1 medium head romaine lettuce, washed and leaves separated

1. Place the carrots, zucchini, and fennel in a medium bowl; set aside.
2. In a medium bowl, combine the orange juice, mustard, olive oil, vinegar, thyme, parsley, salt, and pepper; mix well.
3. Pour the dressing over the vegetables and toss.

Add the walnuts, and mix again. Refrigerate until ready to serve.

4. To serve, line a bowl or plates with lettuce leaves, and spoon ½ cup of salad on top.

*Per Serving:calorie: 201 / fat: 16g / protein: 5g / carbs: 14g / sugars: 6g / fiber: 6g / sodium: 285mg*

## Chickpea Salad

Prep time: 15 minutes / Cook time: 0 minutes / Serves 4

- ½ cup bottled balsamic vinaigrette
- 1 (15-ounce) can chickpeas, rinsed and drained
- 1 cup cherry tomatoes
- 1 small red onion, quartered and sliced
- 2 large cucumbers, peeled and cut into bite-size pieces
- 1 large zucchini, cut into bite-size pieces
- 1 (10-ounce) package frozen shelled edamame, steamed or microwaved
- Chopped fresh parsley, for garnish

1. Pour the vinaigrette into a large bowl. Add the chickpeas, tomatoes, onion, cucumbers, zucchini, and edamame and toss until all the ingredients are coated.
2. Garnish with chopped parsley.

*Per Serving:calorie: 188 / fat: 4g / protein: 10g / carbs: 29g / sugars: 11g / fiber: 8g / sodium: 171mg*

## Edamame and Walnut Salad

Prep time: 10 minutes / Cook time: 0 minutes / Serves 2

- For the vinaigrette
- 2 tablespoons balsamic vinegar
- 1 tablespoon extra-virgin olive oil
- 1 teaspoon grated fresh ginger
- ½ teaspoon Dijon mustard
- Pinch salt
- Freshly ground black pepper, to season
- For the salad
- 1 cup shelled edamame
- ½ cup shredded carrots
- ½ cup shredded red cabbage
- ½ cup walnut halves
- 6 cups prewashed baby spinach, divided

1. In a small bowl, whisk together the balsamic vinegar, olive oil, ginger, Dijon mustard, and salt. Season with pepper. Set aside. To make the salad
2. In a medium bowl, mix together the edamame, carrots, red cabbage, and walnuts.
3. Add the vinaigrette. Toss to coat.
4. Place 3 cups of spinach on each of 2 serving plates.
5. Top each serving with half of the dressed vegetables.
6. Enjoy immediately!

*Per Serving:calorie: 341 / fat: 26g / protein: 13g / carbs: 19g / sugars: 7g / fiber: 8g / sodium: 117mg*

## Chinese Chicken Salad

Prep time: 10 minutes / Cook time: 0 minutes / Serves 4

- 2 cups cooked chicken, diced
- 1 cup finely chopped celery
- 1 cup shredded carrots
- ¼ cup crushed unsweetened pineapple, drained
- 2 tablespoons finely diced pimiento
- Two 8-ounce cans water chestnuts, drained and chopped
- 2 scallions, chopped
- ⅓ cup low-fat mayonnaise
- 1 tablespoon light soy sauce
- 1 teaspoon lemon juice
- 8 large tomatoes, hollowed

1. In a large bowl, combine the chicken, celery, carrots, pineapple, pimiento, water chestnuts, and scallions.
2. In a separate bowl, combine the mayonnaise, soy sauce, and lemon juice. Mix well. Add the dressing to the salad, and toss. Cover, and chill in the refrigerator for 2–3 hours.
3. For each serving, place a small scoop of chicken salad into a hollowed-out tomato.

*Per Serving:calorie: 365 / fat: 16g / protein: 27g / carbs: 32g / sugars: 17g / fiber: 9g / sodium: 476mg*

## Chicken, Cantaloupe, Kale, and Almond Salad

Prep time: 10 minutes / Cook time: 0 minutes / Serves 3

- For The Salad
- 4 cups chopped kale, packed
- 1½ cups diced cantaloupe
- 1½ cups shredded rotisserie chicken
- ½ cup sliced almonds
- ¼ cup crumbled feta
- For The Dressing
- 2 teaspoons honey
- 2 tablespoons extra-virgin olive oil
- 2 teaspoons apple cider vinegar or freshly squeezed lemon juice

1. Divide the kale into three portions. Layer ⅓ of the cantaloupe, chicken, almonds, and feta on each portion.
2. Drizzle some of the dressing over each portion of salad. Serve immediately. Make The Dressing: 3. In a small bowl, whisk together the honey, olive oil, and vinegar.

*Per Serving:calorie: 376 / fat: 23g / protein: 30g / carbs: 16g / sugars: 12g / fiber: 3g / sodium: 415mg*

## Sunflower-Tuna-Cauliflower Salad

Prep time: 30 minutes / Cook time: 0 minutes / Serves 2

- 1 (5-ounce) can tuna packed in water, drained

- ½ cup plain nonfat Greek yogurt
- 1 teaspoon freshly squeezed lemon juice
- 1 teaspoon dried dill
- 1 scallion, chopped
- ¼ cup sunflower seeds
- 2 cups fresh chopped cauliflower florets
- 4 cups mixed salad greens, divided

1. In a medium bowl, mix together the tuna, yogurt, lemon juice, dill, scallion, and sunflower seeds.
2. Add the cauliflower. Toss gently to coat.
3. Cover and refrigerate for at least 2 hours before serving, stirring occasionally.
4. Serve half of the tuna mixture atop 2 cups of salad greens.

*Per Serving:calorie: 251 / fat: 11g / protein: 24g / carbs: 18g / sugars: 8g / fiber: 7g / sodium: 288mg*

## Herbed Spring Peas

Prep time: 10 minutes / Cook time: 15 minutes / Serves 6

- 1 tablespoon unsalted non-hydrogenated plant-based butter
- ½ Vidalia onion, thinly sliced
- 1 cup store-bought low-sodium vegetable broth
- 3 cups fresh shelled peas
- 1 tablespoon minced fresh tarragon

1. In a skillet, melt the butter over medium heat.
2. Add the onion and sauté for 2 to 3 minutes, or until the onion is translucent.
3. Add the broth, and reduce the heat to low.
4. Add the peas and tarragon, cover, and cook for 7 to 10 minutes, or until the peas soften.
5. Serve.

*Per Serving:calorie: 43 / fat: 2g / protein: 2g / carbs: 6g / sugars: 3g / fiber: 2g / sodium: 159mg*

## Fiery Black Bean Salad

Prep time: 10 minutes / Cook time: 0 minutes / Serves 8

- 3 cups cooked black beans
- 2 tomatoes, chopped
- 2 red bell peppers, finely chopped
- 1 cup yellow corn
- 3 garlic cloves, minced
- 1 jalapeño pepper, minced
- ¼ cup fresh lime juice
- 2 tablespoons red wine vinegar
- 1 tablespoon cumin
- 1 tablespoon extra-virgin olive oil
- 2 tablespoons freshly chopped cilantro (optional)

1. Combine all ingredients in a bowl, and chill in the refrigerator for several hours to blend the flavors. Serve.

*Per Serving:calorie: 138 / fat: 3g / protein: 7g / carbs: 23g / sugars: 3g / fiber: 7g / sodium: 8mg*

## Chicken Salad with Apricots

Prep time: 10 minutes / Cook time: 0 minutes / Makes 4 cups

- 1 cup plain Greek yogurt
- 2 tablespoons minced shallots
- 1 teaspoon ground coriander
- 1 teaspoon Dijon mustard (optional)
- 1 tablespoon freshly squeezed lemon juice
- ¼ teaspoon cayenne pepper
- 12 ounces cooked rotisserie chicken, shredded
- 2 cups chopped celery with the leaves
- ¼ cup slivered almonds, toasted
- ¼ cup thinly sliced dried apricots
- 1 bunch fresh parsley, chopped

1. In a medium bowl, mix together the Greek yogurt, shallots, coriander, mustard (if using), lemon juice, and cayenne until well combined.
2. Add the chicken, celery, almonds, apricots, and parsley.
3. Serve on your food of choice (lettuce, crackers, jicama slices, radish slices—you name it).
4. Store any leftovers in an airtight container in the refrigerator for up to 3 days.

*Per Serving:calorie: 232 / fat: 7g / protein: 31g / carbs: 11g / sugars: 7g / fiber: 3g / sodium: 152mg*

## Lobster Salad

Prep time: 10 minutes / Cook time: 45 minutes / Serves 6

- 2 pounds lobster in the shell or 1 pound lobster meat
- ¾ pound small red potatoes
- ½ cup light mayonnaise
- 3 tablespoons plain low-fat yogurt
- 1 tablespoon chopped tarragon
- ¼ cup chopped scallions
- ¼ teaspoon freshly ground black pepper
- 1 small head romaine lettuce, washed and leaves separated

1. To prepare lobster in the shell, place the lobster in boiling water, and boil until the meat is tender, about 20 minutes. Cool the lobster, remove the meat from the shell, and cut into 1-inch cubes. Or buy lobster meat from the seafood department at the supermarket.
2. Wash, but do not peel, the potatoes. Boil the potatoes in water until just tender, about 15–20 minutes. Drain, cool, and quarter.
3. In a bowl, combine mayonnaise, yogurt, tarragon, scallions, and pepper for the dressing.
4. In a separate bowl, combine the lobster and potatoes.
5. Add the dressing to the lobster and potatoes, and mix well. To serve, line plates with lettuce. Spoon lobster salad over the lettuce.

*Per Serving:calorie: 245 / fat: 8g / protein: 29g / carbs: 14g / sugars: 3g / fiber: 4g / sodium: 564mg*

## Crunchy Pecan Tuna Salad

Prep time: 20 minutes / Cook time: 0 minutes / Serves 1

- ½ medium apple, finely chopped
- 2 medium ribs celery, finely chopped
- ¼ large red onion, finely chopped
- 2 tablespoons (16 g) coarsely chopped pecans
- ¼ cup (46 g) canned navy beans, drained, rinsed, and mashed
- 2 ounces (57 g) canned tuna packed in water, drained and rinsed
- 1 tablespoon (14 g) mayonnaise (see Tip)
- ½ tablespoon (8 g) Dijon mustard
- 1 tablespoon (15 ml) fresh lemon juice
- Black pepper, as needed

1. In a large bowl, combine the apple, celery, onion, pecans, beans, and tuna.
2. In a small bowl, mix together the mayonnaise, mustard, lemon juice, and black pepper. Add the mayonnaise mixture to the tuna mixture and stir until the tuna salad is evenly combined.
3. Serve the tuna salad immediately, or refrigerate the tuna salad for 2 to 3 hours or overnight to chill it and allow the flavors to meld.

*Per Serving:calorie: 197 / fat: 11g / protein: 11g / carbs: 16g / sugars: 7g / fiber: 5g / sodium: 179mg*

## Mandarin Orange Chicken Salad

Prep time: 10 minutes / Cook time: 0 minutes / Serves 4

- 1 (8-ounce) container plain Greek yogurt
- ½ teaspoon ground ginger
- 1½ cups cooked cubed chicken
- 1 (8-ounce) package frozen peas in the pod, thawed
- 1 (8-ounce) can water chestnuts, drained and chopped
- 1 (11-ounce) can mandarin orange segments, drained
- ½ cup unsalted peanuts
- 1 (10-ounce) bag chopped romaine lettuce, divided

1. In a large bowl, mix the Greek yogurt with the ground ginger. Add the chicken and mix to coat.
2. Add the pea pods, water chestnuts, mandarin oranges, and peanuts. Stir all the ingredients together until well mixed.
3. Divide ¼ of the bag of romaine into 4 bowls and top with the chicken salad.

*Per Serving:calorie: 338 / fat: 18g / protein: 28g / carbs: 19g / sugars: 10g / fiber: 5g / sodium: 85mg*

## Wild Rice Salad

Prep time: 5 minutes / Cook time: 45 minutes / Serves 6

- 1 cup raw wild rice (rinsed)
- 4 cups cold water
- 1 cup mandarin oranges, packed in their own juice

(drain and reserve 2 tablespoons of liquid)
- ½ cup chopped celery
- ¼ cup minced red bell pepper
- 1 shallot, minced
- 1 teaspoon minced thyme
- 2 tablespoons raspberry vinegar
- 1 tablespoon extra-virgin olive oil

1. Place the rinsed, raw rice and the water in a saucepan. Bring to a boil, lower the heat, cover the pan, and cook for 45–50 minutes until the rice has absorbed the water. Set the rice aside to cool.
2. In a large bowl, combine the mandarin oranges, celery, red pepper, and shallot.
3. In a small bowl, combine the reserved juice, thyme, vinegar, and oil.
4. Add the rice to the mandarin oranges and vegetables. Pour the dressing over the salad, toss, and serve.

*Per Serving:calorie: 134 / fat: 3g / protein: 4g / carbs: 24g / sugars: 4g / fiber: 3g / sodium: 12mg*

## BLT Potato Salad

Prep time: 20 minutes / Cook time: 10 to 15 minutes / Serves 6

- 4 small new red potatoes (about 12 ounces), cut into ½-inch cubes
- ¼ cup reduced-fat mayonnaise or salad dressing
- 1 teaspoon Dijon mustard
- 2 teaspoons chopped fresh or ½ teaspoon dried dill weed
- ¼ teaspoon salt
- ⅛ teaspoon pepper
- ½ cup grape tomatoes or halved cherry tomatoes
- 1½ cups bite-size pieces romaine lettuce
- 2 slices turkey bacon, cooked, crumbled

1. In 2-quart saucepan, place potatoes. Add enough water to cover. Heat to boiling; reduce heat to low. Cover; cook 10 to 15 minutes or until potatoes are tender. Drain; cool about 10 minutes.
2. Meanwhile, in medium bowl, mix mayonnaise, mustard, dill weed, salt and pepper. Stir in potatoes, tomatoes and lettuce until coated. Sprinkle with bacon.

*Per Serving:calorie: 100 / fat: 5g / protein: 3g / carbs: 12g / sugars: 2g / fiber: 1g / sodium: 300mg*

## Three Bean and Basil Salad

Prep time: 10 minutes / Cook time: 0 minutes / Serves 8

- 1 (15 ounces) can low-sodium chickpeas, drained and rinsed
- 1 (15 ounces) can low-sodium kidney beans, drained and rinsed
- 1 (15 ounces) can low-sodium white beans, drained and rinsed
- 1 red bell pepper, seeded and finely chopped
- ¼ cup chopped scallions, both white and green parts
- ¼ cup finely chopped fresh basil
- 3 garlic cloves, minced
- 2 tablespoons extra-virgin olive oil
- 1 tablespoon red wine vinegar
- 1 teaspoon Dijon mustard
- ¼ teaspoon freshly ground black pepper

1. In a large mixing bowl, combine the chickpeas, kidney beans, white beans, bell pepper, scallions, basil, and garlic. Toss gently to combine.
2. In a small bowl, combine the olive oil, vinegar, mustard, and pepper. Toss with the salad.
3. Cover and refrigerate for an hour before serving, to allow the flavors to mix.

*Per Serving:Calorie: 193 / fat: 5g / protein: 10g / carbs: 29g / sugars: 3g / fiber: 8g / sodium: 246mg*

## Strawberry-Spinach Salad

Prep time: 15 minutes / Cook time: 0 minutes / Serves 4

- ½ cup extra-virgin olive oil
- ¼ cup balsamic vinegar
- 1 tablespoon Worcestershire sauce
- 1 (10-ounce) package baby spinach
- 1 medium red onion, quartered and sliced
- 1 cup strawberries, sliced
- 1 (6-ounce) container feta cheese, crumbled
- 4 tablespoons bacon bits, divided
- 1 cup slivered almonds, divided

1. In a large bowl, whisk together the olive oil, balsamic vinegar, and Worcestershire sauce.
2. Add the spinach, onion, strawberries, and feta cheese and mix until all the ingredients are coated.
3. Portion into 4 servings and top each with 1 tablespoon of bacon bits and ¼ cup of slivered almonds.

*Per Serving:calorie: 417 / fat: 29g / protein: 24g / carbs: 19g / sugars: 7g / fiber: 7g / sodium: 542mg*

## Cucumber-Mango Salad

Prep time: 20 minutes / Cook time: 0 minutes / Serves 4

- 1 small cucumber
- 1 medium mango
- ¼ teaspoon grated lime peel
- 1 tablespoon lime juice
- 1 teaspoon honey
- ¼ teaspoon ground cumin
- Pinch salt
- 4 leaves Bibb lettuce

1. Cut cucumber lengthwise in half; scoop out seeds. Chop cucumber (about 1 cup).

2. Score skin of mango lengthwise into fourths with knife; peel skin. Cut peeled mango lengthwise close to both sides of pit. Chop mango into ½-inch cubes.

3. In small bowl, mix lime peel, lime juice, honey, cumin and salt. Stir in cucumber and mango. Place lettuce leaves on serving plates. Spoon mango mixture onto lettuce leaves.

*Per Serving:calorie: 50 / fat: 0g / protein: 0g / carbs: 12g / sugars: 9g / fiber: 1g / sodium: 40mg*

## Pomegranate "Tabbouleh" with Cauliflower

Prep time: 20 minutes / Cook time: 5 minutes / Serves 4 to 6

- ⅓ cup extra-virgin olive oil, divided
- 4 cups grated cauliflower (about 1 medium head)
- Juice of 1 lemon
- ¼ red onion, minced
- 4 large tomatoes, diced
- 3 large bunches flat-leaf parsley, chopped
- 1 large bunch mint, chopped
- ½ cup pomegranate arils
- Kosher salt
- Freshly ground black pepper

1. In a large skillet, heat 2 tablespoons of extra-virgin olive oil. When it's hot, add the cauliflower and sauté for 3 to 5 minutes or until it starts to crisp. Remove the skillet from the heat and allow the cauliflower to cool while you prep the remaining ingredients.

2. In a large bowl, combine the remaining extra-virgin olive oil with the lemon juice and red onion. Mix well, then mix in the tomatoes, parsley, mint, and pomegranate arils.

3. After the cauliflower cools, 5 to 7 minutes, add it to the bowl with the other ingredients. Season with salt and pepper to taste and serve.

4. Store any leftovers in an airtight container in the refrigerator for 3 to 5 days.

*Per Serving:calorie: 205 / fat: 15g / protein: 4g / carbs: 17g / sugars: 9g / fiber: 5g / sodium: 50mg*

## Curried Chicken Salad

Prep time: 15 minutes / Cook time: 40 minutes / Serves 2

- 4 ounces chicken breast, rinsed and drained
- 1 small apple, peeled, cored, and finely chopped
- 2 tablespoons slivered almonds
- 1 tablespoon dried cranberries
- 2 tablespoons chia seeds
- ¼ cup plain nonfat Greek yogurt
- 1 tablespoon curry powder
- 1½ teaspoons Dijon mustard
- ⅛ teaspoon salt
- ¼ teaspoon freshly ground black pepper
- 4 cups chopped romaine lettuce, divided

1. Preheat the oven to 400°F.

2. To a small baking dish, add the chicken. Place the dish in the preheated oven. Bake for 30 to 40 minutes, or until the chicken is completely opaque and registers 165°F on an instant-read thermometer. Remove from the oven. Chop into cubes. Set aside.

3. In a medium bowl, mix together the chicken, apple, almonds, cranberries, and chia seeds.

4. Add the yogurt, curry powder, mustard, salt, and pepper. Toss to coat.

5. On 2 plates, arrange 2 cups of lettuce on each.

6. Top each with one-half of the curried chicken salad.

7. Serve immediately.

*Per Serving:calorie: 240 / fat: 9g / protein: 19g / carbs: 25g / sugars: 14g / fiber: 8g / sodium: 258mg*

## Candied Yams

Prep time: 7 minutes / Cook time: 45 minutes / Serves 8

- 2 medium jewel yams, cut into 2-inch dice
- Juice of 1 large orange
- 2 tablespoons unsalted non-hydrogenated plant-based butter
- 1½ teaspoons ground cinnamon
- ¾ teaspoon ground nutmeg
- ¼ teaspoon ground ginger
- ⅛ teaspoon ground cloves

1. Preheat the oven to 350°F.

2. On a rimmed baking sheet, arrange the diced yam in a single layer.

3. In a medium pot, combine the orange juice, butter, cinnamon, nutmeg, ginger, and cloves and cook over medium-low heat for 3 to 5 minutes, or until the ingredients come together and thicken.

4. Pour the hot juice mixture over the yams, turning them to make sure they are evenly coated.

5. Transfer the baking sheet to the oven, and bake for 40 minutes, or until the yams are tender.

*Per Serving:calorie: 70 / fat: 2g / protein: 70g / carbs: 12g / sugars: 1g / fiber: 2g / sodium: 3mg*

# Chapter 10 Stews and Soups

## Hot and Sour Soup

Prep time: 0 minutes / Cook time: 30 minutes / Serves 6

- 4 cups boiling water
- 1 ounce dried shiitake mushrooms
- 2 tablespoons cold-pressed avocado oil
- 3 garlic cloves, chopped
- 4 ounces cremini or button mushrooms, sliced
- 1 pound boneless pork loin, sirloin, or tip, thinly sliced against the grain into ¼-inch-thick, ½-inch-wide, 2-inch-long strips
- 1 teaspoon ground ginger
- ½ teaspoon ground white pepper
- 2 cups low-sodium chicken broth or vegetable broth
- One 8-ounce can sliced bamboo shoots, drained and rinsed
- 2 tablespoons low-sodium soy sauce
- 1 tablespoon chile garlic sauce
- 1 teaspoon toasted sesame oil
- 2 teaspoons Lakanto Monkfruit Sweetener Classic
- 2 large eggs
- ¼ cup rice vinegar
- 2 tablespoons cornstarch
- 4 green onions, white and green parts, thinly sliced
- ¼ cup chopped fresh cilantro

1. In a large liquid measuring cup or heatproof bowl, pour the boiling water over the shiitake mushrooms. Cover and let soak for 30 minutes. Drain the mushrooms, reserving the soaking liquid. Remove and discard the stems and thinly slice the caps.
2. Select the Sauté setting on the Instant Pot and heat the avocado oil and garlic for 2 minutes, until the garlic is bubbling but not browned. Add the cremini and shiitake mushrooms and sauté for 3 minutes, until the mushrooms are beginning to wilt. Add the pork, ginger, and white pepper and sauté for about 5 minutes, until the pork is opaque and cooked through.
3. Pour the mushroom soaking liquid into the pot, being careful to leave behind any sediment at the bottom of the measuring cup or bowl. Using a wooden spoon, nudge any browned bits from the bottom of the pot. Stir in the broth, bamboo shoots, soy sauce, chile garlic sauce, sesame oil, and sweetener.
4. Secure the lid and set the Pressure Release to Sealing. Press the Cancel button to reset the cooking program, then select the Pressure Cook or Manual setting and set the cooking time for 5

minutes at high pressure. (The pot will take about 10 minutes to come up to pressure before the cooking program begins. )
5. While the soup is cooking, in a small bowl, beat the eggs until no streaks of yolk remain.
6. When the cooking program ends, let the pressure release naturally for at least 15 minutes, then move the Pressure Release to Venting to release any remaining steam.
7. In a small bowl, stir together the vinegar and cornstarch until the cornstarch dissolves. Open the pot and stir the vinegar mixture into the soup. Press the Cancel button to reset the cooking program, then select the Sauté setting. Bring the soup to a simmer and cook, stirring occasionally, for about 3 minutes, until slightly thickened. While stirring the soup constantly, pour in the beaten eggs in a thin stream. Press the Cancel button to turn off the pot and then stir in the green onions and cilantro.
8. Ladle the soup into bowls and serve hot.

*Per Serving:calories: 231 / fat: 13g / protein: 21g / carbs: 14g / sugars: 2g / fiber: 3g / sodium: 250mg*

## Hearty Italian Minestrone

Prep time: 10 minutes / Cook time: 50 minutes / Serves 8

- ½ cup sliced onion
- 1 tablespoon extra-virgin olive oil
- 4 cups low-sodium chicken broth
- ¾ cup diced carrot
- ½ cup diced potato (with skin)
- 2 cups sliced cabbage or coarsely chopped spinach
- 1 cup diced zucchini
- ½ cup cooked garbanzo beans (drained and rinsed, if canned)
- ½ cup cooked navy beans (drained and rinsed, if canned)
- One 14. 5-ounce can low-sodium tomatoes, with liquid
- ½ cup diced celery
- 2 tablespoons fresh basil, finely chopped
- ½ cup uncooked whole-wheat rotini or other shaped pasta
- 2 tablespoons fresh parsley, finely chopped, for garnish

1. In a large stockpot over medium heat, sauté the onion in oil until the onion is slightly browned. Add the chicken broth, carrot, and potato. Cover and cook over medium heat for 30 minutes.
2. Add the remaining ingredients and cook for an additional 15 to 20 minutes, until the pasta is cooked

through. Garnish with parsley and serve hot.

*Per Serving:calories: 101 / fat: 2g / protein: 6g / carbs: 17g / sugars: 4g / fiber: 4g / sodium: 108mg*

## Taco Soup

Prep time: 5 minutes / Cook time: 20 minutes / Serves 4

- Avocado oil cooking spray
- 1 medium red bell pepper, chopped
- ½ cup chopped yellow onion
- 1 pound 93% lean ground beef
- 1 teaspoon ground cumin
- ½ teaspoon salt • ½ teaspoon chili powder
- ½ teaspoon garlic powder
- 2 cups low-sodium beef broth
- 1 (15-ounce) can no-salt-added diced tomatoes
- 1½ cups frozen corn • ⅓ cup half-and-half

1. Heat a large stockpot over medium-low heat. When hot, coat the cooking surface with cooking spray. Put the pepper and onion in the pan and cook for 5 minutes.
2. Add the ground beef, cumin, salt, chili powder, and garlic powder. Cook for 5 to 7 minutes, stirring and breaking apart the beef as needed.
3. Add the broth, diced tomatoes with their juices, and corn. Increase the heat to medium-high and simmer for 10 minutes.
4. Remove from the heat and stir in the half-and-half.

*Per Serving:calories: 487 / fat: 21g / protein: 39g / carbs: 35g / sugars: 8g / fiber: 5g / sodium: 437mg*

## Hearty Hamburger and Lentil Stew

Prep time: 0 minutes / Cook time: 55 minutes / Serves 8

- 2 tablespoons cold-pressed avocado oil
- 2 garlic cloves, chopped • 1 large yellow onion, diced
- 2 carrots, diced • 2 celery stalks, diced
- 2 pounds 95 percent lean ground beef
- ½ cup small green lentils
- 2 cups low-sodium roasted beef bone broth or vegetable broth
- 1 tablespoon Italian seasoning
- 1 tablespoon paprika • 1½ teaspoons fine sea salt
- 1 extra-large russet potato, diced
- 1 cup frozen green peas • 1 cup frozen corn
- One 14½-ounce can no-salt petite diced tomatoes and their liquid
- ¼ cup tomato paste

1. Select the Sauté setting on the Instant Pot and heat the oil and garlic for 3 minutes, until the garlic is bubbling but not browned. Add the onion, carrots, and celery and sauté for 5 minutes, until the onion begins to soften. Add the beef and sauté, using a wooden spoon or spatula to break up the meat as it cooks, for 6 minutes, until cooked through and no streaks of pink remain.
2. Stir in the lentils, broth, Italian seasoning, paprika, and salt. Add the potato, peas, corn, and tomatoes and their liquid in layers on top of the lentils and beef, then add the tomato paste in a dollop on top. Do not stir in the vegetables and tomato paste.
3. Secure the lid and set the Pressure Release to Sealing. Press the Cancel button to reset the cooking program, then select the Pressure Cook or Manual setting and set the cooking time for 20 minutes at high pressure. (The pot will take about 20 minutes to come up to pressure before the cooking program begins. )
4. When the cooking program ends, let the pressure release naturally for at least 15 minutes, then move the Pressure Release to Venting to release any remaining steam. Open the pot and stir the stew to mix all of the ingredients.
5. Ladle the stew into bowls and serve hot.

*Per Serving:calories: 334 / fat: 8g / protein: 34g / carbs: 30g / sugars: 6g / fiber: 7g / sodium: 902mg*

## Buttercup Squash Soup

Prep time: 15 minutes / Cook time: 10 minutes / Serves 6

- 2 tablespoons extra-virgin olive oil
- 1 medium onion, chopped
- 4 to 5 cups Vegetable Broth or Chicken Bone Broth
- 1½ pounds buttercup squash, peeled, seeded, and cut into 1-inch chunks • ½ teaspoon kosher salt
- ¼ teaspoon ground white pepper
- Whole nutmeg, for grating

1. Set the electric pressure cooker to the Sauté setting. When the pot is hot, pour in the olive oil.
2. Add the onion and sauté for 3 to 5 minutes, until it begins to soften. Hit Cancel.
3. Add the broth, squash, salt, and pepper to the pot and stir. (If you want a thicker soup, use 4 cups of broth. If you want a thinner, drinkable soup, use 5 cups. )
4. Close and lock the lid of the pressure cooker. Set the valve to sealing.
5. Cook on high pressure for 10 minutes.
6. When the cooking is complete, hit Cancel and allow the pressure to release naturally.
7. Once the pin drops, unlock and remove the lid.
8. Use an immersion blender to purée the soup right in the pot. If you don't have an immersion blender, transfer the soup to a blender or food processor and purée. (Follow the instructions that came with your machine for blending hot foods. ) 9. Pour the soup into serving bowls and grate nutmeg on top.

*Per Serving:calories: 320 / fat: 16g / protein: 36g / carbs: 7g / sugars: 3g / fiber: 2g / sodium: 856mg*

## Favorite Chili

Prep time: 10 minutes / Cook time: 35 minutes / Serves 5

- 1 pound extra-lean ground beef
- 1 teaspoon salt • ½ teaspoons black pepper
- 1 tablespoon olive oil • 1 small onion, chopped
- 2 cloves garlic, minced
- 1 green pepper, chopped
- 2 tablespoons chili powder
- ½ teaspoons cumin • 1 cup water
- 16-ounce can chili beans
- 15-ounce can low-sodium crushed tomatoes

1. Press Sauté button and adjust once to Sauté More function. Wait until indicator says "hot. " 2. Season the ground beef with salt and black pepper.
3. Add the olive oil into the inner pot. Coat the whole bottom of the pot with the oil.
4. Add ground beef into the inner pot. The ground beef will start to release moisture. Allow the ground beef to brown and crisp slightly, stirring occasionally to break it up. Taste and adjust the seasoning with more salt and ground black pepper.
5. Add diced onion, minced garlic, chopped pepper, chili powder, and cumin. Sauté for about 5 minutes, until the spices start to release their fragrance. Stir frequently.
6. Add water and 1 can of chili beans, not drained. Mix well. Pour in 1 can of crushed tomatoes.
7. Close and secure lid, making sure vent is set to sealing, and pressure cook on Manual at high pressure for 10 minutes.
8. Let the pressure release naturally when cooking time is up. Open the lid carefully.

*Per Serving:calories: 213 / fat: 10g / protein: 18g / carbs: 11g / sugars: 4g / fiber: 4g / sodium: 385mg*

## Comforting Chicken and Mushroom Soup

Prep time: 5 minutes / Cook time: 20 minutes / Serves 6
- 1 quart low-sodium chicken broth
- 1 tablespoon light soy sauce
- 1 cup sliced mushrooms, stems removed
- 1 tablespoon finely chopped scallions
- 1 tablespoon dry sherry
- ½ pound boneless, skinless chicken breast, cubed

1. In a stockpot, simmer all ingredients except the chicken for 10 minutes.
2. Add the chicken cubes, and simmer for 6–8 minutes more. Serve with additional soy sauce if desired (but be aware that this will raise the sodium level of the soup).

*Per Serving:calories: 88 / fat: 4g / protein: 10g / carbs: 2g / sugars: 1g / fiber: 0g / sodium: 88mg*

## Beef, Mushroom, and Wild Rice Soup

Prep time: 0 minutes / Cook time: 55 minutes / Serves 6
- 2 tablespoons extra-virgin olive oil or unsalted butter

- 2 garlic cloves, minced
- 8 ounces shiitake mushrooms, stems removed and sliced
- 1 teaspoon fine sea salt
- 2 carrots, diced
- 2 celery stalks, diced
- 1 yellow onion, diced
- 1 teaspoon dried thyme
- 1½ pounds beef stew meat, larger pieces halved, or beef chuck, trimmed of fat and cut into ¾-inch pieces
- 4 cups low-sodium roasted beef bone broth
- 1 cup wild rice, rinsed
- 1 tablespoon Worcestershire sauce
- 2 tablespoons tomato paste

1. Select the Sauté setting on the Instant Pot and heat the oil and garlic for about 1 minute, until the garlic is bubbling but not browned. Add the mushrooms and salt and sauté for 5 minutes, until the mushrooms have wilted and given up some of their liquid. Add the carrots, celery, and onion and sauté for 4 minutes, until the onion begins to soften. Add the thyme and beef and sauté for 3 minutes more, until the beef is mostly opaque on the outside. Stir in the broth, rice, Worcestershire sauce, and tomato paste, using a wooden spoon to nudge any browned bits from the bottom of the pot.
2. Secure the lid and set the Pressure Release to Sealing. Press the Cancel button to reset the cooking program, then select the Pressure Cook or Manual setting and set the cooking time for 25 minutes at high pressure. (The pot will take about 15 minutes to come up to pressure before the cooking program begins. )
3. When the cooking program ends, let the pressure release naturally for at least 15 minutes, then move the Pressure Release to Venting to release any remaining steam. Open the pot. Ladle the soup into bowls and serve hot.

*Per Serving:calories: 316 / fat: 8g / protein: 29g / carbs: 32g / sugars: 6g / fiber: 8g / sodium: 783mg*

## Pasta e Fagioli with Ground Beef

Prep time: 0 minutes / Cook time: 30 minutes / Serves 8
- 2 tablespoons extra-virgin olive oil
- 4 garlic cloves, minced
- 1 yellow onion, diced
- 2 large carrots, diced
- 4 celery stalks, diced
- 1½ pounds 95 percent extra-lean ground beef
- 4 cups low-sodium vegetable broth
- 2 teaspoons Italian seasoning
- ½ teaspoon freshly ground black pepper
- 1¼ cups chickpea-based elbow pasta or whole-wheat elbow pasta

- 1½ cups drained cooked kidney beans, or one 15-ounce can kidney beans, rinsed and drained
- One 28-ounce can whole San Marzano tomatoes and their liquid
- 2 tablespoons chopped fresh flat-leaf parsley

1. Select the Sauté setting on the Instant Pot and heat the oil and garlic for 2 minutes, until the garlic is bubbling but not browned. Add the onion, carrots, and celery and sauté for 5 minutes, until the onion begins to soften. Add the beef and sauté, using a wooden spoon or spatula to break up the meat as it cooks, for 5 minutes; it's fine if some streaks of pink remain, the beef does not need to be cooked through.
2. Stir in the broth, Italian seasoning, pepper, and pasta, making sure all of the pasta is submerged in the liquid. Add the beans and stir to mix. Add the tomatoes and their liquid, crushing the tomatoes with your hands as you add them to the pot. Do not stir them in.
3. Secure the lid and set the Pressure Release to Sealing. Press the Cancel button to reset the cooking program, then select the Pressure Cook or Manual setting and set the cooking time for 2 minutes at low pressure. (The pot will take about 15 minutes to come up to pressure before the cooking program begins. )
4. When the cooking program ends, let the pressure release naturally for 10 minutes, then move the Pressure Release to Venting to release any remaining steam. Open the pot and stir the soup to mix all of the ingredients.
5. Ladle the soup into bowls, sprinkle with the parsley, and serve right away.

*Per Serving:calories: 278 / fat: 9g / protein: 26g / carbs: 25g / sugars: 4g / fiber: 6g / sodium: 624mg*

## Mexican Tortilla Soup

Prep time: 10 minutes / Cook time: 40 minutes / Serves 8
- 2 tablespoons extra-virgin olive oil
- 1 onion, chopped
- 2 cloves garlic, minced
- ¼ cup freshly chopped cilantro
- 1 tablespoon cumin
- 1 teaspoon cayenne pepper
- 1 quart low-sodium chicken broth
- One 15-ounce can low-sodium whole tomatoes, drained and coarsely chopped
- 1 medium zucchini, sliced
- 1 medium yellow squash, sliced
- 1 cup yellow corn
- Six 6-inch corn tortillas
- ½ cup reduced-fat shredded cheddar cheese

1. Preheat the oven to 350 degrees.
2. In a large saucepan, heat the oil, and sauté the onion and garlic for 5 minutes.
3. Add the cilantro, cumin, and cayenne pepper; sauté for 3 more minutes. Add the remaining ingredients except the tortillas and cheese. Bring to a boil; cover and let simmer for 30 minutes.
4. Cut each tortilla into about 10 strips (use a pizza cutter to do this easily). Place the strips on a cookie sheet and bake for 5–6 minutes at 350 degrees until slightly browned and toasted. Remove from the oven.
5. To serve the soup, place strips of tortilla into each bowl. Ladle the soup on top of the tortilla strips. Top with cheese.

*Per Serving:calories: 193 / fat: 4g / protein: 9g / carbs: 31g / sugars: 3g / fiber: 3g / sodium: 172mg*

## Chicken Tortilla Soup

Prep time: 10 minutes / Cook time: 35 minutes / Serves 4
- 1 tablespoon extra-virgin olive oil
- 1 onion, thinly sliced
- 1 garlic clove, minced
- 1 jalapeño pepper, diced
- 2 boneless, skinless chicken breasts
- 4 cups low-sodium chicken broth
- 1 roma tomato, diced
- ½ teaspoon salt
- 2 (6-inch) corn tortillas, cut into thin strips
- Nonstick cooking spray
- Juice of 1 lime
- Minced fresh cilantro, for garnish
- ¼ cup shredded cheddar cheese, for garnish

1. In a medium pot, heat the oil over medium-high heat. Add the onion and cook for 3 to 5 minutes until it begins to soften. Add the garlic and jalapeño, and cook until fragrant, about 1 minute more.
2. Add the chicken, chicken broth, tomato, and salt to the pot and bring to a boil. Reduce the heat to medium and simmer gently for 20 to 25 minutes until the chicken breasts are cooked through. Remove the chicken from the pot and set aside.
3. Preheat a broiler to high.
4. Spray the tortilla strips with nonstick cooking spray and toss to coat. Spread in a single layer on a baking sheet and broil for 3 to 5 minutes, flipping once, until crisp.
5. When the chicken is cool enough to handle, shred it with two forks and return to the pot.
6. Season the soup with the lime juice. Serve hot, garnished with cilantro, cheese, and tortilla strips.

*Per Serving:calories: 191 / fat: 8g / protein: 19g / carbs: 13g / sugars: 2g / fiber: 2g / sodium: 482mg*

## Chock-Full-of-Vegetables Chicken Soup

Prep time: 5 minutes / Cook time: 15 minutes / Serves 2
- 1 tablespoon extra-virgin olive oil

- 8 ounces chicken tenders, cut into bite-size chunks
- 1 small zucchini, finely diced
- 1 cup sliced fresh button mushrooms
- 2 medium carrots, thinly sliced
- 2 celery stalks, thinly sliced
- 1 large shallot, finely chopped
- 1 garlic clove, minced
- 1 tablespoon dried parsley
- 1 teaspoon dried marjoram
- ⅛ teaspoon salt
- 2 plum tomatoes, chopped
- 2 cups reduced-sodium chicken broth
- 1½ cups packed baby spinach

1. In a large saucepan set over medium-high heat, heat olive oil.
2. Add the chicken. Cook for 3 to 4 minutes, stirring occasionally, or until browned. Transfer to a plate. Set aside.
3. To the saucepan, add the zucchini, mushrooms, carrots, celery, shallot, garlic, parsley, marjoram, and salt. Cook for 2 to 3 minutes, stirring frequently, until the vegetables are slightly softened.
4. Add the tomatoes and chicken broth. Increase the heat to high. Bring to a boil, stirring occasionally. Reduce the heat to low. Simmer for 5 minutes, or until the vegetables are tender.
5. Stir in the spinach, cooked chicken, and any accumulated juices on the plate. Cook for about 2 minutes, stirring, until the chicken is heated through.
6. Serve hot and enjoy!

*Per Serving:calories: 262 / fat: 10g / protein: 32g / carbs: 16g / sugars: 3g / fiber: 6g / sodium: 890mg*

## Green Ginger Soup

Prep time: 10 minutes / Cook time: 30 minutes / Serves 2
- ½ cup chopped onion
- ½ cup peeled, chopped fennel
- 1 small zucchini, chopped
- ½ cup frozen lima beans
- ¼ cup uncooked brown rice
- 1 bay leaf
- 1 teaspoon dried basil
- ⅛ teaspoon freshly ground black pepper
- 2 cups water
- 1 cup frozen green beans
- ¼ cup fresh parsley, chopped
- 1 (3-inch) piece fresh ginger, peeled, grated, and pressed through a strainer to extract the juice (about 2 to 3 tablespoons)
- Salt, to season
- 2 tablespoons chopped fresh chives

1. In a large pot set over medium-high heat, stir

together the onion, fennel, zucchini, lima beans, rice, bay leaf, basil, pepper, and water. Bring to a boil. Reduce the heat to low. Simmer for 15 minutes.
2. Add the green beans. Simmer for about 5 minutes, uncovered, until tender.
3. Stir in the parsley.
4. Remove and discard the bay leaf.
5. In a blender or food processor, purée the soup in batches until smooth, adding water if necessary to thin.
6. Blend in the ginger juice.
7. Season with salt. Garnish with the chives.
8. Serve hot and enjoy immediately!

*Per Serving:calories: 189 / fat: 2g / protein: 7g / carbs: 39g / sugars: 3g / fiber: 7g / sodium: 338mg*

## Pumpkin Soup

Prep time: 15 minutes / Cook time: 30 minutes / Serves 6
- 2 cups store-bought low-sodium seafood broth, divided
- 1 bunch collard greens, stemmed and cut into ribbons
- 1 tomato, chopped
- 1 garlic clove, minced
- 1 butternut squash or other winter squash, peeled and cut into 1-inch cubes
- 1 teaspoon paprika
- 1 teaspoon dried dill
- 2 (5-ounce) cans boneless, skinless salmon in water, rinsed

1. In a heavy-bottomed large stockpot, bring ½ cup of broth to a simmer over medium heat.
2. Add the collard greens, tomato, and garlic and cook for 5 minutes, or until the greens are wilted and the garlic is softened.
3. Add the squash, paprika, dill, and remaining 1½ cups of broth. Cover and cook for 20 minutes, or until the squash is tender.
4. Add the salmon and cook for 3 minutes, or just enough for the flavors to come together.

*Per Serving:calories: 161 / fat: 6g / protein: 24g / carbs: 5g / sugars: 1g / fiber: 1g / sodium: 579mg*

## Vegetarian Chili

Prep time: 25 minutes / Cook time: 10 minutes / Serves 6
- 2 teaspoons olive oil
- 3 garlic cloves, minced
- 2 onions, chopped
- 1 green bell pepper, chopped
- 1 cup textured vegetable protein (T. V. P. )
- 1-pound can beans of your choice, drained
- 1 jalapeño pepper, seeds removed, chopped
- 28-ounce can diced Italian tomatoes

- 1 bay leaf
- 1 tablespoon dried oregano
- ½ teaspoons salt
- ¼ teaspoons pepper

1. Set the Instant Pot to the Sauté function. As it's heating, add the olive oil, garlic, onions, and bell pepper. Stir constantly for about 5 minutes as it all cooks. Press Cancel.
2. Place all of the remaining ingredients into the inner pot of the Instant pot and stir.
3. Secure the lid and make sure vent is set to sealing. Cook on Manual mode for 10 minutes.
4. When cook time is up, let the steam release naturally for 5 minutes and then manually release the rest.

*Per Serving:calories: 242 / fat: 2g / protein: 17g / carbs: 36g / sugars: 9g / fiber: 12g / sodium: 489mg*

## Thai Corn and Sweet Potato Stew

Prep time: 10 minutes / Cook time: 20 minutes / Serves 4

- 1 small can (5. 5 ounces) light coconut milk
- 1 cup chopped onion
- ½ cup chopped celery
- 2 cups cubed sweet potato (can use frozen)
- ¾ to 1 teaspoon sea salt
- 2 cups water
- 1½ tablespoons Thai yellow or red curry paste
- 1½ cups frozen corn kernels
- 1½ cups chopped red bell pepper
- 1 package (12 to 14 ounces) tofu, cut into cubes, or 1 can (14 ounces) black beans, rinsed and drained
- 2½ tablespoons freshly squeezed lime juice
- 4 to 5 cups baby spinach leaves
- ⅓ to ½ cup fresh cilantro or Thai basil, chopped
- Lime wedges (optional)

1. In a soup pot over high heat, warm 2 tablespoons of the coconut milk. Add the onion, celery, sweet potato, and ¾ teaspoon of the salt, and sauté for 4 to 5 minutes. Add the water, Thai paste, and remaining coconut milk. Increase the heat to high to bring to a boil. Cover and reduce the heat to medium-low, and let the mixture simmer for 8 to 10 minutes, or until the sweet potato has softened. Turn off the heat, and use an immersion blender to puree the soup base. Add the corn, bell pepper, and tofu or beans, and turn the heat to medium-low. Cover and cook for 3 to 4 minutes to heat through. Add the lime juice, spinach, and cilantro or basil, and stir until the spinach has just wilted. Taste, and season with the remaining ¼ teaspoon salt, if desired. Serve with the lime wedges (if using).

*Per Serving:calorie: 223 / fat: 7g / protein: 10g / carbs: 36g / sugars: 11g / fiber: 6g / sodium: 723mg*

## Herbed Chicken Stew with Noodles

Prep time: 10 minutes / Cook time: 40 minutes / Serves 8

- 1 tablespoon extra-virgin olive oil
- 1 onion, chopped
- 2 garlic cloves, minced
- 1 pound boneless, skinless chicken breast, cubed
- 2 tablespoons flour
- 3 cups low-sodium chicken broth
- 1 cup dry white wine
- 1 tablespoon chopped fresh thyme (or 1 teaspoon dried)
- 4 cups cooked egg noodles, hot (from 1/2 pound dry egg noodles)
- ½ cup minced parsley

1. In a large saucepan, heat the oil and sauté the onion and garlic for about 5 minutes. Add the chicken cubes, and sauté until the chicken is cooked (about 10 minutes).
2. Sprinkle the flour over the chicken. Add the chicken broth, wine, and thyme. Bring to a boil, and then lower the heat and simmer for 30 minutes.
3. Toss together the noodles and the parsley in a large bowl. Pour the stew over the noodles and serve.

*Per Serving:calories: 285 / fat: 9g / protein: 14g / carbs: 37g / sugars: 4g / fiber: 2g / sodium: 419mg*

## Instantly Good Beef Stew

Prep time: 20 minutes / Cook time: 35 minutes / Serves 6

- 3 tablespoons olive oil,divided
- 2 pounds stewing beef, cubed
- 2 cloves garlic, minced • 1 large onion, chopped
- 3 ribs celery, sliced • 3 large potatoes, cubed
- 2–3 carrots, sliced
- 8 ounces no-salt-added tomato sauce
- 10 ounces low-sodium beef broth
- 2 teaspoons Worcestershire sauce
- ¼ teaspoon pepper • 1 bay leaf

1. Set the Instant Pot to the Sauté function, then add in 1 tablespoon of the oil. Add in ⅓ of the beef cubes and brown and sear all sides. Repeat this process twice more with the remaining oil and beef cubes. Set the beef aside.
2. Place the garlic, onion, and celery into the pot and sauté for a few minutes. Press Cancel.
3. Add the beef back in as well as all of the remaining ingredients.
4. Secure the lid and make sure the vent is set to sealing. Choose Manual for 35 minutes.
5. When cook time is up, let the pressure release naturally for 15 minutes, then release any remaining pressure manually.
6. Remove the lid, remove the bay leaf, then serve.

*Per Serving:calories: 401 / fat: 20g / protein: 35g / carbs: 19g / sugars: 5g / fiber: 3g / sodium: 157mg*

## Chicken Rice Soup

Prep time: 10 minutes / Cook time: 10 minutes / Serves 8

- 1 teaspoon vegetable oil
- 2 ribs celery, chopped in ½"-thick pieces
- 1 medium onion, chopped
- 1 cup wild rice, uncooked
- ½ cup long-grain rice, uncooked
- 1 pound boneless skinless chicken breasts, cut into ¾" cubes
- 5¼ cups fat-free, low-sodium chicken broth
- 2 teaspoons dried thyme leaves
- ¼ teaspoon red pepper flakes

1. Using the Sauté function on the Instant Pot, heat the teaspoon of vegetable oil. Sauté the celery and onion until the onions are slightly translucent (3–5 minutes). Once cooked, press Cancel.
2. Add the remaining ingredients to the inner pot.
3. Secure the lid and make sure the vent is set to sealing. Using the Manual function, set the time to 10 minutes.
4. When cook time is over, let the pressure release naturally for 10 minutes, then perform a quick release.

*Per Serving:calories: 160 / fat: 2g / protein: 16g / carbs: 18g / sugars: 2g / fiber: 1g / sodium: 375mg*

## Comforting Summer Squash Soup with Crispy Chickpeas

Prep time: 10 minutes / Cook time: 20 minutes / Serves 4

- 1 (15-ounce) can low-sodium chickpeas, drained and rinsed
- 1 teaspoon extra-virgin olive oil, plus 1 tablespoon
- ¼ teaspoon smoked paprika
- Pinch salt, plus ½ teaspoon
- 3 medium zucchini, coarsely chopped
- 3 cups low-sodium vegetable broth
- ½ onion, diced
- 3 garlic cloves, minced
- 2 tablespoons plain low-fat Greek yogurt
- Freshly ground black pepper

1. Preheat the oven to 425°F. Line a baking sheet with parchment paper.
2. In a medium mixing bowl, toss the chickpeas with 1 teaspoon of olive oil, the smoked paprika, and a pinch salt. Transfer to the prepared baking sheet and roast until crispy, about 20 minutes, stirring once. Set aside.
3. Meanwhile, in a medium pot, heat the remaining 1 tablespoon of oil over medium heat.
4. Add the zucchini, broth, onion, and garlic to the pot, and bring to a boil. Reduce the heat to a simmer, and cook until the zucchini and onion are tender, about 20 minutes.
5. In a blender jar, or using an immersion blender, purée the soup. Return to the pot.
6. Add the yogurt, remaining ½ teaspoon of salt, and pepper, and stir well. Serve topped with the roasted chickpeas.

*Per Serving:calories: 188 / fat: 7g / protein: 8g / carbs: 24g / sugars: 7g / fiber: 7g / sodium: 528mg*

## Nancy's Vegetable Beef Soup

Prep time: 25 minutes / Cook time: 8 hours / Serves 8

- 2 pounds roast, cubed, or 2 pounds stewing meat
- 15 ounces can corn     • 15 ounces can green beans
- 1 pound bag frozen peas
- 40 ounces can no-added-salt stewed tomatoes
- 5 teaspoons salt-free beef bouillon powder
- Tabasco, to taste     • ½ teaspoons salt

1. Combine all ingredients in the Instant Pot. Do not drain vegetables.
2. Add water to fill inner pot only to the fill line.
3. Secure the lid, or use the glass lid and set the Instant Pot on Slow Cook mode, Low for 8 hours, or until meat is tender and vegetables are soft.

*Per Serving:calories: 229 / fat: 5g / protein: 23g / carbs: 24g / sugars: 10g / fiber: 6g / sodium: 545mg*

## Fresh Fish Chowder

Prep time: 10 minutes / Cook time: 50 minutes / Serves 6

- 2 tablespoons extra-virgin olive oil
- 1 large garlic clove, minced
- 1 small onion, chopped
- 1 large green bell pepper, chopped
- One 14½-ounce can no-salt-added crushed tomatoes
- 1 tablespoon tomato paste
- ½ teaspoon dried basil
- ½ teaspoon dried oregano
- ¼ cup dry red wine     • ½ teaspoon salt
- ½ teaspoon freshly ground black pepper
- ½ cup uncooked brown rice
- ½ pound fresh halibut, cubed
- 2 tablespoons freshly chopped parsley

1. In a 3-quart saucepan, heat the olive oil over medium-high heat. Add the garlic, onion, and green pepper; sauté for 10 minutes over low heat until the vegetables are just tender.
2. Add the tomatoes, tomato paste, basil, oregano, wine, salt, and pepper. Let simmer for 15 minutes. Add the rice and continue to cook for 15 minutes.
3. Add the halibut, and cook for about 5–7 minutes, until the fish is cooked through. Garnish the stew with chopped parsley and serve.

*Per Serving:calories: 166 / fat: 7g / protein: 8g / carbs: 17g / sugars: 3g / fiber: 3g / sodium: 430mg*

# Chapter 11 Desserts

## Grilled Peach and Coconut Yogurt Bowls

Prep time: 5 minutes / Cook time: 10 minutes / Serves 4

- 2 peaches, halved and pitted
- ½ cup plain nonfat Greek yogurt
- 1 teaspoon pure vanilla extract
- ¼ cup unsweetened dried coconut flakes
- 2 tablespoons unsalted pistachios, shelled and broken into pieces

1. Preheat the broiler to high. Arrange the rack in the closest position to the broiler.
2. In a shallow pan, arrange the peach halves, cut-side up. Broil for 6 to 8 minutes until browned, tender, and hot.
3. In a small bowl, mix the yogurt and vanilla.
4. Spoon the yogurt into the cavity of each peach half.
5. Sprinkle 1 tablespoon of coconut flakes and 1½ teaspoons of pistachios over each peach half. Serve warm.

*Per Serving:calories: 102 / fat: 5g / protein: 5g / carbs: 11g / sugars: 8g / fiber: 2g / sodium: 12mg*

## Baked Pumpkin Pudding

Prep time: 5 minutes / Cook time: 20 minutes / Serves 4

- 1½ cups mashed pumpkin
- 1 egg
- 2½ tablespoons agave nectar
- ½ teaspoon vanilla extract
- 1 teaspoon pumpkin pie spice
- ¼ cup slivered almonds
- ¼ cup raisins

1. Preheat the oven to 350 degrees.
2. In a large bowl, combine the pumpkin, egg, agave nectar, vanilla, and pumpkin pie spice, and mix well. Stir in the almonds and raisins, leaving a few for garnish.
3. Spoon the mixture into 4 ramekins, and garnish with the remaining almonds and raisins.
4. Bake at 350 degrees for approximately 20 minutes, or until golden on top.
5. Serve warm or at room temperature.

*Per Serving:calories: 130 / fat: 5g / protein: 4g / carbs: 20g / sugars: 13g / fiber: 2g / sodium: 18mg*

## Chewy Chocolate-Oat Bars

Prep time: 20 minutes / Cook time: 30 minutes / Makes 16 bars

- ¾ cup semisweet chocolate chips

- ⅓ cup fat-free sweetened condensed milk (from 14-oz can)
- 1 cup whole wheat flour
- ½ cup quick-cooking oats
- ½ teaspoon baking powder
- ½ teaspoon baking soda
- ¼ teaspoon salt
- ¼ cup fat-free egg product or 1 egg
- ¾ cup packed brown sugar
- ¼ cup canola oil
- 1 teaspoon vanilla
- 2 tablespoons quick-cooking oats
- 2 teaspoons butter or margarine, softened

1. Heat oven to 350°F. Spray 8-inch or 9-inch square pan with cooking spray.
2. In 1-quart saucepan, heat chocolate chips and milk over low heat, stirring frequently, until chocolate is melted and mixture is smooth. Remove from heat.
3. In large bowl, mix flour, ½ cup oats, the baking powder, baking soda and salt; set aside. In medium bowl, stir egg product, brown sugar, oil and vanilla with fork until smooth. Stir into flour mixture until blended. Reserve ½ cup dough in small bowl for topping.
4. Pat remaining dough in pan (if dough is sticky, spray fingers with cooking spray or dust with flour). Spread chocolate mixture over dough. Add 2 tablespoons oats and the butter to reserved ½ cup dough; mix with pastry blender or fork until well mixed. Place small pieces of mixture evenly over chocolate mixture.
5. Bake 20 to 25 minutes or until top is golden and firm. Cool completely, about 1 hour 30 minutes. For bars, cut into 4 rows by 4 rows.

*Per Serving:1 Bar: calorie: 180 / fat: 7g / protein: 3g / carbs: 27g / sugars: 18g / fiber: 1g / sodium: 115mg*

## Chocolate Tahini Bombs

Prep time: 20 minutes / Cook time: 8 minutes / Makes 15 each

- 15 whole dates, pits removed (date intact, not split in half completely)
- 2½ tablespoons tahini, divided
- ½ cup canned coconut milk
- 4 ounces dark chocolate, chopped
- 1 tablespoon toasted sesame seeds

1. Line a baking sheet with parchment paper.
2. Fill each date with a small amount of the tahini,

roughly ¼ teaspoon, and place them on the prepared baking sheet. Put the filled dates in the freezer for 10 to 15 minutes.

3. Meanwhile, heat the coconut milk in a small saucepan over medium-low until simmering.

4. Place the chocolate in a medium heatproof bowl, and when the milk is simmering, pour it into the bowl and let stand for 3 minutes to soften the chocolate.

5. Stir the mixture until it is smooth and the chocolate is completely melted.

6. Remove the dates from the freezer and dip one date at a time into the chocolate. Coat evenly using a fork and place them back on the baking sheet. Sprinkle the dates with the sesame seeds and repeat until all dates are coated in chocolate.

7. Allow to cool completely for the chocolate to harden, or eat immediately.

*Per Serving:calories: 98 / fat: 6g / protein: 1g / carbs: 9g / sugars: 6g / fiber: 2g / sodium: 6mg*

## Banana N'Ice Cream with Cocoa Nuts

Prep time: 10 minutes / Cook time: 12 minutes / Serves 4 to 6

- For the Cocoa Nuts:
- ¼ cup freshly squeezed orange juice
- 1 tablespoon coconut oil
- 2 teaspoons cocoa powder
- ½ teaspoon kosher salt
- ¼ teaspoon ground cinnamon
- ¼ teaspoon ground cardamom
- ½ teaspoon orange zest
- 1 cup raw almonds
- For the Banana N'ice Cream:
- 2 frozen, diced bananas

1. Preheat the oven to 350°F. Line a baking sheet with parchment paper.

2. In a small saucepan, bring the orange juice to a boil over medium-high heat, reduce the heat to low, and simmer until the juice is reduced to about 2 tablespoons, 5 to 7 minutes. Add the coconut oil, stir until well combined, and remove from the heat. Whisk in the cocoa powder, salt, cinnamon, cardamom, and zest. Then add the almonds and stir to coat them. Spread the mixture onto the prepared baking sheet.

3. Bake the nuts for 10 to 12 minutes, stirring halfway through, until toasted. Allow to cool.

4. Store the nuts in an airtight container at room temperature for up to 2 weeks. Make the Banana N'ice Cream: 5. Put the frozen bananas in a food processor and pulse. Scrape down the sides, then pulse once more. Continue to do this for several minutes until the texture resembles ice cream.

Serve immediately with the cooled nuts.

*Per Serving:calories: 199 / fat: 14g / protein: 6g / carbs: 16g / sugars: 7g / fiber: 4g / sodium: 195mg*

## Mixed-Berry Snack Cake

Prep time: 15 minutes / Cook time: 28 to 33 minutes / Serves 8

- ¼ cup low-fat granola
- ½ cup buttermilk
- ⅓ cup packed brown sugar
- 2 tablespoons canola oil
- 1 teaspoon vanilla
- 1 egg
- 1 cup whole wheat flour
- ½ teaspoon baking soda
- ½ teaspoon ground cinnamon
- ⅛ teaspoon salt
- 1 cup mixed fresh berries (such as blueberries, raspberries and blackberries)

1. Heat oven to 350°F. Spray 8- or 9-inch round pan with cooking spray. Place granola in resealable food-storage plastic bag; seal bag and slightly crush with rolling pin or meat mallet. Set aside.

2. In large bowl, stir buttermilk, brown sugar, oil, vanilla and egg until smooth. Stir in flour, baking soda, cinnamon and salt just until moistened. Gently fold in half of the berries. Spoon into pan. Sprinkle with remaining berries and the granola.

3. Bake 28 to 33 minutes or until golden brown and top springs back when touched in center. Cool in pan on cooling rack 10 minutes. Serve warm.

*Per Serving:calorie: 160 / fat: 5g / protein: 3g / carbs: 26g / sugars: 12g / fiber: 1g / sodium: 140mg*

## Mixed-Berry Cream Tart

Prep time: 20 minutes / Cook time: 0 minutes / Serves 8

- 2 cups sliced fresh strawberries
- ½ cup boiling water
- 1 box (4-serving size) sugar-free strawberry gelatin
- 3 pouches (1½ ounces each) roasted almond crunchy granola bars (from 8. 9-oz box)
- 1 package (8 ounces) fat-free cream cheese
- ¼ cup sugar
- ¼ teaspoon almond extract
- 1 cup fresh blueberries
- 1 cup fresh raspberries
- Fat-free whipped topping, if desired

1. In small bowl, crush 1 cup of the strawberries with pastry blender or fork. Reserve remaining 1 cup strawberries.

2. In medium bowl, pour boiling water over gelatin; stir about 2 minutes or until gelatin is completely dissolved. Stir crushed strawberries into gelatin.

Refrigerate 20 minutes.

3. Meanwhile, leaving granola bars in pouches, crush granola bars with rolling pin. Sprinkle crushed granola in bottom of 9-inch ungreased glass pie plate, pushing crumbs up side of plate to make crust.

4. In small bowl, beat cream cheese, sugar and almond extract with electric mixer on medium-high speed until smooth. Drop by spoonfuls over crushed granola; gently spread to cover bottom of crust.

5. Gently fold blueberries, raspberries and remaining 1 cup strawberries into gelatin mixture. Spoon over cream cheese mixture. Refrigerate about 3 hours or until firm. Serve topped with whipped topping.

*Per Serving:calorie: 170 / fat: 3g / protein: 8g / carbs: 27g / sugars: 17g / fiber: 3g / sodium: 340mg*

## Avocado Chocolate Mousse

Prep time: 5 minutes / Cook time: 0 minutes / Serves 4

- 2 avocados, mashed
- ¼ cup canned coconut milk
- 2 tablespoons unsweetened cocoa powder
- 2 tablespoons pure maple syrup
- ½ teaspoon espresso powder
- ½ teaspoon vanilla extract

1. In a blender, combine all of the ingredients. Blend until smooth.
2. Pour the mixture into 4 small bowls and serve.

*Per Serving:calories: 222 / fat: 18g / protein: 3g / carbs: 17g / sugars: 7g / fiber: 8g / sodium: 11mg*

## Fudgy Walnut Brownies

Prep time: 10 minutes / Cook time: 1 hour / Serves 12

- ¾ cup walnut halves and pieces
- ½ cup unsalted butter, melted and cooled
- 4 large eggs
- 1½ teaspoons instant coffee crystals
- 1½ teaspoons vanilla extract
- 1 cup Lakanto Monkfruit Sweetener Golden
- ¼ teaspoon fine sea salt
- ¾ cup almond flour
- ¾ cup natural cocoa powder
- ¾ cup stevia-sweetened chocolate chips

1. In a dry small skillet over medium heat, toast the walnuts, stirring often, for about 5 minutes, until golden. Transfer the walnuts to a bowl to cool.

2. Pour 1 cup water into the Instant Pot. Line the base of a 7 by 3-inch round cake pan with a circle of parchment paper. Butter the sides of the pan and the parchment or coat with nonstick cooking spray.

3. Pour the butter into a medium bowl. One at a time, whisk in the eggs, then whisk in the coffee crystals, vanilla, sweetener, and salt. Finally, whisk in the flour and cocoa powder just until combined. Using a rubber spatula, fold in the chocolate chips and walnuts.

4. Transfer the batter to the prepared pan and, using the spatula, spread it in an even layer. Cover the pan tightly with aluminum foil. Place the pan on a long-handled silicone steam rack, then, holding the handles of the steam rack, lower it into the Instant Pot.

5. Secure the lid and set the Pressure Release to Sealing. Select the Cake, Pressure Cook, or Manual setting and set the cooking time for 45 minutes at high pressure. (The pot will take about 10 minutes to come up to pressure before the cooking program begins. )

6. When the cooking program ends, let the pressure release naturally for 10 minutes, then move the Pressure Release to Venting to release any remaining steam. Open the pot and, wearing heat-resistant mitts, grasp the handles of the steam rack and lift it out of the pot. Uncover the pan, taking care not to get burned by the steam or to drip condensation onto the brownies. Let the brownies cool in the pan on a cooling rack for about 2 hours, to room temperature.

7. Run a butter knife around the edge of the pan to make sure the brownies are not sticking to the pan sides. Invert the brownies onto the rack, lift off the pan, and peel off the parchment paper. Invert the brownies onto a serving plate and cut into twelve wedges. The brownies will keep, stored in an airtight container in the refrigerator for up to 5 days, or in the freezer for up to 4 months.

*Per Serving:calories: 199 / fat: 19g / protein: 5g / carbs: 26g / sugars: 10g / fiber: 20g / sodium: 56mg*

## Broiled Pineapple

Prep time: 5 minutes / Cook time: 5 minutes / Serves 4

- 4 large slices fresh pineapple
- 2 tablespoons canned coconut milk
- 2 tablespoons unsweetened shredded coconut
- ¼ teaspoon sea salt

1. Preheat the oven broiler on high.
2. On a rimmed baking sheet, arrange the pineapple in a single layer. Brush lightly with the coconut milk and sprinkle with the coconut.
3. Broil until the pineapple begins to brown, 3 to 5 minutes.
4. Sprinkle with the sea salt.

*Per Serving:calories: 110 / fat: 3g / protein: 1g / carbs: 23g / sugars: 15g / fiber: 3g / sodium: 16mg*

## Blackberry Yogurt Ice Pops

Prep time: 10 minutes / Cook time: 0 minutes / Serves 4

- 12 ounces plain Greek yogurt
- 1 cup blackberries
- Pinch nutmeg
- ¼ cup milk
- 2 (1-gram) packets stevia

1. In a blender, combine all of the ingredients. Blend until smooth.
2. Pour the mixture into 4 ice pop molds. Freeze for 6 hours before serving.

*Per Serving:calories: 71 / fat: 1g / protein: 10g / carbs: 8g / sugars: 5g / fiber: 2g / sodium: 37mg*

## Blender Banana Snack Cake

Prep time: 5 minutes / Cook time: 30 to 32 minutes / Serves 9

- ¼ cup coconut nectar or pure maple syrup
- ¼ cup water
- 2 teaspoons vanilla
- 1 teaspoon cinnamon
- ½ teaspoon nutmeg
- ¼ teaspoon sea salt
- 3½ cups sliced, well-ripened bananas
- 1 cup whole grain spelt flour
- ½ cup rolled oats
- 2 teaspoons baking powder

1. Preheat the oven to 350°F. Lightly coat an 8" x 8" pan with cooking spray and line the bottom of the pan with parchment paper.
2. In a blender, combine the nectar or syrup, water, vanilla, cinnamon, nutmeg, salt, and 3 cups of the sliced bananas. Puree until smooth. Add the flour, oats, baking powder, and the remaining ½ cup of bananas. Pulse a couple of times, until just combined. (Don't puree; you don't want to overwork the flour. ) Transfer the mixture into the baking dish, using a spatula to scrape down the sides of the bowl. Bake for 30 to 32 minutes, until fully set. (Insert a toothpick in the center and see if it comes out clean. ) Transfer the cake pan to a cooling rack. Let cool completely before cutting.

*Per Serving:calorie: 141 / fat: 1g / protein: 3g / carbs: 32g / sugars: 14g / fiber: 4g / sodium: 177mg*

## Almond Butter Blondies

Prep time: 10 minutes / Cook time: 20 minutes / Serves 8

- ½ cup creamy natural almond butter, at room temperature
- 4 large eggs
- ¾ cup Lakanto Monkfruit Sweetener Golden
- 1 teaspoon pure vanilla extract
- ½ teaspoon fine sea salt
- 1¼ cups almond flour
- ¾ cup stevia-sweetened chocolate chips

1. Pour 1 cup water into the Instant Pot. Line the base of a 7 by 3-inch round cake pan with a circle of parchment paper. Butter the sides of the pan and the parchment or coat with nonstick cooking spray.
2. Put the almond butter into a medium bowl. One at a time, whisk the eggs into the almond butter, then whisk in the sweetener, vanilla, and salt. Stir in the flour just until it is fully incorporated, followed by the chocolate chips.
3. Transfer the batter to the prepared pan and, using a rubber spatula, spread it in an even layer. Cover the pan tightly with aluminum foil. Place the pan on a long-handled silicone steam rack, then, holding the handles of the steam rack, lower it into the Instant Pot.
4. Secure the lid and set the Pressure Release to Sealing. Select the Cake, Pressure Cook, or Manual setting and set the cooking time for 40 minutes at high pressure. (The pot will take about 10 minutes to come up to pressure before the cooking program begins. )
5. When the cooking program ends, let the pressure release naturally for 10 minutes, then move the Pressure Release to Venting to release any remaining steam. Open the pot and, wearing heat-resistant mitts, grasp the handles of the steam rack and lift it out of the pot. Uncover the pan, taking care not to get burned by the steam or to drip condensation onto the blondies. Let the blondies cool in the pan on a cooling rack for about 5 minutes.
6. Run a butter knife around the edge of pan to make sure the blondies are not sticking to the pan sides. Invert the blondies onto the rack, lift off the pan, and peel off the parchment paper. Let cool for 15 minutes, then invert the blondies onto a serving plate and cut into eight wedges. The blondies will keep, stored in an airtight container in the refrigerator for up to 5 days, or in the freezer for up to 4 months.

*Per Serving:calories: 211 / fat: 17g / protein: 8g / carbs: 20g / sugars: 10g / fiber: 17g / sodium: 186mg*

## Strawberry Chia Pudding

Prep time: 5 minutes / Cook time: 0 minutes / Serves 2

- 1½ cups frozen whole strawberries
- 3 tablespoons white chia seeds
- 1 tablespoon coconut nectar or pure maple syrup
- 1 teaspoon lemon juice
- Pinch of sea salt

- ½ cup + 2–3 tablespoons plain low-fat nondairy milk

1. In a blender, combine the strawberries, chia seeds, nectar or syrup, lemon juice, salt, and ½ cup plus 2 tablespoons of the milk. Puree until the seeds are fully pulverized and the pudding begins to thicken. (It will thicken more as it cools. ) Add the extra 1 tablespoon milk if needed to blend. Transfer the mixture to a large bowl or dish and refrigerate until chilled, about an hour or more. (It will thicken more with chilling, but really can be eaten right away. )

*Per Serving:calorie: 185 / fat: 5g / protein: 4g / carbs: 33g / sugars: 16g / fiber: 9g / sodium: 182mg*

## Pineapple-Peanut Nice Cream

Prep time: 10 minutes / Cook time: 0 minutes / Serves 6
- 2 cups frozen pineapple
- 1 cup peanut butter (no added sugar, salt, or fat)
- ½ cup unsweetened almond milk

1. In a blender or food processor, combine the frozen pineapple and peanut butter and process.
2. Add the almond milk, and blend until smooth. The end result should be a smooth paste.

*Per Serving:calories: 143 / fat: 3g / protein: 10g / carbs: 15g / sugars: 7g / fiber: 3g / sodium: 22mg*

## Creamy Orange Cheesecake

Prep time: 35 minutes / Cook time: 35 minutes / Serves 10
- Sauce:
- ¾ cup graham cracker crumbs
- 2 tablespoons sugar
- 3 tablespoons melted, light, soft tub margarine
- Sauce:
- 2 (8-ounce) packages fat-free cream cheese, at room temperature
- ⅔ cup sugar
- 2 eggs
- 1 egg yolk
- ¼ cup frozen orange juice concentrate
- 1 teaspoon orange zest
- 1 tablespoon flour
- ½ teaspoon vanilla
- 1½ cups water

1. Combine crust ingredients. Pat into 7" springform pan.
2. Cream together cream cheese and sugar. Add eggs and yolk. Beat for 3 minutes.
3. Beat in juice, zest, flour, and vanilla. Beat 2 minutes.
4. Pour batter into crust. Cover with foil.
5. Place the trivet into your Instant Pot and pour in

1½ cups water. Place a foil sling on top of the trivet, then place the springform pan on top.
6. Secure the lid and make sure lid is set to sealing. Press Manual and set for 35 minutes.
7. When cook time is up, press Cancel and allow the pressure to release naturally for 7 minutes, then release the remaining pressure manually.
8. Carefully remove the springform pan by using hot pads to lift the pan up by the foil sling. Uncover and place on a cooling rack until cool, then refrigerate for 8 hours.

*Per Serving:calories: 159 / fat: 3g / protein: 9g / carbs: 25g / sugars: 19g / fiber: 0g / sodium: 300mg*

## Apple Cinnamon Bread Pudding

Prep time: 5 minutes / Cook time: 1 hour / Serves 10
- 9 slices whole-wheat bread, cubed (about 5–6 cups)
- 2 cups cubed apples (Granny Smith apples work well)
- 4 cups fat-free milk
- 1 cup egg substitute
- 2 teaspoon vanilla
- 2 teaspoon cinnamon
- ¼ cup agave nectar
- ½ cup raisins

1. Preheat the oven to 350 degrees.
2. In a large baking dish, combine the bread and apples.
3. In a bowl, whisk together the milk, egg substitute, vanilla, cinnamon, and agave nectar. Add the raisins. Pour the milk mixture over the bread, and let stand for 15 minutes so the bread can absorb some of the liquid.
4. Bake at 350 degrees for 40–45 minutes, until the bread pudding is set and firm. Cut into squares, and serve warm with whipped topping or low-fat ice cream.

*Per Serving:calories: 175 / fat: 1g / protein: 10g / carbs: 28g / sugars: 15g / fiber: 3g / sodium: 232mg*

## Creamy Pineapple-Pecan Dessert Squares

Prep time: 25 minutes / Cook time: 0 minutes / Serves 18
- ¾ cup boiling water
- 1 package (4-serving size) lemon sugar-free gelatin
- 1 cup unsweetened pineapple juice
- 1½ cups graham cracker crumbs
- ½ cup sugar
- ¼ cup shredded coconut
- ¼ cup chopped pecans
- 3 tablespoons butter or margarine, melted
- 1 package (8 ounces) fat-free cream cheese
- 1 container (8 ounces) fat-free sour cream
- 1 can (8 ounces) crushed pineapple, undrained

1. In large bowl, pour boiling water over gelatin; stir about 2 minutes or until gelatin is completely dissolved. Stir in pineapple juice. Refrigerate about 30 minutes or until mixture is syrupy and just beginning to thicken.
2. Meanwhile, in 13x9-inch (3-quart) glass baking dish, toss cracker crumbs, ¼ cup of the sugar, the coconut, pecans and melted butter until well mixed. Reserve ½ cup crumb mixture for topping. Press remaining mixture in bottom of dish.
3. In medium bowl, beat cream cheese, sour cream and remaining ¼ cup sugar with electric mixer on medium speed until smooth; set aside.
4. Beat gelatin mixture with electric mixer on low speed until foamy; beat on high speed until light and fluffy (mixture will look like beaten egg whites). Beat in cream cheese mixture just until mixed. Gently stir in pineapple (with liquid). Pour into crust-lined dish; smooth top. Sprinkle reserved ½ cup crumb mixture over top. Refrigerate about 4 hours or until set. For servings, cut into 6 rows by 3 rows.

*Per Serving:calorie: 120 / fat: 5g / protein: 3g / carbs: 18g / sugars: 11g / fiber: 0g / sodium: 180mg*

## Chocolate Almond Butter Fudge

Prep time: 10 minutes / Cook time: 0 minutes / Makes 9 Pieces

- 2 ounces unsweetened baking chocolate
- ½ cup almond butter
- 1 can full-fat coconut milk, refrigerated overnight, thickened cream only
- 1 teaspoon vanilla extract
- 4 (1-gram) packets stevia (or to taste)

1. Line a 9-inch square baking pan with parchment paper.
2. In a small saucepan over medium-low heat, heat the chocolate and almond butter, stirring constantly, until both are melted. Cool slightly.

3. In a medium bowl, combine the melted chocolate mixture with the cream from the coconut milk, vanilla, and stevia. Blend until smooth. Taste and adjust sweetness as desired.
4. Pour the mixture into the prepared pan, spreading with a spatula to smooth. Refrigerate for 3 hours. Cut into squares.

*Per Serving:1 piece: calories: 169 / fat: 11g / protein: 8g / carbs: 11g / sugars: 7g / fiber: 3g / sodium: 64mg*

## Cherry Almond Cobbler

Prep time: 10 minutes / Cook time: 25 minutes / Serves 4

- 2 cups water-packed sour cherries
- ¼ teaspoon fresh lemon juice
- ⅛ teaspoon almond extract
- ½ cup almond flour, sifted
- ⅛ teaspoon salt
- ¼ cup flaxseeds
- ¾ teaspoon baking powder
- 1 tablespoon canola oil
- ¼ cup egg substitute
- 2 tablespoons fat-free milk
- ¼ cup granulated sugar substitute (such as stevia)

1. Preheat the oven to 425 degrees. Drain the cherries, reserving ⅔ cup of liquid, and place the cherries in a shallow 9-inch glass or porcelain cake pan.
2. In a small mixing bowl, combine the lemon juice, almond extract, and drained cherry liquid; mix well. Spoon over the cherries.
3. In a mixing bowl, combine the almond flour, flaxseeds, and baking powder. Mix thoroughly. Stir in the oil, egg substitute, milk, and sugar substitute, mixing well.
4. Spoon the mixture over the cherries, and bake at 425 degrees for 25–30 minutes or until the crust is golden brown.

*Per Serving:calories: 216 / fat: 14g / protein: 7g / carbs: 19g / sugars: 10g / fiber: 6g / sodium: 132mg*

# 30-Day Meal Plan

| | Breakfast | Lunch | Dinner | Snack/Dessert |
|---|---|---|---|---|
| Day 1 | Veggie-Stuffed Omelet | Chicken Paprika | Open-Faced Pulled Pork | Lemon Artichokes |
| Day 2 | Breakfast Hash | Traditional Beef Stroganoff | Sesame-Crusted Tuna Steak | Creamy Cheese Dip |
| Day 3 | Sausage, Sweet Potato, and Kale Hash | Roasted Salmon with Salsa Verde | Red Wine Pot Roast with Winter Vegetables | Vegetable Kabobs with Mustard Dip |
| Day 4 | Vanilla Steel-Cut Oatmeal | Sautéed Chicken with Artichoke Hearts | Red Beans | Lemon Cream Fruit Dip |
| Day 5 | Berry–French Toast Stratas | Bacon-Wrapped Vegetable Kebabs | Creole Braised Sirloin | Instant Popcorn |
| Day 6 | Easy Breakfast Chia Pudding | Beef and Pepper Fajita Bowls | Pork Chops Pomodoro | Low-Sugar Blueberry Muffins |
| Day 7 | Mini Breakfast Quiches | Saffron-Spiced Chicken Breasts | Texas Caviar | Spinach and Artichoke Dip |
| Day 8 | Bacon-and-Eggs Avocado | Pork Tacos | Peppercorn-Crusted Baked Salmon | Baked Scallops |
| Day 9 | Savory Grits | Kung Pao Chicken and Zucchini Noodles | Parmesan-Crusted Pork Chops | Grilled Peach and Coconut Yogurt Bowls |
| Day 10 | Breakfast Panini | Butterflied Beef Eye Roast | Seafood Stew | Baked Pumpkin Pudding |
| Day 11 | Cherry, Chocolate, and Almond Shake | Mexican-Style Shredded Beef | Whole-Wheat Linguine with Kale Pesto | Chewy Chocolate-Oat Bars |
| Day 12 | Ginger Blackberry Bliss Smoothie Bowl | Cilantro Lime Chicken Thighs | Taco Stuffed Sweet Potatoes | Chocolate Tahini Bombs |
| Day 13 | Pumpkin–Peanut Butter Single-Serve Muffins | Spice-Rubbed Pork Loin | Coconut-Ginger Rice | Banana N'Ice Cream with Cocoa Nuts |
| Day 14 | Coddled Eggs and Smoked Salmon Toasts | Greek Scampi | Broiled Dijon Burgers | Mixed-Berry Snack Cake |
| Day 15 | Plum Smoothie | Quinoa Vegetable Skillet | Herb-Crusted Lamb Chops | Mixed-Berry Cream Tart |

|  | Breakfast | Lunch | Dinner | Snack/Dessert |
|---|---|---|---|---|
| Day 16 | Pumpkin Walnut Smoothie Bowl | Bavarian Beef | Sage-Parmesan Pork Chops | Avocado Chocolate Mousse |
| Day 17 | Mandarin Orange–Millet Breakfast Bowl | Turkey Chili | Southwestern Quinoa Salad | Fudgy Walnut Brownies |
| Day 18 | Cynthia's Yogurt | Open-Faced Philly Cheesesteak Sandwiches | Beef Burgundy | Broiled Pineapple |
| Day 19 | Tropical Fruit 'n Ginger Oatmeal | Rosemary Lamb Chops | Chicken Patties | Blackberry Yogurt Ice Pops |
| Day 20 | Green Eggs and Ham | Pork Carnitas | Easy Beef Curry | Blender Banana Snack Cake |
| Day 21 | Spaghetti Squash Fritters | Edamame-Tabbouleh Salad | Homey Pot Roast | Almond Butter Blondies |
| Day 22 | Biscuits | Halibut Supreme | Baked Monkfish | Strawberry Chia Pudding |
| Day 23 | Sausage Egg Cup | Creole Steak | Jerk Chicken Thighs | Pineapple-Peanut Nice Cream |
| Day 24 | Blueberry Cornmeal Muffins | Walnut-Crusted Halibut with Pear Salad | Slow Cooker Ropa Vieja | Creamy Orange Cheesecake |
| Day 25 | Polenta Porridge with Berry Swirl | Wild Rice with Blueberries and Pumpkin Seeds | Creamy Cod with Asparagus | Apple Cinnamon Bread Pudding |
| Day 26 | Cottage Cheese Almond Pancakes | Mustard Herb Pork Tenderloin | One-Pan Chicken Dinner | Creamy Pineapple-Pecan Dessert Squares |
| Day 27 | Breakfast Meatballs | Quinoa Pilaf with Salmon and Asparagus | Grilled Steak and Vegetables | Chocolate Almond Butter Fudge |
| Day 28 | Veggie And Egg White Scramble With Pepper Jack Cheese | Ground Turkey Tetrazzini | Air Fryer Fish Fry | Cherry Almond Cobbler |
| Day 29 | Crepe Cakes | Steak with Bell Pepper | Garlic Galore Rotisserie Chicken | Broiled Asparagus |
| Day 30 | Coconut Pancakes | Asian-Style Grilled Beef Salad | Broiled Sole with Mustard Sauce | Sweet Potato Crisps |

# INDEX

# MEASUREMENT CONVERSION CHART

## VOLUME EQUIVALENTS(DRY)

| US STANDARD | METRIC (APPROXIMATE) |
|---|---|
| 1/8 teaspoon | 0.5 mL |
| 1/4 teaspoon | 1 mL |
| 1/2 teaspoon | 2 mL |
| 3/4 teaspoon | 4 mL |
| 1 teaspoon | 5 mL |
| 1 tablespoon | 15 mL |
| 1/4 cup | 59 mL |
| 1/2 cup | 118 mL |
| 3/4 cup | 177 mL |
| 1 cup | 235 mL |
| 2 cups | 475 mL |
| 3 cups | 700 mL |
| 4 cups | 1 L |

## WEIGHT EQUIVALENTS

| US STANDARD | METRIC (APPROXIMATE) |
|---|---|
| 1 ounce | 28 g |
| 2 ounces | 57 g |
| 5 ounces | 142 g |
| 10 ounces | 284 g |
| 15 ounces | 425 g |
| 16 ounces (1 pound) | 455 g |
| 1.5 pounds | 680 g |
| 2 pounds | 907 g |

## VOLUME EQUIVALENTS(LIQUID)

| US STANDARD | US STANDARD (OUNCES) | METRIC (APPROXIMATE) |
|---|---|---|
| 2 tablespoons | 1 fl.oz. | 30 mL |
| 1/4 cup | 2 fl.oz. | 60 mL |
| 1/2 cup | 4 fl.oz. | 120 mL |
| 1 cup | 8 fl.oz. | 240 mL |
| 1 1/2 cup | 12 fl.oz. | 355 mL |
| 2 cups or 1 pint | 16 fl.oz. | 475 mL |
| 4 cups or 1 quart | 32 fl.oz. | 1 L |
| 1 gallon | 128 fl.oz. | 4 L |

## TEMPERATURES EQUIVALENTS

| FAHRENHEIT(F) | CELSIUS(C) (APPROXIMATE) |
|---|---|
| 225 °F | 107 °C |
| 250 °F | 120 °C |
| 275 °F | 135 °C |
| 300 °F | 150 °C |
| 325 °F | 160 °C |
| 350 °F | 180 °C |
| 375 °F | 190 °C |
| 400 °F | 205 °C |
| 425 °F | 220 °C |
| 450 °F | 235 °C |
| 475 °F | 245 °C |
| 500 °F | 260 °C |

# The Dirty Dozen and Clean Fifteen

The Environmental Working Group (EWG) is a nonprofit, nonpartisan organization dedicated to protecting human health and the environment Its mission is to empower people to live healthier lives in a healthier environment. This organization publishes an annual list of the twelve kinds of produce, in sequence, that have the highest amount of pesticide residue-the Dirty Dozen-as well as a list of the fifteen kinds ofproduce that have the least amount of pesticide residue-the Clean Fifteen.

| THE DIRTY DOZEN | THE CLEAN FIFTEEN |
|---|---|
| • The 2016 Dirty Dozen includes the following produce. These are considered among the year's most important produce to buy organic: | • The least critical to buy organically are the Clean Fifteen list. The following are on the 2016 list: |

THE DIRTY DOZEN:

| | |
|---|---|
| Strawberries | Spinach |
| Apples | Tomatoes |
| Nectarines | Bell peppers |
| Peaches | Cherry tomatoes |
| Celery | Cucumbers |
| Grapes | Kale/collard greens |
| Cherries | Hot peppers |

THE CLEAN FIFTEEN:

| | |
|---|---|
| Avocados | Papayas |
| Corn | Kiw |
| Pineapples | Eggplant |
| Cabbage | Honeydew |
| Sweet peas | Grapefruit |
| Onions | Cantaloupe |
| Asparagus | Cauliflower |
| Mangos | |

• *The Dirty Dozen list contains two additional itemskale/collard greens and hot peppers-because they tend to contain trace levels of highly hazardous pesticides.*

• *Some of the sweet corn sold in the United States are made from genetically engineered (GE) seedstock. Buy organic varieties of these crops to avoid GE produce.*

91125002R00059